The
TEXAS
Military Experience

**Number 43: Williams-Ford
Texas A&M University Military History Series**

The TEXAS Military Experience
From the Texas Revolution through World War II

Edited by
Joseph G. Dawson III

Texas A&M University Press
College Station

Copyright © 1995 by Joseph G. Dawson III
Manufactured in the United States of America
All rights reserved
Second Printing, 2010

The paper used in this book meets the minimum requirements
of the American National Standard for Permanence
of paper for Printed Library Materials, Z39.48-1984.
Binding materials have been chosen for durability.
∞

Library of Congress Cataloging-in-Publication Data

The Texas military experience : from the Texas Revolution through
   World War II / editor, Joseph G. Dawson III.
       p. cm. — (Texas A&M University military history series ; 43)
   Includes bibliographical references and index.
   ISBN 978-1-60344-197-1 (pbk.)
   1. Texas—History, Military. I. Dawson, Joseph G., 1945-
II. Series.
F386.5.T483   1995   95-3321
355'.009764—dc20   CIP

CONTENTS

Illustrations   vii
Acknowledgments   ix
Introduction, by Joseph G. Dawson III   3

1. The Alamo as Icon,   14
   by Paul Andrew Hutton

2. Race, Revolution, and the Texas Republic: 32
   Toward a Reinterpretation, by James E. Crisp

3. "In This Way We Did the Country   49
   Some Service": Ben McCulloch
   and the War with Mexico, 1846–47,
   by Thomas W. Cutrer

4. Texas in the Southern War   71
   for Independence, by Ralph A. Wooster

5. Black Regulars on the Texas Frontier,   86
   1866–85, by William H. Leckie

6. Women and the Texas Military Experience: 97
   The Nineteenth Century, by Sandra L. Myres

7. "The American Congo":   113
   Captain John G. Bourke and the Texas
   Military Experience, by Joseph C. Porter

8. The 36th Infantry Division in World War II,   128
    by Martin Blumenson

 9. Man against Fire: Audie Murphy   137
    and His War, by Roger J. Spiller

10. The Texas Military Experience   155
    in Films, by Don Graham

11. The Texas Military Experience   167
    in Literature, by Tom Pilkington

Epilogue: The Texas Military Experience,   184
    by Roger Beaumont

Notes   193
Contributors   237
Index   241

ILLUSTRATIONS

The Alamo, ca. 1935	16
Juan Seguín, by Jefferson Wright	42
Ben McCulloch	53
The Struggle for Devil's Den, by Alfred R. Waud	75
Captain Dodge's Colored Troops to the Rescue, by Frederic Remington	90
General George and Mrs. Elizabeth Custer at Austin, Texas	108
John G. Bourke	125
Thirty-sixth Infantry Division occupying Schweigen, Germany, 1945	132
Audie Murphy	140
Death of Davy Crockett and fall of the Alamo	159

ACKNOWLEDGMENTS

I AM PLEASED TO ACKNOWLEDGE THE SUPPORT AND ENCOURagement of numerous people who have helped turn symposium proceedings into a book of essays.

The Military Studies Institute (MSI) was established at Texas A&M University in 1984 to encourage the research and study of military history and defense issues, particularly as pertaining to Texas, the Southwest, and the United States. Since 1984 the institute has fulfilled its charter by (1) establishing a Speakers Series, thus creating a forum of expression for retired and active-duty military officers, historians, sociologists, political scientists, and defense analysts; (2) encouraging research into defense and military matters; and (3) hosting a series of symposia on selected topics. This book is the result of one of those symposia.

The Military Studies Institute has been fortunate to have a talented Advisory Council that has ably supported its activities and goals over the years. I am especially grateful to my friend and colleague R. J. Q. Adams, who, as chair of the council, has so often lent his good humor and sound advice to MSI's projects. Thanks, too, to Roger A. Beaumont for his worthwhile suggestions and numerous kindnesses. Other members of the council have, from time to time, all contributed in various ways, leading to improvements in MSI and its programs. The council members have included James C. Bradford, James Burk, Larry D. Hill, Alex Mintz, Brian M. Linn, and John Robertson.

Of utmost importance has been Laura Ampol Hall, MSI secretary *extraordinaire*, who entered the manuscript into the word processor and kept up with the inevitable changes and corrections that brought the work to completion.

I give special thanks to Archie P. McDonald and Walter L. Buenger for their help and suggestions on the project.

I also wish to thank Robert A. Calvert, who served as coordinator of the MSI symposium at which all but one of these papers were originally presented. Thanks, too, are in order to David Farmer and the DeGolyer Library of Southern Methodist University, which kindly extended permission to republish a revised version of Paul Andrew Hutton's introduction to the book *Alamo Images*. I am also indebted to Steve Smith of the Archives and Special Collections department, Sterling Evans Library, who made helpful suggestions on illustrations. And finally, I must express my gratitude to the contributors to this volume; without them this evaluation of the Texas military experience could not have been made.

Joseph G. Dawson III

# The TEXAS Military Experience

INTRODUCTION

Joseph G. Dawson III

TEXAS AND TEXANS HAVE ACHIEVED AN EXTRAORDINARY place in American history and popular culture. To reveal the state's history and influence, readers may turn to books with such titles as *The Seven Keys to Texas, The Texas Literary Tradition, Texas Myths,* and *The Folklore of Texan Cultures*.[1] Yet, despite these and many other published works about the state, one aspect—the Texas military experience—has not received appropriate attention. This book offers an introduction to that subject.

The Texas Revolution of 1835-36 forms the foundation of the Texas military experience, just as the North American colonial wars and the American Revolution form the basis of the American military tradition.[2] Fundamental to Texas and its history is one of the most celebrated sieges in military annals: the fall of the Alamo. In his chapter, Paul Andrew Hutton shows that the battle has become legendary, the primary participants on the Texas side—such as Davy Crockett, William B. Travis, and Jim Bowie—have become heroes to many Texans and Americans, and the place itself has virtually achieved the status of a patriotic shrine.[3] Although debunking heroes and heroics has long been an accepted practice in American writing, revisionist historians of whatever stripe have learned that challenging the traditional view of the battle at the Alamo and its stalwart defenders imperils their professional and personal reputations. After reading Hutton's chapter, one can wonder if the historiography of the Alamo has reached a point that an objective and thorough analysis of the battle would be greeted dispassionately.

Viewing the Alamo's defenders as heroic, self-sacrificing, and noble-minded has been a longstanding aspect of writings about the Texas military experience. However, as James Crisp demonstrates in his extensive interpretive survey of the historiography of the Texas Revolution, historians debate the motivations and attitudes of those involved in that war.

Crisp asserts that racism did not cause the Revolution but instead that the conflict fixed racism in the minds of most Anglo-Texans in the years following. Although Crisp's controversial interpretation is at odds with a number of other historians, it helps place the military events of 1836 in a better context and may prompt further analysis of the Revolution, its leaders, and their followers.[4]

Ironically, as Don Graham points out in his chapter on Texas history in film, so much attention has been paid to the stunning defeat at the Alamo and James Fannin's surrender of his entire army at Goliad that those Texas military losses detract from the victory at San Jacinto. That battle revenged the Alamo, culminated the Revolution on a high note, and gained Texas's independence from Mexico. Furthermore, it propelled Sam Houston into the heroic pantheon of Crockett, Travis, and Bowie.[5]

Following the Revolution, the years of the Texas Republic add another facet to the Texas military experience. From 1836 to 1845 Texas functioned as an independent nation with elected officials, diplomats, and a military establishment. In the Gulf of Mexico, Commodore Edwin N. Moore adopted the example of the Revolution's naval commanders, created a squadron, and patrolled the Gulf Coast from the late 1830s to the early 1840s. In 1843, Moore and his vessels countered an offensive strike by the Mexican navy and thus contributed significantly to maintaining an independent Texas.[6] On land, the Texas army used regulars, militia, and volunteers to watch for Indian attacks, guard against incursions by the Mexican army, and mount offensive counterattacks. Nevertheless, Mexican forces twice captured San Antonio in 1842. One of the Texan counteroffensives, the expedition to Mier on the Rio Grande, turned out to be a disaster that ranked near to that of Fannin's surrender at Goliad in 1836. The survivors of the Mier Expedition suffered a terrible humiliation. Drawing lots, they had to turn over every tenth soldier of the 176 Texan prisoners to be executed. The decimation of the Mier prisoners lit a burning flame of revenge among many Texans.[7]

The famous Texas Rangers often are cast in a heroic mold and associated with rounding up cattle rustlers in the 1870s or chasing modern outlaws of the twentieth century, such as Bonnie Parker and Clyde Barrow. In his chapter on Ben McCulloch and the Ranger units serving with General Zachary Taylor's American army during the Mexican-American War, Thomas Cutrer relates a lesser-known aspect of the Rangers: their service as volunteer soldiers during wartime. Cutrer describes how the Rangers enlisted and then applied their skills of frontier patrolling and Indian fighting directly to the needs of American conventional forces operating in enemy territory. Moreover, Cutrer shows that the fearsome reputation the Rangers already had established by 1846 was well deserved. As he points out, however, the Rangers also added a stain to Texas military history because of their poor discipline and extraneous violence against Mexicans during the war. Some Texans tried to justify or excuse such conduct as revenge for Mexican raids from 1837 to 1845 and the execution of the Mier prisoners. Others again raised the cry "Remember the Alamo." Cutrer's chapter links McCulloch and the Rangers to a broader Texas military history. Although his work supplements the studies of individual Ranger leaders, their image as hardy individualists probably will continue to rank above their service in units.[8]

Texas contributed many conventional regiments and brigades to the Confederacy in the Civil War. In his chapter, Ralph A. Wooster provides an excellent summary of units and leaders. He also details campaigns and battles in Texas during the Civil War, including Terry's Texas Rangers, officially the 8th Texas Cavalry Regiment, which carried on the hell-for-leather tradition of Ben McCulloch. Of greater national renown was General John Bell Hood and the famous Texas Brigade, which served with exceptional distinction as part of Robert E. Lee's Army of Northern Virginia in the war's eastern theater. Wooster also discusses the antics of General Henry Hopkins Sibley, who mounted an expedition from Texas designed to capture Santa Fe, New Mexico. The expedition turned out to be disastrous for Sibley, disappointing for the Confederacy, and deadly for many of the Texas recruits. Other general officers who led their Texas units with distinction were Lawrence Sullivan Ross, Hiram Granbury, and John G. Walker. Albert Sidney Johnston, former secretary of war for the Republic of Texas, became one of the highest-ranking Confederate army officers but was killed in action at the battle of Shiloh in 1862. Overall, Texas officers and soldiers emerged from the Civil War closely identified—or stigmatized—with the Confederacy and its failed war for independence.[9]

The affiliation of Texas with the Confederacy has left an indelible mark on the history of the state, but historians have argued over whether Texas was a southern or a western state. In his history of slavery in Texas, Randolph B. Campbell has argued persuasively that Texas is more southern than western, but the debate is sure to continue. If it is categorized as southern, then Texas would be a part of what John Hope Franklin has characterized as the "militant South."[10] It can be argued that this "militancy" rested on two pillars. First, Anglo leaders in the nineteenth-century South encouraged and enjoyed fostering the image of *regional* military prowess. This included the reputation of high enrollments of southern men at military schools, especially the U.S. Military Academy at West Point, New York; the rapid recruitment of southern volunteers into national service in time of American wars; and the claim that southern militia companies were viable when those outside the South were mere empty shells. The second pillar was the image of the belligerent *individual* southerner who was quick to take offense (particularly in regard to matters of personal honor and the defense of slavery, issues which often overlapped); ready to resort to personal violence by dueling or less formal means; and familiar with weapons and used to carrying them. Therefore, a meld of organized preparation for warfare (sometimes with an ambivalence or hostility toward regular military discipline), pride in national or regional military service, and individual inclination toward the use of violence all seemed to typify the South—and, therefore, by implication, Texas.[11]

In an extensive critique of Dixie's martial image, historian Robert E. May counteracts "the stereotype of a militant white society in the South" and stresses that the stereotype has been "a major theme in our [American] history." May's analysis also demonstrates how the South's military stereotype has held on as an enduring myth.[12]

On the other hand, writers assigning Texas to the West instead of the South sometimes seem to draw upon the same arguments to conclude that the state's belligerence and fascination with weapons is a result of the frontier heritage. That heritage certainly has its own stereotypes, including the violent cattle town, vigilante justice, the individualistic lawman, and the near-constant threat from Indian attacks. This introductory essay is not the place to resolve such debates, merely to indicate that these arguments are longstanding ones.[13] The South and the West both had violent underpinnings, and it is open to debate how each influenced the American military tradition or the Texas military experience.

Regardless of the section with which Texas is identified, one can contend that after the Reconstruction period of the 1860s and 1870s Texas—along with the rest of the states—began a long transition toward becoming more homogeneous, more broadly "American," and less sectional. One aspect of such a transition is the subject of William H. Leckie's chapter, "Black Regulars on the Texas Frontier, 1866–85." After the Civil War, for the first time in American history, African Americans were recruited from several states into the regular U.S. Army. As Leckie describes, many of those path-breaking soldiers were stationed in Texas, where they garrisoned a succession of forts and participated in a series of campaigns against Indian tribes in the Southwest. They established a creditable record as soldiers in Texas and elsewhere. Despite suffering from discrimination and racist violence, such as the incidents at Brownsville in 1906 and in Houston in 1917, their devoted service sustained the idea of keeping blacks in the regular armed forces into the twentieth century.[14]

An overlooked feature of military service in Texas was the role of women who accompanied soldiers to their posts. Sandra Myres was an authority on the subject. In her chapter on army wives in the nineteenth century, Myres provides a valuable summary of her own research. The diaries, letters, and published memoirs of soldiers' wives have contributed to a more complete picture of life in the army from the 1860s to the 1890s. This is especially true in such matters as interpersonal relationships, daily routines at army posts, and attitudes—particularly of officers—toward Hispanics, Indians, and African Americans. Since the 1970s, when she helped pioneer the field, Myres and other scholars have conducted significant new research that has underscored the place of families in the lives of military personnel and added much to what has been called the "new military history."[15]

Exploring another trail of the new military history, Joseph Porter's chapter describes U.S. Army captain John G. Bourke, a scientist-author as well as a tactician. Bourke's careful ethnological writings are vital to the understanding of both the Apache Indians and Texas Hispanics late in the nineteenth century. Porter's portrait of Bourke reveals the captain as an extraordinary officer for his day, one for whom science and writing were more important than field duty with troops. Bourke took advantage of his assignment in Texas to record his observations on the folkways of the people he found and to maintain the concept that some officers could be scientists as well as soldiers. Porter's chapter on Bourke appropriately focuses on the captain's time in Texas but also widens the view of subjects that can be incorporated into the Texas military experience.[16]

Many would agree that the 36th Infantry Division epitomizes the modern Texas military. Martin Blumenson effectively describes the campaigns of this division in World War II. He persuasively argues, however, that the 36th was a Texas division more by origin and tradition than in fact. Blumenson points out that its composition started changing soon after the war began. Recruits from all over the United States joined the division, transforming it from a National Guard unit into a standard U.S. infantry division. Blumenson's conclusion is an important correction of the long-standing notion that the T-Patchers were strictly a Texas outfit. However, the 36th retained a strong Texas flavor, not only because of its origin and place of training but also because of the number of its officers from Texas. General Fred Walker did not need to change the clublike staff and line officers until after the battle of Salerno in 1943.

Although many enlisted men and junior officers from outside Texas had joined the division before Salerno, the 36th lost much of its Texas flavor after the battle. Several officers were relieved from their posts. Replacements arrived for the assistant division commander, the division artillery officer, and four senior staff officers; in addition, six battalion commanders were relieved and two were captured.[17] Consequently, these changes produced a marked shift of the division away from its Texas heritage.

The most controversial episode in the history of the 36th Division was the battle at the Rapido River in mid-January, 1944. The division history called the attempt to cross the Rapido a "two-day nightmare," which Blumenson treats in detail in his book, *Bloody River: The Real Tragedy of the Rapido*.[18] He concludes that the division was caught in "perhaps a no-win situation," but also emphasizes that higher commanders complimented the unit by choosing it to make the Rapido crossing. Certainly the division commander, General Walker, did not see the operation as a compliment. In 1944 he was skeptical about the crossing and years later recalled it bitterly. "It was a tragedy that this fine Division had to be wrecked ... in an attempt to do the impossible. It was ordered to cross the Rapido River directly in front of the strongest German positions under conditions that violated sound tactical principles." According to Walker, the river was "unfordable" at the assigned location, and the crossing equipment given to the division was "unsuitable." Walker concluded that the heavy casualties the division suffered meant "unnecessary losses of fine men to no purpose."[19]

In war it is unfortunate but true that diversionary attacks seldom receive the same attention given the main effort. In this case, the Americans fought their main battle at the Anzio beachhead, and the Rapido diversion was one of the most difficult of all combat operations: crossing a river at a point well defended by the enemy. But it is up to the senior commanders to explain their plans to their subordinates so that a great effort will be made to fulfill every part of the plan. General Geoffrey Keyes, commander of the II Corps, did not convincingly describe to General Walker the need for an assault. General Mark Clark, Keyes's superior and leader of the Fifth Army, failed to impress on Walker how the attack on the Rapido would support the planned beachhead by drawing away German units that might otherwise reinforce Anzio. Any compliment that Clark paid to the division or appreciation he had for its soldiers was lost on the T-Patchers. After the war, in fact, antagonistic officers of the 36th criticized Clark so strongly that they forced a congressional investigation and held up Clark's promotion to the rank of major general in the regular army.[20] Perhaps the battle at the Rapido can be compared to the Alamo: a battle that could be viewed as a sacrifice to serve the larger cause elsewhere.

The 36th Division suffered severe losses in several battles: Salerno, the Rapido, and San Pietro, to name a few. The division has one of the longest battle records of any U.S. division in the European Theater of Operations in World War II. By the end of the war it was also one of the most battered divisions in the American army.

Roger Spiller reminds us that twentieth-century war is not neat lines on a headquarters map but soldiers against machines and individual soldiers against one another. Spiller shows why Audie Murphy became the best known of all Medal of Honor winners. Douglas MacArthur, for example, is remembered best as a general, not for the heroic acts that won him the medal. It is no wonder that Robert Kemble put Murphy on a short list of notable American soldiers, a list that included George C. Marshall, Dwight D. Eisenhower, and Omar N. Bradley.[21] By winning his medals, Murphy became a symbol: the archetype of the American combat soldier.

John Wayne's long movie career meant that he was not only a heroic symbol for servicemen in World War II but, as Richard Holmes points out, a symbol for American servicemen in Vietnam as well.[22] The Duke's towering stature comes as no surprise, but what about that of diminutive Audie Murphy? Ron Kovic, in his bitter Vietnam memoir, *Born on the Fourth of July*, recalled that as he shook hands with Marine recruiters "and stared up into their eyes, I couldn't help but feel I was shaking hands with John Wayne and Audie Murphy."[23] Lieutenant William Calley, infamous for his role in the My Lai massacre, also had recollections of Audie Murphy. "We thought we will go to Vietnam and be Audie Murphys. Kick in the door, run in the hooch, give it a good burst—kill!"[24] In the fires of war, however, Calley turned out to be quite unlike his hero. Murphy proved himself many times a resourceful leader, a sergeant who warranted promotion to the rank of lieutenant. On the other hand, Calley stands out as an example of the type of individual who would not have become an officer in previous wars, according to Guenter Lewy.[25]

Two other leaders of World War II represented the best qualities that Texans could claim for military officers from their state. One was Fleet Admiral Chester W. Nimitz. A native of Fredericksburg, Nimitz was a graduate of the U.S. Naval Academy and a professional naval officer who entered the navy in 1905. Nimitz rose to command the U.S. Pacific Fleet and Pacific Ocean areas. Through E. B. Potter's excellent biography, it is understandable why Nimitz became one of the most highly regarded American commanders of the Second World War. The other prominent Texan leader was Major General James Earl Rudder from Eden. A graduate of Texas A&M College in 1932, Rudder was called to active duty in 1941. He became associated with the development of the U.S. Army's Rangers. Holding the rank of lieutenant colonel, Rudder led the 2nd Ranger Battalion in the assault up Pointe du Hoc at Normandy on D-Day, June 6, 1944. Rudder's Rangers destroyed five large German artillery pieces that could have devastated American troops landing on Omaha and Utah beaches. Prestigious military officers such as Nimitz and Rudder preserved what many Texans regarded as the state's military tradition into the twentieth century.[26]

Moving from the individual in combat to a broader view, Don Graham and Tom Pilkington do a fine job introducing readers to the image of Texas and Texans in film and fiction. Graham asserts that Texas in general and its martial activities in particular have created rich fodder for Hollywood. Ironically, Graham contrasts how Texans have mythologized their defeats as well as celebrated their victories. Indeed, they have eulogized the fall of the Alamo alongside such signal victories as those over the Mexicans at San Jacinto, over several tribes of Indians in numerous skirmishes, and over the Nazis in Europe through the gripping story of Audie Murphy. Both Graham and Pilkington warn us to be skeptical of Texan stereotypes. They advise us to pay attention to the insightful exceptions to those stereotypes on screen and in novels that provide greater understanding about Texas and how it might fit into southern or American military traditions. Taken together, their chapters go beyond mere discussions of movies and books to link those expressions of popular culture to the larger issues of politics, society, and military history.

Although this book focuses on some important aspects of the Texas military experience, others also bear investigation. One such aspect is the interaction between cities and military posts and the proliferation of such installations, especially during World War II and the Cold War era. Numerous Texas cities, including San Antonio, Fort Worth, Wichita Falls, Lubbock, San Angelo, and El Paso, as well as entire counties, have reaped long-term benefits from hosting major military bases. Such relationships are not new, of course. For example, an article by Thomas T. Smith discusses the crucial relationship between Fort Inge and Uvalde from 1849 to 1869, and Robert Wooster's book surveys garrison life on the Texas frontier. During the years 1846–1900 the federal government established eighteen major U.S. Army posts and several small camps in Texas; some of them survived into the twentieth century.²⁷

In the 1930s and 1940s, a new wave of construction of military bases replaced several old frontier posts that had been closed five or six decades earlier. As air power became one of the measurements of national military strength, U.S. Army air bases popped up like cactus flowers to give pilots the advantage of excellent flying conditions in Texas. San Antonio, in particular, distinguished itself by hosting four army airfields (Brooks, Kelly, Lackland, and Randolph) as well as Fort Sam Houston (established in 1879, classified as a fort in 1890); serving as headquarters for one of the army's continental commands; and eventually housing a cluster of hospital facilities. The U.S. Navy picked Dallas, Corpus Christi, and Beeville as sites for naval air stations. Some of the principal aircraft companies located large manufacturing plants in Texas, especially near Dallas. Carswell Air Force Base, near Fort Worth, was the headquarters for major training and administrative commands.

These examples are by no means exhaustive, especially regarding military-related businesses and industries, but indicate the type and numbers of military-industrial and military-urban connections in twentieth-century Texas that would benefit from further scholarly examination. Questions abound. For instance, was Texas more receptive than other states to hosting a plethora of military bases? Did the selection of such bases simply come about through the astute politics of influential members of the state's congressional delegation? How did politics combine with climate, geography, the needs of the expanding American military services, and plans by corporations to locate in anti-union areas with cheap labor? These and other questions need to be covered as elements of the Texas military experience.²⁸

In both world wars of the twentieth century, Texas preserved an aspect of the "southern military tradition" by sending high numbers of volunteers (as well as thousands of draftees) into military service. Nearly two hundred thousand Texans enlisted or were drafted during the Great War, and of those approximately five thousand died while in service—10 percent of service deaths from a state with less than 5 percent of the nation's population. In the Second World War, Texas contributed 7 percent of the American armed services, and Texans also suffered disproportionately in service deaths—more than 7 percent of the total losses from 1941 to 1945. Perhaps too much can be made of these figures, but traditionalists would assert that they indicate a continuing commitment, even a devotion, to military matters well above that of the rest of the United States. They lend credence to historian Char Miller's recitation of conventional wisdom when he says that Texas is considered "one of the most martial of states."²⁹

How do the military experiences of other states compare with Texas? Two authors have advanced a claim for Oklahoma's military tradition, but greater weight can be given to such states as Virginia and New York. Using criteria such as a state's important military leaders, number and longevity of military posts and installations, and battles fought within its borders, Virginia and New York certainly have significant military histories.[30] Although some Texans might blanch at the idea of comparing the military credentials of the Lone Star and Empire states, even the vaunted tradition of Texas A&M University—providing more officers than any other college or university for the American military services between 1941 and 1945—has been challenged by a neighboring rival, Louisiana State University.[31]

Another major issue worthy of examination involves Hispanics and the Texas military experience. The legacies of Spanish colonialism (1519–1821) are evident in many ways in modern Texas: place names, locations of cities, food, laws and legal practices, architecture, music, and religion, to list some obvious ones.[32] From 1821 to 1836, after the end of Spanish rule, Texas was a province in the Republic of Mexico. Mexican military forces engaged rebellious Texans in the Texas Revolution (1835–36) and U.S. military forces (including Texans) in the Mexican War (1846–48). Many cross-border raids and skirmishes occurred during the next century. It is logical to ask, How did Spanish and Mexican examples influence Texas military development? One way was the continuing use of sites established by the Spanish for major military posts, with San Antonio as the foremost example.[33] Beyond that, other influences are open to question.

Although it is clear that Spanish and Mexican culture permeated Texas life in many ways, establishing a military model was not one of them. Anglo-Texans sometimes remarked on the bravery of individual Mexican soldiers or officers and acknowledged that some Mexican army units were well trained and well led. Overall, however, most Anglo-Texans have taken a "rather disdainful view of Hispanics and Mexicans," according to historian Donald Chipman. Two other scholars, Arnoldo De León and David Montejano, support Chipman's conclusion. De León emphasizes that from 1821 to 1900 a central theme in Texas history has been the general lack of respect displayed by Anglo-Texans toward Hispanics. Montejano's work reinforces De León's and carries the same theme through 1936.[34] Therefore, it appears that a combination of Anglo-Texan disdain for Hispanics and strong Anglo-European military traditions have won out over Hispanic influence.

The twentieth-century roles of Texas women, African Americans, and Hispanics in the military need closer investigation. These and other questions await the attention of students and scholars as they explore other avenues of the Texas military experience.

THE ALAMO AS ICON

Paul Andrew Hutton

ON MARCH 6, 1836, THE GARRISON OF THE FORTRESS ALAMO, in San Antonio de Béxar, Texas, numbering just under two hundred, was overwhelmed and slaughtered by a vastly superior force of Mexican troops under General Antonio López de Santa Anna. Although in a military sense the battle was of little significance, it nevertheless became a symbolic rallying point for the Texan revolutionaries. It provided a battle cry that has become world famous: "Remember the Alamo!"

Similar battles, in which one side is annihilated, have of course long fascinated mankind. Peoples in many nations point proudly to such events in their history. The story is often the same, although the details may differ. The heroes are always vastly outnumbered by a vicious enemy from a culturally inferior nation bent on the utter destruction of the heroic band's people. These men fight for their way of life in a battle that is clearly hopeless. They know that they are doomed but go willingly to their deaths in order to bleed the enemy and buy time for their people. Often they are betrayed, sometimes by the failure of their countrymen to rescue them, and usually a lone survivor carries the tale of their sublime sacrifice to the world. They perish with a fierce élan that turns their defeat into a spiritual victory. The leader of the defeated band is often elevated to the status of a national hero, while the battle becomes a point of cultural pride: an example of patriotism and self-sacrifice. Such was the case with Saul at Mount Gilboa, Leonidas at Thermopylae, Roland at Roncesvalles, Custer at the Little Big Horn, and Gordon at Khartoum. Such is clearly the case with the Alamo and its trinity of heroes: William Barret Travis, Jim Bowie, and Davy Crockett.

There have always been two Alamos: the Alamo of historical fact, and the Alamo of our collective imagination. One was a mission and a fortress and is now a shrine. The other has become a cultural and political symbol, an icon to be revered. But symbols have many uses and can be portrayed in many ways. Thus, a name enshrined in historical memory has also been used to sell dog food and rental cars, banking services and real estate, history and propaganda.

The line between the Alamo of fact and the Alamo of popular fancy is often blurred. Although an amazingly large body of historical and popular literature has been generated on the battle, there has never been an adequate serious study of it by a professional academic historian. Therefore, competent popular historians such as Walter Lord, who has written the best book on the battle, have not had the usual body of solid secondary materials to draw upon. Academic historians have deserted the field, leaving the battle to the popularizers and propagandists. Those who have written about the Alamo, for the most part, have often repeated false stories recounted in books, articles, and newspapers. The written historical record is a disappointing one.[1]

One of the reasons that academic historians have not written on the Alamo is because it is so popular a topic. So much has been produced on the battle and its heroes that many assume everything has already been covered. Others dismiss the subject as too trivial to warrant their attention. As a result, the Alamo of our collective imagination has become dominant, assuming an importance in the national mind that is greater than the historical Alamo.

From popular histories, novels, poems, children's books, paintings, songs, television shows, and movies has emerged the Alamo that we know today. For the most part this body of material has treated the Alamo in a hagiographic manner, perpetuating false notions but also developing powerful cultural symbols. The lives of heroes are a testament to the values and aspirations of those who admire them. If their images change over time, they may act as a barometer of fluctuating societal values. By looking at a symbolic event like the Alamo as it has been portrayed in popular culture, we can learn much about the character of the people who create, nourish, and cherish the image. Thus, if we can understand what the Alamo means to Texans, and to Americans generally, we can discover much about their changing values, character, and self-image as a people.

Although the Alamo is an important national symbol, it is far more vital as a creation myth for Texas. Myth is used here in its folkloric sense, not as a word meaning falsehood. Although a true myth may indeed bear little resemblance to historical fact, that is irrelevant to its folkloric function. A powerful mythic saga like the Alamo tale is embraced by a people and characterizes them, expressing shared beliefs and cultural symbols. As

The Alamo, circa 1935. Courtesy Zintgraff Photographers, San Antonio.

a creation myth for Texans, the Alamo story helps define them as a people, making them distinct from other Americans.

The tale embraces powerful themes of courage, sacrifice, betrayal, and redemption. Its trinity of heroes—Travis, Bowie, and Crockett—have since been deified beyond recognition as mere mortals. This was not necessarily a gradual development. Contemporaries immediately saw the mythic potential of the battle. The *Telegraph and Texas Register* for March 24, 1836, proclaimed as much in an early account of the battle. "Spirits of the mighty, though fallen! Honors and rest are with ye: the spark of immortality which animated your forms, shall brighten into a flame, and Texas, the whole world, shall hail ye like demi-gods of old, as founders of new actions, and as patterns of imitation!"[2]

Texans quickly recognized the parallels that existed between the Alamo and similar struggles in antiquity. Americans have long been burdened by an inferiority complex toward Europe and often point proudly to national achievements that compare favorably, or surpass, similar European events or cultural landmarks. Texans were anxious to see elements of a unique regional identity coming out of their revolutionary struggle, but they could not help comparing it to an equally powerful symbolic battle from the past.

On March 26, 1836, the citizens of Nacogdoches issued a resolution in praise of the defense of the Alamo that harkened back to ancient days. "The tongue of every noble spirit of whom we speak is silent in death and we anticipate in succinct and imperfect narrative the future Glory of their fame. They died martyrs to liberty; and on the altar of their sacrifice will be made many a vow that shall break the shackles of tyranny. Thermopylae, is no longer without a parallel, and when time shall consecrate the dead of the Alamo, Travis and his companions will be named in rivalry with Leonidas and his Spartan band."[3]

Thomas Jefferson Green, one of the leaders of the tragic Mier Expedition,[4] improved on that sentiment with a famous quote that was inscribed on the first Alamo monument in Austin: "Thermopylae had her messenger of defeat—the Alamo had none."

Thermopylae was, of course, the battle in northern Greece during which a small band of Spartan warriors sacrificed themselves to stall the onslaught of Xerxes' Persian hordes in 480 B.C. Although all but one were killed, the battle gave the other Greek city-states time to mobilize their forces and drive the Persians out of Greece, thus ensuring the survival of western civilization and the birth of democracy. The Alamo had now matched that ancient struggle and gone it one better. No one, according to the myth, survived the battle of the Alamo. As with the struggle at Thermopylae, the early Texans viewed the conflict at the Alamo as a contest of civilizations: freedom versus tyranny, democracy versus despotism, Protestantism versus Catholicism, the New World culture of the United States versus the Old World culture of Mexico, Anglo-Saxons versus the mongrelized mixture of Indian and Spanish races, and ultimately, the forces of good over evil.

A creation myth draws lines of good and evil that are always razor sharp. The story is meant to give to a people a strong and unique self-image. It does not cater to the enemy in any way. Thus the myth of the Alamo is often stunningly racist. The myth is a nineteenth-century creation, and it reflects the racial sensibilities of that time. This racial mentality lasted well into the twentieth century, although in more muted form.

The fact that *tejanos*, Hispanic Texans, had died fighting against the centralist government of Santa Anna at the Alamo was generally ignored in the historical and popular literature on the battle until the 1960s. Until then, writers tended to share Colonel Travis's opinion of the Hispanic residents of Béxar. "The citizens of this municipality are all our enemies, except those who have joined us heretofore. We have three Mexicans now in the fort; those who have not joined with us in this extremity, should be declared public enemies, and their property should aid in paying the expenses of the war."[5]

At least seven *tejanos* died fighting with Travis in the Alamo, and another, Brigido Guerrero, may well have talked his way out of the Alamo during the battle by claiming to be a prisoner of the Texans. Three *tejanos* were sent from the Alamo as messengers before the final assault. The leader of the *tejanos* in the Alamo, Juan Seguín, was one of these messengers.

Seguín, scion of a wealthy and influential Hispanic family, had long been a friend of the Anglo settlers in Texas. His liberal sensibilities bridled at the centralist dictatorship of Santa Anna. His father, Erasmo, was a warm friend to Stephen F. Austin and Jim Bowie and had been elected as delegate to the convention that ultimately declared Texas independent. Juan Seguín's company of *tejano* cavalry had proven invaluable as scouts in the early days of the war.

Seguín, who held the rank of captain in the Texas army, had scouted with Travis to ensure that General Martín Perfecto de Cos's defeated army withdrew from Texas late in 1835, and they later rode into the Alamo together. On the night of February 25, accompanied by his aide Antonio Cruz y Arocha, Seguín made a daring ride through the encircling Mexicans to carry a message from Travis to Sam Houston. After delivering his message, Seguín raised a company of twenty-five *tejanos* and hurried to Cíbolo to await the arrival of James Fannin's men from Goliad in order to march with them to rescue the Alamo. But the inept, timid Fannin never came, while Seguín waited impatiently and time ran out for the defenders of the Alamo. Texas has since raised monuments to the diffident Fannin, who eventually surrendered his army and was executed by the Mexicans, while the bold patriot Seguín has been ignored, despite his heroic participation in the battle of San Jacinto.

During the liberal revival of the 1960s, with interest in ethnic minorities, civil rights, and pluralism on the rise, Seguín was suddenly rediscovered. He became the standard Hispanic pictured in school texts and popular histories on Texas. He was featured in John Wayne's 1960 epic film, *The Alamo;* in a program on the Public Broadcasting Service in 1982; in the 1987 NBC television movie *The Alamo: Thirteen Days to Glory;* and in the 1988 IMAX spectacle *Alamo: The Price of Freedom*. A fine pictorial biography in 1982 by the noted Texas graphic artist Jack Jackson, entitled *Los Tejanos: The True Story of Juan Seguín and the Texas-Mexicans during the Rising of the Lone Star,* presented Seguín as a heroic and tragic figure.[6]

To the Hispanic left, however, Seguín was anything but an acceptable hero. Rudy Acuña, a well-known Chicano historian, resigned from the advisory board of the PBS program on Seguín, protesting that "to make heroes of the Mexican people defending the Alamo is like making heroes of the Vichy government . . . *Seguín* represents an accommodationist point of view that promotes the wrong kind of assimilation." David J. Weber, noted historian of the Southwest and the Spanish Borderlands frontier and the leading member of the PBS advisory board, disagreed. Weber preferred to view Seguín as "a tragic figure in Mexican-American history caught between two cultures in collision."[7]

Even after the liberal renaissance of the 1960s, Seguín remained visible as a symbol of the Hispanics who fought for Texas independence. More conservative writers then could point to Seguín in answer to charges that the Revolution was nothing but a racial conflict and an Anglo theft of Mexican land. According to these writers, the participation of Seguín and others, such as Lorenzo de Zavala, proved that the Texas Revolution was a struggle for liberty against despotism, as traditionalists had long claimed.

One standard myth of the Alamo portrayed the defenders as fighting and dying for their rights as citizens under the Mexican Constitution of 1824. The flag of the Alamo pictured in books, paintings, and movies reinforced that view. It was a Mexican tricolor with the date 1824 replacing the Mexican eagle. There is no evidence to support the belief that such a flag ever flew over the Alamo. Reuben M. Potter seems to have made up the flag in 1860.[8] Although Juan Seguín and his *tejanos* may have been fighting for a more liberal Mexico, the Anglos in the Alamo were fighting for independence. They agreed with Travis, who wrote from the Alamo on March 3: "Let the Convention go on and make a declaration of independence, and we will then understand, and the world will understand, what we are fighting for. If independence is not declared, I shall lay down my arms, and so will the men under my command. But under the flag of independence, we are ready to peril our lives a hundred times a day."⁹

Travis, who was ardently anti-Mexican, was not about to fight for his rights as a Mexican citizen under a modified Mexican banner, and neither were the men under his command. Almost all of them were recent emigrants to Texas, and it was unlikely that many of them knew anything about the Mexican Constitution. The only flag captured at the Alamo (or at least the only one reported by Santa Anna) was the blue banner of a band of Louisiana volunteers, the New Orleans Greys. Santa Anna sent it back to Mexico City as evidence that he was battling Anglo filibusters. His characterization of the Anglo defenders of the Alamo is probably just as close to the truth as the Texan vision of them as a heroic band dedicated to the defense of liberty. After all, one of the Texans' major grievances with the Mexican Constitution was that it banned slavery. In 1836, the Texas Revolution was generally regarded north of the Mason-Dixon line as a conspiracy on the part of the Southern slavocracy to extend its power westward. The defenders of the Alamo certainly fought for freedom, but it was the freedom to economically prosper without Mexican economic or political interference.

Nevertheless, defenders of the Alamo myth have been quick to point to the *tejanos* as proof that the battle was part of the eternal struggle for liberty and not a racial conflict, a land grab, or an effort to expand slavery. When Arizona governor Bruce Babbitt dared to suggest in a 1979 speech in San Antonio that the "Alamo is a symbol of the problem in our relationship with Mexico . . . a sacred symbol to Texans and an extension of the American ideal. But to Mexico, it's a symbol of territory lost, a nation plundered by overbearing gringo neighbors," he was loudly attacked by Texans who pointed to the *tejanos* of the Alamo as proof that race had nothing to do with the battle.¹⁰

"The Alamo stands as one of the most cherished examples in recorded history of mankind's eternal struggle for human rights," thundered an editorial in the *Lubbock Avalance-Journal*. "It is not a racial symbol, nor even a nationalist symbol as Gov. Babbitt's ignorance would have him believe, but a beacon for all the world to see that man's struggle against repression is never in vain. Gov. Babbitt overlooks, if he ever knew, that many Mexicans living in what is now Texas joined in—and gave their lives for—the Revolution against a totalitarian regime personified by Santa Anna."¹¹

"The heroes of the Alamo don't need defending against a politician two states away," huffed then–Texas attorney general Mark White. "The Alamo was part of Texas' fight for liberty, which was backed by Mexicans and anglos alike and decided in 1836 at San Jacinto."[12]

The Bryan *Eagle* angrily pointed out that the Alamo was "a shrine representing, not war with Mexico, but a Texas struggle for liberty which was endorsed by most Mexicans as well."[13] Juan Seguín and his handful of *tejanos*, so long ignored by Texans, had by 1979 been magnified in numbers to represent "most Mexicans" in Texas.

Ruben Bonilla, national president of the League of United Latin-American Citizens, defended Babbitt's statement. "Texas suffers from an Alamo mentality," Bonilla declared. "As a result of that, Mexican-Americans have been denied access to political and social systems of this state and country." Bonilla said that Mexican-American leaders in Texas agreed with the Arizona governor's viewpoint. "We support Gov. Babbitt's statements. We have our pride as Texans in the Alamo, but we also recognize that the United States has a paternalistic attitude toward Mexico." Bonilla, a Corpus Christi attorney, was surprised by the sudden interest in *tejano* defenders of the Alamo as expressed by critics of Babbitt. "American and Texas history books have held up Hispanics for ridicule, embarrassment and humiliation," Bonilla said. "Contributions of Hispanics are lost in the back pages of history, like patriots such as Juan Seguín who fought valiantly for Texas' freedom."[14]

If, for some, the "Alamo mentality" symbolizes racial repression, for most Texans and Americans the old mission remains symbolic of democracy triumphant through defeat. The most cherished moment of the Alamo myth perfectly captures that democratic spirit: Travis's line in the dust.

According to tradition, Travis called the weary garrison together during a lull in the Mexican bombardment the evening of March 3, 1836. James Butler Bonham had brought word that Fannin was not coming, and Travis then fully realized that the Alamo was doomed. He faced his men and shared with them the news that Fannin would not be sending reinforcements. Although there was no hope of victory, Travis was determined to stay in the Alamo and sell his life as dearly as possible in order to buy more time for Texans to the north and east to organize an army. Drawing his saber, he drew a line in the pale dust before him and asked those who would stand with him and die for liberty to cross over.

It was a moment of sublime democratic choice as, one by one, every member of the garrison made his personal decision to die for freedom instead of live under tyranny. Jim Bowie, too ill to lift himself from his cot, asked his friends to carry him across. Finally, only one man remained on the other side of the line, a friend of Bowie's from France named Louis "Moses" Rose. Later that night, he climbed the wall and vanished into the darkness beyond.

The line that Travis drew became the most dramatic moment in the Alamo saga. The men of the Alamo voted with their physical beings—with their lives—for the cause of freedom, choosing death willingly with Texan determination. The symbolic power of the line and the men's bold decision is overpowering. Painters, novelists, popular historians, and film makers all embraced it as part of the Alamo story. The legend appears in various forms: sometimes the men are asked to cross the line if they wish to leave, and often all the men choose to stay. In the 1955 film *The Last Command*, Travis speaks to his men in a driving rainstorm and they all cross the line. In John Wayne's *The Alamo*, five years later, Travis speaks to Jim Bowie's volunteers who have decided to depart and does not draw the line. After his speech, Bowie and his men all move over to join him and stay. In whatever form the story takes the message is always the same: the defenders of the Alamo willingly chose to sacrifice themselves so that Texas might live. "But nobody forgets the line," wrote J. Frank Dobie in 1939. "It is drawn too deep and straight."[15]

But did Travis really draw the line? For years historians found it a difficult tale to accept. It had not appeared until 1873, when William P. Zuber's article "An Escape from the Alamo" appeared in the *Texas Almanac*. According to Zuber, Louis Rose staggered up to his father's cabin in Grimes County a few days after the fall of the Alamo. They took in the exhausted man, and he related the story of the line to them, complete with a fulsome version of Travis's speech to the defenders of the Alamo. Even though Zuber later admitted that he made up much of the speech, the story of the line was quickly appropriated by poets, novelists, and historians. The most influential of the latter was Anna J. Hardwicke Pennybacker, whose *History of Texas for Schools* contained an even more embellished version of Zuber's story. First published in 1888, Pennybacker's history of Texas went through six editions and was historical gospel to generations of Texas schoolchildren.[16]

Although the story never lost its fascination for poets and novelists, it has not fared as well with historians in the twentieth century. The revised edition of Pennybacker's history that appeared in 1908 dropped Zuber's story. Clarence Wharton's 1932 school text, which became the standard Texas history for years, ignored the story. Finally Amelia Williams, for years considered the final authority on the Alamo, dismissed the story of the line as "the creation of a vivid imagination" in her 1931 doctoral dissertation on the Alamo.[17]

But then, in 1939, a Texas history buff named R. B. Blake rummaged through court and land records in Nacogdoches County and discovered proof that Louis Rose had indeed lived and had been in the Alamo. Rose had testified in several cases concerning land claims for relatives of Alamo victims. Furthermore, Blake discovered that it was common knowledge among old-timers in Nacogdoches, where Rose operated a meat market, that the old Frenchman had been in the Alamo and had left the garrison. People frequently asked Rose why he had not stayed with the others in the Alamo, to which the reply invariably came, "By God, I wasn't ready to die."[18]

Walter Lord, in *A Time to Stand*, concluded that although the story of the line was basically true, it had been garbled in Rose's original tale to Zuber or, more likely, greatly embellished by Zuber. Lord turned up an 1876 interview with Susannah Dickinson, the only adult Anglo survivor, in which she stated that on the night before the final Mexican assault Travis had called the men together, explained that the situation was hopeless, and offered any who wished to depart the opportunity to do so. One man, she called him Ross, stepped out of the ranks and was gone before dawn.[19]

So the shining legend has a basis in truth, even though the actual line was never drawn across the dusty ground of the Alamo compound. But it happened on March 5 instead of March 3, which explains why the Alamo's two final couriers, John W. Smith and James Allen, never mentioned it. Even without the line, however, that sublime moment of democratic choice occurred in all its triumphant glory. Of course, the line will eternally live in the popular imagination whether or not it was drawn. And ultimately, that is more important than the historical record. J. Frank Dobie understood this when he wrote: "It is a line that nor all the piety nor wit of research will ever blot out. It is a Grand Canyon cut into the bedrock of human emotions and heroical impulses."[20]

Even though the story of the line is central to the symbolic power of the Alamo, it has never caused as much argument or bitter controversy as another part of the traditional tale of the Alamo: the death of Davy Crockett. This controversy would seem ridiculously unimportant if so many people did not get regularly exercised over it. After all, no matter what the exact details of his death, Crockett still perished as the same martyr for freedom. Nevertheless, a grand debate continues to rage over whether he went down fighting like a tiger at bay or was overpowered and surrendered with several others, only to be executed by direct order of Santa Anna.

Interestingly, the story of Crockett's surrender was quite common in the nineteenth century and seemed to upset no one. Contemporary newspaper accounts of the battle often stated that Crockett had surrendered and was then executed by the Mexicans. This was often used by the press in 1836 as further evidence of Santa Anna's barbarity. Even Crockett's oldest son, Congressman John Wesley Crockett, accepted the surrender story as true, writing in 1840 that "while Santa Anna was a prisoner in Texas, I am informed, he stated to a number of gentlemen, that he [Crockett] was saved alive by Alcuante [Almonte], and that he, Santa Anna, ordered him to be put to death after it was all over." The story was retold repeatedly in early popular histories of the frontier. Theodore Roosevelt included it in his "Remember the Alamo" story in *Hero Tales from American History* (1895). It was not considered to be a negative reflection on Crockett.[21]

Edward S. Ellis, whose popular *The Life of Colonel David Crockett* was published in 1884 and went through numerous editions, also recounted the surrender story in such a way as to cast Crockett in a heroic light.

> At last only six of the garrison were left alive. They were surrounded by General Castrillon and his soldiers. The officer shouted to them to surrender, promising that their lives should be spared. In the little group of Spartans were Davy Crockett and Travis, so exhausted they were scarcely able to stand....
>
> There were a few brave and humane officers, and among them were General Castrillon and Burdillon. They spoke sympathizingly to Crockett and Travis, and with several other officers walked to where the scowling Santa Anna stood and asked that the surrender of the few survivors might be received.
>
> The reply was an order that all should be shot. Seeing his treachery, the enraged Crockett roused himself, and swinging his Bowie aloft, made a furious rush for the Mexican Nan Sahib. The intrepid Tennessean was riddled with bullets before he could pass half the intervening distance. Almost at the same moment, the other five were shot down.[22]

This version of Crockett's death is certainly fanciful. We know with some certainty, for instance, that Travis was killed on the north wall early in the final assault. Ellis copied his version of Crockett's death from Richard Penn Smith's spurious Crockett autobiography, *Col. Crockett's Exploits and Adventures in Texas* (1836), which in turn got it from early newspaper accounts based on the eyewitness statement of a Mexican soldier. The point to be made here is not that the Ellis or Smith versions are correct in every detail but that they were accepted by most readers without argument. As late as the early 1950s, juvenile histories and comic books were repeating this version of Crockett's death.

Then, in December, 1954, the "Disneyland" television program on ABC aired the first episode of a three-part series on Davy Crockett. By the time Fess Parker as Crockett went down swinging his rifle, Old Betsy, at the advancing Mexicans in the final episode, a craze of unprecedented proportions was sweeping the nation.

After seven incredible months of a merchandising bonanza in which every conceivable kind of item carried the Davy Crockett label—coonskin caps, toy soldier sets, toy guns, bicycles, towels, pajamas, soap, wallets, pillows, bedspreads, purses, and even ladies' underwear—the Crockett craze began a sharp decline. But the Disney version of Crockett was fixed in the minds of a whole generation of Americans. Seven million copies of "The Ballad of Davy Crockett" record were sold, and every one of those buyers now knew for certain just how Davy had died—fighting to the bitter end with his rifle as a club—though the audience never actually saw Crockett die in the Disney show. There is a slow fade as he wades into the Mexicans—the last defender of the Alamo.

Both the 1955 film *The Last Command* and the 1960 film *The Alamo* depict Crockett blowing up the powder magazine as the Mexicans rush upon him. This is a version of Crockett's death that is based upon nothing except a Hollywood scriptwriter's imagination. Robert Evans, the Texan in charge of the Alamo's powder, reportedly attempted such an act near the end of the battle but was shot before he could torch the magazine.

When Walter Lord wrote *A Time to Stand,* the best book to date on the Alamo, he trod a careful middle ground concerning Crockett's death. He included the story of the execution of the captured Texans but did not identify any of them. In an appendix, he addressed the question of Crockett's end and noted that several reliable Mexican eyewitnesses agreed that the famous frontiersman was captured and then executed on order of Santa Anna.[23]

Of the Mexican sources on the Alamo battle, none was more reliable than the diary of José Enrique de la Peña, an officer on Santa Anna's staff. First published in Mexico in 1955, a new translation of de la Peña's diary was published in 1975 entitled *With Santa Anna in Texas: A Personal Narrative of the Revolution.* Translated and edited by Carmen Perry, former director of the Daughters of the Republic of Texas Library at the Alamo, the 202-page book contained a single page relating the execution of Crockett. Said de la Peña:

> Some seven men had survived the general carnage and, under the protection of General Castrillón, they were brought before Santa Anna. Among them was one of great stature, well proportioned, with regular features, in whose face there was the imprint of adversity, but in whom one also noticed a degree of resignation and nobility that did him honor. He was the naturalist David Crockett, well known in North America for his unusual adventures, who had undertaken to explore the country and who, finding himself in Béjar at the very moment of surprise, had taken refuge in the Alamo, fearing that his status as a foreigner might not be respected. Santa Anna answered Castrillón's intervention in Crockett's behalf with a gesture of indignation and, addressing himself to the sappers, the troops closest to him, ordered his execution. . . . Though tortured before they were killed, these unfortunates died without complaining and without humiliating themselves before their torturers.[24]

Perry's book set off quite a controversy as journalists picked up on the Crockett death scene as a quick way to get a headline. "Students of American history and John Wayne fans take note. The legendary story of the Alamo may need revision," declared the *Denver Post*. "Has the King of the Wild Frontier been relieved of his coon-skin crown?" asked the *Jackson [Tennessee] Sun*. "Naturally, it will be hard for a generation that grew up singing 'Born on a mountain-top in Tennessee' to accept the mental image of a cowardly Crockett groveling in the Alamo corner," noted the *Jackson Sun* reporter, who had obviously not even bothered to read the one page in the book that she was writing about.[25]

"Did Crockett die at the Alamo? Historian Carmen Perry says no," read the headline in the October 13, 1975, issue of *People* magazine. Above a picture of Perry the magazine ran a photo of John Wayne as Crockett. The press, absolutely ignorant of any historical works on the Alamo, consistently used movie versions of Crockett's death as a reference point for their readers. That, of course, made perfect sense, since most people know nothing about Crockett or the Alamo except what they have seen on television or in the movies. They react to such controversies from the perspective of the films they have seen. Perry was uncomfortable with all the publicity, and especially with the anonymous hate mail and late-night phone calls. Nevertheless, she staunchly defended de la Peña's account. "People don't believe his account because they don't want to believe it," she stoically noted. They "prefer to live by legend." Soon enough, however, the

Daughters of the Republic of Texas rallied to support their former librarian, and another organization, the Sons of the Republic of Texas, gave *With Santa Anna in Texas* its prestigious Summerfield G. Roberts Award as the outstanding Texas book of 1975. Noted Texas historian Joe Frantz was perplexed as to what all the shouting was about. "I think its significance is of detail," said Frantz. It was, he asserted, "whether I die now or whether I die a half-hour later."[26]

Partly in response to the controversy over the diary, Dan Kilgore, a certified public accountant in Corpus Christi who served as president of the Texas State Historical Association in 1977, delivered a speech on Crockett's death as his presidential address. He expanded that speech into a carefully researched and intelligent monograph published in 1978 entitled *How Did Davy Die?* Kilgore concluded that the mass of evidence supported the de la Peña account of Crockett's death.[27]

The reaction to Perry's book was mild compared to the ravings directed at Kilgore. "Them's Fightin' Words. Davy's Legend Smudged," ran the headline in Kilgore's hometown newspaper, the *Corpus Christi Times*. "Any Texan worth his lizard skin cowboy boots and Willie Nelson albums knows better than to smear the legend of Davy Crockett." Critics seemed to lump intellectuals and Communists together in their defense of Crockett. A letter to Kilgore from Alabama labeled the author "a mealy-mouthed intellectual" who deserved to "have his mouth washed out with soap." A letter to Kilgore from Fort Myers, Florida, agreed. "We know the reason for this. This is one of the Communists' plans to degrade our heroes. . . . He's still king of the Wild Frontier."[28]

Peggy Dibrell, who chaired the Daughters of the Republic of Texas Alamo Committee, disputed Kilgore's version of Crockett's death and then amazingly suggested that the version in the John Wayne movie was correct. "There were plans made before the battle to blow up the gunpowder stored in the main shrine if it was overrun," Dibrell remarked in the San Antonio *Express News* of March 6, 1985, "and Davy Crockett was attempting to do that when he was killed." Such a ridiculous statement is reflective of the triumph of popular culture over historical fact, even among those entrusted with preserving an accurate record of the Texas Revolution. Dan Kilgore watched in amazement as the controversy swirled around him. He remained good-natured about it all but did note sarcastically: "I wouldn't have minded all this if they'd bought my books. Nobody even read the damn book."[29]

With the celebration of the Texas sesquicentennial in 1986, there was a flurry of publications, museum exhibits, and film projects. All of these further established the important place the Alamo as icon holds in both Texas and American culture. Noted artist Eric von Schmidt completed a massive painting of the battle that was the centerpiece of an Alamo exhibit at San Antonio's Witte Museum and was later featured in *Smithsonian* magazine. Southern Methodist University's DeGolyer Library developed an Alamo exhibit in 1985 that was first displayed at the library in Dallas and then, in an abbreviated format, traveled throughout Texas. Susan Prendergast Schoelwer's lavish catalog of that exhibit, *Alamo Images: Changing Perceptions of a Texas Experience,* quickly became a classic of Alamo literature. The Smithsonian Institution's National Portrait Gallery and the Tennessee State Museum put together an impressive exhibit to commemorate the 200th anniversary of David Crockett's birth that stood in both Washington, D.C., and Nashville.[30]

Several television productions focusing on the Alamo were also planned to mark the sesquicentennial. Two of these, Rex Sparger's twenty-hour miniseries *Going to the Alamo* and Lorimar's *Roll Call at the Alamo,* received considerable publicity but never made it into production. Two television films, however, were completed: *Houston: The Legend of Texas* on CBS in 1986 and *The Alamo: Thirteen Days to Glory* on NBC in January, 1987. In March, 1988, *Alamo: The Price of Freedom* opened at the Alamo IMAX Theater at the San Antonio Rivercenter Mall. This forty-eight-minute, highly patriotic docudrama has played continually ever since on its sixty-one-and-a-half by eighty-four-and-a-half-foot screen. As patrons wait in line for each screening, they can gaze wistfully out huge picture windows at the grounds of the real Alamo just below them.[31]

Both the University of Nebraska Press and the University of Tennessee Press marked the sesquicentennial with new paperback editions of David Crockett's autobiography. The former also reissued Virgil E. Baugh's lame 1960 book, *Rendezvous at the Alamo: Highlights in the Lives of Bowie, Crockett, and Travis,* and Richard Boyd Hauck's masterful 1982 bibliographic guide, *David Crockett: A Handbook.* Two new Crockett biographies also appeared: James Wakefield Burke's fanciful and novelistic *David Crockett: The Man behind the Myth* and Gary Foreman's fine pictorial compilation *Crockett: The Gentleman from the Cane.* The University of North Carolina Press reissued James Shackford's 1956 Crockett biography, with a new introduction by Michael Lofaro, and Walter Blair's folksy *Davy Crockett: Legendary Frontier Hero* was reprinted by Lincoln-Herndon Press.[32]

Perhaps the best of the sesquicentennial Crockett books, Michael Lofaro's anthology *Davy Crockett: The Man, the Legend, the Legacy, 1786–1986,* was also the most controversial. Some of the heat was taken off Perry and Kilgore as the defenders of the "true historical faith" assailed this latest revisionist. "Professor shoots holes in Crockett myth," ran the headline in the April 17, 1986, *Knoxville Journal*. "Davy Crockett never wore a coonskin cap, didn't go to Texas to fight for independence, and wasn't killed clubbing Mexicans to death at the Alamo." A column by that paper's city editor accused Lofaro of "turning our own East Tennessee hero into a frontier streaker." Knoxville columnist Doug Morris hoped it was not true, pleading: "Our heroes are precious few. Don't make us learn history all over again."[33]

South of the Red River there was no such worry that history might need to be relearned. "Davy Crockett died fighting at the Alamo. He did not surrender. He did not ask for quarter," railed San Angelo *Standard Times* city editor Bob Boyd. Such tales, he claimed, were concocted "by revisionist and sloppy historians eager to make a name by claiming spurious proof that Crockett tried to surrender after the Mexicans broke into the Alamo." A spokesperson for the Daughters of the Republic of Texas dismissed the book, noting that "I think we have a few invaders whose sole intention is to destroy any of the heroism of the Alamo."[34]

I was bemused by the furor over Lofaro's excellent book, having felt some mild stings from outraged traditionalists over an article on the Alamo I had written for the March, 1986, *American History Illustrated*. It was a rather straightforward, heroic, and traditional narrative piece, but because it included the Crockett capture story it raised the hackles of a few readers. I had been contemplating writing a biography of Crockett for some time when Stephen Harrigan and Gregory Curtis of *Texas Monthly* asked me to write a sesquicentennial piece on the Alamo hero for their magazine. This, I thought, would be a great way to get started on my Crockett biography project, so I promptly agreed. I wrote what could be considered a slavishly adoring essay, which was lavishly presented as their November, 1986, cover story. I could not imagine that my essay would upset anyone, even though Harrigan, knowing the citizens of his state better than I, had wryly warned me to be prepared.[35]

Harrigan was right. "I am a Texas history teacher in McAllen," thundered a letter to *Texas Monthly*, "and what Mr. Hutton wrote amounts to blasphemy. In this sesquicentennial year Texas heroes should be revered, not destroyed. They should be held in esteem at all times, but especially so this year. If Mr. Hutton has a problem with heroes, then he should take care of it alone. . . . I will never teach my students what he wrote. A real Texan would not." Added another reader: "I have just finished reading the latest witch-hunt on David Crockett . . . and unlike the author of what is actually repetitious, warmed-over myth about how Crockett died at the Alamo the real David Crockett would not have written a dime-store comic book on hearsay."[36]

"You news media people have done it again! Some guy, out to make a buck, hacks to death another national hero! It's too bad Custer, Patton, Elvis, and ole Davy aren't alive to defend themselves," chimed in an outraged reader from Austin. And so it went, with a veritable avalanche of mail reaching my New Mexico office protesting this base revision of history. None quite matched the vitriol of a lady in Algood, Tennessee, who wrote: "Why don't you find something or somebody to write about (You call it research?) besides Americans who were *real men*, not like you gutless wonders of today, who call yourselves *men*. What would you have kids of today have for their heroes? The longhaired, dirty stinking, foul-mouthed noise makers who call themselves singers but are a bunch of garbage. 'Historians' such as you could never measure up to these great *men*, so stop trying." I was, quite naturally, encouraged by this response to realize that our citizens cared so deeply about their history.[37]

Kent Biffle, noted columnist for the *Dallas Morning News*, found my discomfort delightful and got right to the point in his morning column about just where I had gone wrong.

> Davy Crockett's name in inch-high letters is all over the cover of the November *Texas Monthly* magazine above the headline: "Hero or Hype?" The lower deck demands: "Should we still believe in a man who wasn't born on a mountaintop, hardly ever wore a coonskin cap, and surrendered at the Alamo?" Well, nobody gives a rat's tail about Davy's altitude at birth. And his fans could probably adjust to the notion of Davy in a tractor hat or a Bosox cap. But the *surrender* part warms them to incandescence.

Biffle, tongue firmly in cheek, noted that the author of the article had approached the subject of Crockett's surrender "as if he were undressing in public" and then went on to present arguments both pro and con. He ended by commenting, and perhaps rightly so, that such haggling was useless anyway for "nearly everybody knows that Davy Crockett died while blowing up the powder magazine in the old chapel. And he looked a lot like John Wayne."[38]

As Carmen Perry, Dan Kilgore, Michael Lofaro, and I have all discovered, the Alamo is a near-religious icon to many people. Any attempt to tamper with the iconographic Alamo of the popular imagination will meet with staunch resistance by defenders of the historical faith. Such a defense from an organization like the Daughters of the Republic of Texas is certainly understandable. Their membership is based on genealogy, and their primary reason for existence is to protect the heroic myth that surrounds the building they so lovingly guard. Such ancestor worship, of course, makes it exceedingly difficult to interpret history frankly. Many other Americans, however, embrace the same heroic myth of the Alamo as the DRT because it has become a vital part of their own self-identification. To suggest that some in the Alamo fought in defense of slavery, or that racism helped bring on the battle, or that Davy Crockett was captured and executed is to attack a powerfully symbolic icon embraced by many Americans as a defining moment in their own history as well as the history of the nation. To attack the traditional story of the Alamo is thus to attack a patriotic touchstone of the republic's soul. The myth will undoubtedly triumph over the facts, and the icon will remain intact.

RACE, REVOLUTION, AND THE TEXAS REPUBLIC:

Toward a Reinterpretation

James E. Crisp

IN 1979, FROM BENEATH THE WALLS OF THE ALAMO, JOHN H. Jenkins issued a challenge to all historians of Texas. No one, he reminded us, had ever written "a comprehensive history of the most important event in Texas' past."[1] This amazing state of affairs—the absence of a complete study of the Texas Revolution—persists despite (or perhaps because of) a greater abundance and availability of pertinent archival materials than ever before. Scholars also have access to the extensive publication and dissemination of hitherto rare and scattered primary sources, for which Jenkins can take as much credit as anyone. There was no definitive history of the conflict even by its sesquicentennial year, and the Texas Revolution stands as defiant of its would-be masters as were those Texian warriors at Gonzales and the Alamo. Numerous historians have discovered firsthand the accuracy of John Jenkins's assertion that "no events in [Texas] history are more unexplained and more misinterpreted than those of the . . . Revolution."[2]

The historian who tackles the Texas Revolution faces not only a formidable task of synthesis but an even more daunting challenge of revision and reinterpretation. According to Jenkins, the basic premises of virtually every historical study about the war written in the first century after Texas independence "must be re-examined, questioned, and . . . mostly rejected." There has been, he notes, a "complete revolution in historiographical and biographical methodology" since 1936. The drastic changes in our standards of objectivity, attitudes toward minority groups, and understanding of social processes and human motivation—in addition to the mass of newly available archival materials (especially those of Mexican provenance)—require the Revolution's historian to attack some of the most "hallowed shibboleths" of Texas history. Speaking as a direct descendent of "the youngest man in Sam Houston's army," Jenkins puts it this way:

"Our Texas heroes can no longer be considered Simon pure, and they can no longer be exclusively white Anglo-Saxon Protestants. We are aware now that our forbears were not always on the side of the Lord, that they made colossal blunders and almost all had motives that are now suspect."[3]

In his 1979 call for a new synthesis and reinterpretation, Jenkins made it clear that intensive archival research, considerable linguistic accomplishment, and a degree of scholarly detachment uncommon in Texas historiography would be prerequisites for the long-overdue delineation of the Revolution. Only three years earlier, historian David J. Weber issued a strikingly similar call for an overall restoration of historiographic balance in the Mexican period of Borderlands history (of which the Texas Revolution is an integral part). Weber's survey of this literature revealed a field that remained wide open to those who could "combine linguistic skill with interdisciplinary training and impartiality necessary to understand" the complexities of this era. And Weber, like Jenkins, emphasized that the protagonists of the revised drama could no longer all be white Anglo-Saxon Protestants: insufficient attention had been paid to the actions and motivations of the Hispanic inhabitants of northern Mexico during the years of Anglo settlement, revolt, and conquest.[4] The *mexicanos* could no longer be treated merely as docile drudges, obstacles to "progress," or cardboard villains.

What has been the response over the past decade to these challenges to scholarship? How well, after a hundred and fifty years, do we understand the context, causes, and consequences of the conflict in Texas? How far have we come in the painful but rewarding process of revising our views toward the Revolution and the republic to which it gave birth? There is, it seems, both good and bad news.

The good news is that a handful of scholars have been hard at work, bringing to their tasks the skills and the spirit demanded by Jenkins and Weber. We are beginning to see the fruits of their labors, the foremost among which is Weber's own impressive book *The Mexican Frontier, 1821–1846: The American Southwest under Mexico*.[5] But Weber's volume is also indicative of the bad news: with regard to the Texas Revolution, recent scholarship has been (despite its strengths) fragmentary, disjointed, narrowly focused, and, in some respects, mutually contradictory. Both the contributions and the limitations of *The Mexican Frontier* may best be seen within the larger context of the problematic historiography of the Texan revolt.

In 1979 John Jenkins cited the probing, demythologizing studies of Archie McDonald on Travis and of Dan Kilgore on Crockett as examples of the kind of work that needed to be done on the Revolution as a whole.⁶ To this honor roll can be added the name of Margaret Swett Henson for her reappraisal of Travis's nemesis, Juan Davis Bradburn. Yet her work on Bradburn is necessarily peripheral to the Revolution itself, and like these other biographical studies, it neither approaches nor aspires to the comprehensiveness we seek.⁷

Another kind of narrowness, if one may dare to use that term in describing such an ambitious work, is shown in Malcolm D. McLean's delightful multivolume resurrection of the Texas colonization project of Sterling C. Robertson. Despite its usefulness to all historians of Anglo-Texan settlement, *Papers Concerning Robertson's Colony in Texas* was never intended as a new synthesis, however revisionist in spirit. Moreover, when McLean does examine the causes of the Texas Revolution, it is with the assumption that all Mexico was as obsessed as is McLean himself with the chicanery and duplicity of Samuel May Williams and his eminent employer, Stephen F. Austin. But surely no one—not even the impresario Robertson—has equaled McLean's tenacious fervor in this regard. The very doggedness of his exhumation of the dubious land transactions that preceded the Revolution may even have led McLean into what David Hackett Fischer calls "the reductive fallacy."⁸

Smashing shibboleths in a style that John Jenkins would have to applaud, McLean asserts that

> most Texas historians, writing from the point of view of the Texans, and without examining the official correspondence in Spanish that gives the Mexican point of view, have been so eager to get to the blood and thunder of the Texas Revolution, . . . that they have failed to look beneath the surface and discover what really brought the Mexican army into Texas. . . .
>
> The Mexican army was actually sent into Texas to arrest those land speculators, but the Texans refused to surrender them, so that is what precipitated the Texas Revolution. . . .⁹

And, with tongue in cheek, he adds: "Who knows? If they had given them up, there might not have been any need to 'Remember the Alamo!' or Goliad, and we might still be Mexican citizens today."¹⁰

A tendency toward reductionism more subtle than McLean's, yet also more serious and troublesome, may be found in the writings of another active Texas historian whose views of the revolt of 1835–36 demand consideration. Arnoldo De León embodies much of the recent revolution in historical approach to which John Jenkins has referred. Like Jenkins,

McLean, and Weber, De León believes that Hispanics have been given inadequate attention in Texas history. Sharply critical of the attitudes and actions of nineteenth-century Anglo-Texans, De León shares Jenkins's conviction that many scholars have been reluctant to denigrate the state's pantheon of revolutionary heroes. The founding fathers of Anglo-American Texas, writes De León, saw Mexicans as "degenerate, depraved, and questionably human. The haunting prospect of being ruled by such people indefinitely explains in part the Texian movement for independence in 1836. Historians, however, have not paid due attention to these attitudes as factors in the movement for independence, for to do so is to come close to labeling the first generation of Texans as racists."[11]

But racism, contends De León, while perhaps "not *the* cause of the Texas Revolution, . . . certainly . . . was *very* prominent as a promoting and underlying cause."[12] The revolt in Texas, he concludes, was a revolution "of racial adjustment. For Anglo-Texans to have accepted anything other than 'white supremacy and civilization' was to submit to Mexican do-mination and to admit that Americans were willing to become like Mexicans. The prospect of being dominated by such untamed, uncivil, and disorderly creatures made a contest for racial hegemony almost inevitable."[13]

De León's work, along with that of David J. Weber, was cited by Walter Nugent in 1985 as providing evidence that Borderlands history is still alive and well and that the very concept of the Borderlands remains a valid one beyond the political changes of 1821 and 1846.[14] Nugent is certainly correct on both counts, but his pairing of these two scholars is nevertheless ironic. In their most recent works, Weber and De León bring very different perspectives, if not wholly divergent interpretations, to the Texas Revolution, and especially to the role of racism and ethnic conflict in the origin of that revolt.

This contrast previously was not so sharp. In the 1970s, both historians portrayed negative Anglo-American attitudes toward Mexicans in the Southwest as virtually guaranteeing conflict between the two groups.[15] In his 1974 doctoral dissertation, De León faulted Weber only for giving inadequate attention to the role of racial prejudice toward nonwhites in producing what Weber still described (to use De León's words) as an "instant negative reaction" that occurred "whenever and wherever whites met Mexicans." Although Weber did take note of the presence of racial bias among Anglo-Americans, he stressed instead the enduring influence of the "Black Legend": the traditional Anglo-Protestant image of Spanish bigotry, brutality, and perfidy. By emphasizing that Mexicans had "inherited the bad reputation of their Spanish forefathers," suggested De

León, Weber had given support to a "clash of cultures" thesis instead of acknowledging the central role played by color-conscious racism in shaping the Anglo response toward Mexicans and, ultimately, in promoting the Texas Revolution.[16]

Contrary to the conclusions of both Weber and De León, however, it may be argued with considerable support from a wide range of scholarship that neither white racism nor the Black Legend offers an adequate explanation of the origins of the Texas revolt: that the wellsprings of the Revolution must be sought beyond a clash of cultures or of complexions. Is this to suggest that cultural and racial prejudices did not exist or that they did not profoundly shape the course of the conflict? Certainly not. But their function and their influence deserve a careful reappraisal. Any comprehensive reinterpretation of the Texas Revolution must avoid perpetuating the stark dichotomies of racial and cultural cleavage that have for so long dominated both scholarly and popular understanding.

Ironically, the strength of the Black Legend actually became one of the chief sources of American sympathy and tolerance for Mexicans in the decade following the overthrow of Spanish rule. Americans generally (and simplistically) interpreted the achievement of Mexican independence as an imitation of their own struggle against Britain and naturally looked upon the Mexicans more favorably after they had broken free from Spain's dominion. Although a few critics did view postrevolutionary Mexico's deficiencies as evidence that her people had been permanently "blighted" by centuries of despotic rule,[17] the more prevalent opinion was that the influence of "free institutions" would gradually erase the vestigial reminders of the banished colonial regime.[18]

One might even say that the more terrible the initial image of the Spaniard, the greater the degree of forbearance shown by Anglo-Americans in the face of perceived Mexican faults. In 1825, after a little more than three months in Mexico, American diplomatic aide Edward Thornton Tayloe made the following assessment:

> Whatever may be said of the bad blood of the Mexicans, I cannot but view them as a mild and amiable people . . . for their state of degradation and ignorance they are indebted not to any natural deficiencies of their own, but to the miserable and timid policy of their former Spanish masters. They are superstitious, but that arises from their education; they are jealous of strangers—the policy of Spain made them so; and they are ignorant, for in ignorance alone could they be retained under blind subjection to the mother country. If

they are vicious, their vices arise from the same cause—the ignorance of virtue. . . .

These are serious defects, but the improvement of the Mexican people is daily taking place. They are beginning to be enlightened with the rays of the rising sun of liberty; . . . The effects of a daily increasing intercourse with foreigners are even now perceptible, and lead me to believe that before many years roll over a remarkable change must take place.[19]

David J. Weber argued in the early 1970s that "Mexicans and Americans in Texas and across the [north Mexican] frontier . . . found much to dislike about one another" and that "in a way, they had always known they would."[20] Americans went into Mexico, he suggested, with a preconstructed negative stereotype of the Mexican, incorporating "the worst qualities of Spaniards and Indians." "Not surprisingly," wrote Weber, "the Anglo-Americans' expectations were fulfilled."[21]

On the contrary, one can argue that the evidence will not sustain the proposition that most of the thousands of Americans who settled in Texas in the 1820s and early 1830s entered Mexico expecting to dislike the Mexicans. It would be more accurate to say that the Anglo-Texans experienced a measure of initial disillusionment, instead of a confirmation of their preconceptions, when Mexican realities did not meet their high but often narrowly ethnocentric expectations.

It should be acknowledged at this point that Weber, De León, and other scholars who have cataloged Americans' first impressions of Mexicans are essentially correct in labeling these reactions as negative.[22] It is also true that Anglo indictments of Mexican character, whether couched in terms of color, culture, or in an undifferentiated amalgam of insults, could and did serve in various times and places as a rationale for an assumption of superiority, for disdain toward Mexican law and authority, and ultimately for callous discrimination and exploitation.

It should also be stressed, however, that negative first impressions—whether they were in response to the color of the Mexicans' skin or to specific elements of their culture—did not always harden into permanently negative attitudes. Nor did they necessarily determine the sort of interaction that developed between Mexicans and Anglo-Americans. The record of Americans' exposure to Mexico suggests instead that between 1821 and 1835, they were reacting more out of ignorance and provincialism than according to negative expectations. It also reveals that there was a good deal of initial surprise, shock, and even disgust upon the settlers' first arrival in Mexico. But where circumstances allowed Americans to become familiar with the Mexicans and their way of life—to see them on their own terms instead of merely as one-dimensional obstacles, threats, or targets of opportunity—the Anglos' opinions often changed, their attitudes mellowed, and their evaluations of Mexico and Mexicans became more positive as they gradually came to understand more fully an unfamiliar people and culture.

A similar pattern emerges from the impressive work of Glenda Riley and Sandra Myres on the attitudes of white women toward racial and ethnic minorities in the West.[23] Both of these scholars have found that women who had the opportunity to get beyond superficial and second-hand contact with Indians and other groups tended to like and accept them far more than we have been led to believe. Even when women's preconceptions had been formed by sensationalist celebrations of the Indians' savagery, writes Riley, "terror was routinely replaced by equanimity, aversion by acceptance, and hatred by affection."[24] The key to the development of friendship, and even love, was the opportunity to engage in an "educational process" of nonexploitative interaction leading to cultural understanding. Where that opportunity was absent, or was lost in a sudden rush of advancing Anglo immigration, or was spurned by those who allowed nothing to interfere with the pursuit of gain, the result—among women and men alike—was a pattern of distrust, misunderstanding, and mutual hostility.[25]

There were, in other words, some circumstances that were more likely than others to promote the "learning process" necessary for the development of cross-cultural understanding and cordiality. Such favorable circumstances often prevailed for Americans who visited or immigrated to Mexico. They were certainly not entirely absent in prerevolutionary Texas, where, as Malcolm McLean tells us, "the lives of the Anglo-Americans, the Mexicans, and the Indians became intimately intertwined, in a more humane, sympathetic, and understanding atmosphere than the usual Texas histories would lead us to believe ever existed. . ."[26]

A rare opportunity to see this learning process in action comes from an unlikely source: the *Journal and Correspondence* of Edward Thornton Tayloe, private secretary to Joel Roberts Poinsett, U.S. minister to Mexico. Tayloe and Poinsett—the only Anglo-Americans to write book-length descriptions of Mexico in the 1820s—were cited by David Weber in the 1970s as exemplifying the almost universally negative, even "contemptuous," reaction of Americans to Mexicans "wherever they encountered them."[27]

Weber's reading of Tayloe's view of Mexicans is one-dimensional; it is nothing more than a list of vices.[28] And indeed, Tayloe saw little else in the first weeks of his Mexican adventure. A month after his arrival in Mexico City in the late spring of 1825, Tayloe was still somewhat in shock from the "filth, vice, and ignorance" he saw in the capital city's populace. "I have filled this letter with the vices of the people," he wrote his brother in Virginia, "[and] I might add many more—wishing they had virtues to compensate in some degree their defects. Should I attempt to find them out, I fear that I shall fail."[29]

Tayloe's extended stay in Mexico, however, and the considerable time available to him for inquiry and exploration allowed him to begin to see beyond superficialities and to find the Mexicans less strange. We have already seen Tayloe's expression of optimism for Mexico's future, as he employed the language of the Black Legend to place the blame for Mexican vices on the departed Spanish regime. That particular entry in his journal was made on August 14, 1825, roughly three months after his introduction to the capital city. On the following day, he wrote his brother that he would have to "qualify the doubt I expressed in a former letter, whether the Mexican people are purely republicans. . . . [T]he great body of the people," he now concluded, "are patriotic and ready to serve in the cause of their country."[30]

As fall turned to winter on the central Mexican plateau, Tayloe's admiration for the Mexicans and their nation continued to grow. The Christmas holidays brought words of praise for his new Mexican friends and the warmth with which he was welcomed into their homes. On New Year's Eve he wrote to a kinsman in Virginia that "the more I see of [the Mexican people], the more I am pleased—and though they have a great many vices, I am disposed to make allowances for them."[31]

By the time he left Mexico in 1828, Edward Tayloe was by no means uncritical of the country he had come to know. Like Stephen F. Austin and many of the Anglo-American settlers of Texas, he lamented Mexico's political instability, decried the corruption and mismanagement he saw in her government, and warned of the still-formidable power of the forces of political reaction in the church and the army. But though he may never have become totally reconciled to ladies smoking cigars or priests betting on cockfights, his chief complaints were no longer directed at either the character or the complexions of the Mexican people.[32]

As Tayloe was learning and changing, the shift in his attitudes extended to the critical area of race. It is true that like most visitors to Mexico from the United States, from Harvard undergraduate Richard Henry Dana to the "unschooled trapper" James Ohio Pattie, Tayloe's first reaction was to the Mexicans' nonwhite color.[33] As he disembarked at Vera Cruz, he was revolted at the sight of what he termed "squalid" mestizo soldiers; yet only three days later he was describing the many mestizo soldiers he had met on the road to Mexico City as "generally good-looking men." He added parenthetically, I "have become reconciled to their yellow skins."[34] By the time he had been in Mexico for two years, this Virginia gentleman was a social intimate and ardent admirer of the liberal politician Vicente Guerrero, whom he understood to be of "some African blood," and who, he remarked to his brother, looked like a mulatto. Tayloe also confided that he looked forward with some enthusiasm to the prospect of the election of Guerrero—in whom he saw "strong natural powers, shrewdness, and sound judgment"—to the Mexican presidency.[35]

The surprising flexibility of Tayloe's racial sensibilities should not, in fact, surprise us. Substantial evidence indicates that for individuals as well as for groups and even whole societies, racial prejudice should not be considered a fixed element—a "given"—in any historical situation. The specific circumstances of interaction are, as in the case of women and Indians on the frontier, of more critical importance than the different attributes or expectations that either side might possess. And especially on the societal level, demographic and economic patterns are likely to be far more important than variations of skin color or cultural norms in determining the status of a group and the character of its relations with others.[36] One must acknowledge, with historian George M. Fredrickson, that there *are* at work "subliminal and deeply rooted psychological factors" in the reactions of many whites to alien peoples of dark colors and strange habits. But Fredrickson does not believe that such factors can explain the very great "situational variations in intensity and character" of race relations in America over the last four centuries. He concludes that specific social and economic forces have been paramount in shaping not only explicit, articulated, *ideological* racism but also "the implicit or *societal* racism that can be inferred from actual social relationships."[37]

The history of American-Mexican contact in the Southwest offers many examples wherein shifts in specific "race relations situations"—changes in attitudes, behavior, and public policy—have been much more closely related to variables of population and economic development than to either cultural dissonances or prevailing racial orthodoxies. In a variety of locales, social historians have documented the establishment, after some initial distrust, of harmonious relations between Hispanic inhabitants and Anglo immigrants, accompanied by significant degrees of mutual acculturation. Intermarriage was frequent and in many instances resulted in the apparent "Mexicanization" of the newcomers. The disruption of such compatibility usually occurred with the population surges and changing economies brought about by mineral discoveries, the arrival of railroads, warfare, or other sudden turn of events. And even as such dramatic changes provoked ethnic conflict or precipitated a decline in the status and fortunes of most Mexicans, interethnic alliances along class lines based on mutual economic interests at times proved stronger than the pride and prejudice of race.[38]

Although our knowledge of Anglo-Mexican relations in prerevolutionary Texas remains incomplete, it is certain that on the eve of the revolt peace and interethnic cooperation, not conflict, was the norm across most of the province. Even as violence erupted in 1835, the opposing sides failed to divide neatly along ethnic lines, though some participants belatedly tried to define the collision as "one between white and colored races."[39] In fact, the programs of both the "peace" and "war" parties in Texas were predicated on some form of cooperation with Mexicans. As the consensus emerged for participation in a civil war against the central government of Mexico, it included many Hispanic soldiers and citizens. Some of these, like Juan N. Seguín and his company of *bejareño* volunteers, persisted in their alliance with the Anglos even when independence from Mexico became the revolt's overt aim.

Moreover, it should be remembered that those who opposed revolution and independence were by no means all native Mexicans. Motivated by political principle as well as economic considerations, probably a majority of the Anglo-Texan settlers hoped to avoid violence in 1835. A considerable number of the revolutionary leaders, even as late as February of 1836, continued to view their fight as part of a larger struggle *within* Mexico instead of one *with* Mexico. Furthermore, contrary to Texan historiographical tradition, some Anglos persisted to the bitter end in their support of the Mexican government. A company of perhaps two dozen of these East Texas "Tories" were prepared to join Santa Anna as late as the day before Houston's victory at San Jacinto![40]

Given these facts, and the impressive body of historical and sociological scholarship suggesting that the role of racism may be in large part epiphenomenal—a functional adjustment to changing circumstances instead of a principal cause in itself—how should we assess the widely held and time-honored view that the Texas Revolution was a product of racial antipathy and ethnic cleavage?[41]

Arnoldo De León, as one of the most emphatic recent proponents of

"Juan Seguin," painting by Jefferson Wright. Courtesy Archives Division, Texas State Library.

this interpretation, would have us believe that the Anglo-Texans were able to cooperate closely and comfortably with the *criollo* elite among the *tejanos* both before and after the Revolution only because the latter were essentially Caucasian in ancestry. He implies that Americans who blended successfully into the midst of local Mexican majorities simply "adjusted" to Hispanic culture even as they "harbored racist feelings" (and, one must suppose, bided their time).[42] This attempt to reconcile a psychohistorical thesis of determinative racism with the realities of early Anglo-Mexican relations leads De León to what may be a distorted and oversimplified portrayal of the Texas Revolution as a "war of racial adjustment."[43]

A more persuasive argument is that the Revolution is demonstrative of George M. Fredrickson's thesis that racism, both "societal" and "ideological," is a phenomenon more symptomatic than causal. The revolt may be more accurately viewed as "a war of racial disruption": creating new competitive alignments, accelerating and redirecting economic and population growth, and providing the environment of danger and uncertainty in which racism has historically flourished. Paul D. Lack, in his ground-breaking reexamination of slavery's role in the Revolution, is certainly correct when he suggests that a combination of growing Mexican abolitionism, the destruction of the federal system, and the presence of nonwhite troops in the advancing Mexican armies helped to generate among at least some Anglo-Texans a vision of the conflict as a war between the races.[44]

In other words, De León's interpretation of the Revolution as a conflict between *peoples* instead of *principles* is hardly new. It is almost as old as the Revolution itself. The Texan struggle was born in the midst of a Mexican civil war and portrayed by its earliest leaders as the "last rallying point of liberty" for the "republicans of Mexico": as part of "the great work of laying the cornerstone of liberty in the great Mexican republic." Such sentiments became harder to maintain, however, as the rebels found the success of their cause more dependent on the aid of American volunteers than of Mexican federalists.[45] Even as the General Council of the provisional revolutionary government of Texas was endorsing cooperation with "any Mexican Liberal, whose cause is our cause, as opposed to military despotism,"[46] an aggressive minority of pro-independence men within the government were trying to redefine the issue. "The Mexican people and the Anglo-Americans in Texas," they insisted, "never can be one and the same people. A civil compact can never bind together long [sic] people who differ so widely in their pursuits, their religion, their Languages and their ideas of civil liberty."[47]

There is no doubt that the difficult circumstances of the Revolution, as well as the blatantly anti-Mexican views of a minority of the Texan officials, exacerbated ethnic divisions among a rebel force that was losing Mexican allies as rapidly as it was gaining recruits from the United States. But there can also be no doubt that the leaders of the rebellion distorted reality when, desperately appealing for American help in the darkest hours of the war, they used the dramatic language of racial warfare to describe their situation. Even Stephen F. Austin, who had so often defended the Mexicans against criticism, contributed to this radical redefinition of the cause. Traveling on the East Coast of the United States in May of 1836, still unaware of the turn of events at San Jacinto on April 21 and frantically seeking aid for the struggle in Texas, he declared that the conflict there was "a war of barbarian and of despotic principles, waged by the mongrel Spanish-Indian and Negro race, against civilization and the Anglo-American race."[48]

What should we make of such statements? De León interprets them as revealing under conditions of crisis what had been present all along: admissions of "latent racist feelings" that "surely contributed to [the] strike for independence."[49] There is some truth to this view, but it is not the whole truth. One can consider Austin's infamous declaration—so uncharacteristic of his lifelong approach to Mexico—as an effort to appeal as quickly and forcefully as possible to an American public who only vaguely understood the origins of the war in Texas. Americans were, however, especially susceptible to such rhetoric in a decade that saw the race-related issues of slave revolt, abolitionism, and Indian removal advance to the center of public consciousness.

In any case, after the passions of battle had cooled and Austin had returned home, he would modify this starkly racial interpretation of the turmoil in Mexico and Texas. A few months before his death late in 1836, Austin wrote that Mexico's "state of chaos, [was] produced by the sudden transition from extreme Spanish slavery and ignorance, to extreme republican liberty."[50] More important, despite bitter postrevolutionary clashes over land and property ownership between natives and newcomers in Goliad, Victoria, and other areas, the Texas Republic to which Austin returned was by no means the scene of unmitigated ethnic conflict. There was *tejano* participation in the new nation's regular military, in the Ranger companies, and in the political and judiciary systems.[51] Moreover, not only was a steady immigration (and repatriation) from Mexico into South Texas taking place following the Revolution, but as late as 1839 this increase in the Hispanic population was welcomed by leading Anglo spokesmen as beneficial to the prosperity and security of the Texas Republic.[52] This is hardly what one would expect following a "war between the races."

Perhaps the symbolic high-water mark of Anglo-Mexican cooperation in the Texas Republic came as President Mirabeau B. Lamar visited San Antonio in 1841 to promote his forthcoming Santa Fe Expedition. The president hoped that this mission, to which he had appointed the leading *tejano* José Antonio Navarro as one of three special commissioners, would bring New Mexico's population (as well as her trade connections and mineral riches) within Texan jurisdiction. In a festive celebration held in "Mrs. Yturri's long room," Lamar and the wife of San Antonio's mayor Juan N. Seguín "opened the ball with a waltz."[53]

Less than a year later, however, disaster had shattered the dreams of all of these men. The armed forces of Mexico had captured the expedition, imprisoned Navarro, and retaliated against Texas by briefly occupying San Antonio. In the renewed border warfare which followed, Seguín was falsely accused of treason by both sides and was forced into exile. By 1843 his fate was indicative of the plight of most Hispanics in the Texas Republic, where the constitutional linkage of loyalty, citizenship, and the rights of land ownership made them vulnerable to those who would use war hysteria to snatch away *tejano* titles. More and more people in Texas had a direct interest in labeling all Mexicans as "enemies."[54]

The new intensity of the warfare with Mexico, which found Texas financially bankrupt and militarily weak, also contributed to a reemerging Texan self-image as a besieged bastion of white civilization surrounded by barbarians. Anglo-Texans writing the history of their Revolution in this context had remarkably short memories of their recent cooperation with Mexicans. Their one-dimensional interpretation of the war for independence depicting hearty Anglo-Saxons battling against enslavement by their semi-savage racial and cultural inferiors soon dominated literary and artistic portrayals of the conflict. It also strongly influenced scholarly interpretation of the Revolution throughout the remainder of the nineteenth century and into the twentieth.[55]

This paradigm of racial conflict as an explanation of the past, perhaps most vividly exemplified by D. W. Griffith's film epics, *The Birth of Texas* and *The Birth of a Nation,* closely paralleled, of course, the bitter path of Texan and American race relations in the century following annexation.[56] When historian Seymour V. Connor in the 1960s searched in vain for a pattern of Anglo-Mexican animosity in prerevolutionary Texas, he concluded that historians who saw inevitable racial friction at the root of the conflict had been misled by the rabid anti-Mexican prejudice of their own day, which they anachronistically projected onto the Anglo-Texan colonial experience.[57]

Is this, in fact, what Eugene C. Barker and William C. Binkley had done when they concurred that "at bottom the Texas Revolution was the product of the racial and political inheritances of the two peoples"?[58] Not exactly. Although there is much ambiguity and imprecision in their use of the terms *racial and political inheritances*, the implicit theme that emerges from the works of these two eminent historians of the Texas Revolution is not one of persistent prerevolutionary ethnic conflict. It is, instead, one of a general aura of misunderstanding and distrust between Americans and Mexicans that made compromise impossible when the crisis came in 1835.[59]

This theme of mutual misunderstanding was explicitly developed in the 1930s by sociologist Samuel H. Lowrie, whose thesis of "culture conflict" in Texas was endorsed and lucidly restated by Cecil Robinson in 1968.[60] Having noted the basically friendly relations between Anglos and Hispanics in early Texas, Lowrie and Robinson argued that there were nevertheless deep-seated, even unconscious, cultural differences between the two groups. These differences created fundamental disparities in the two sides' "assumptions in essential areas of human behavior."[61] The cultural gap was most clearly manifested, suggested Lowrie and Robinson, in the political realm, where the two peoples held divergent views regarding religious freedom, slavery and racial proscription, and administrative justice.

It is against this background of debate over the role of racial and cultural conflict in the origins of the Texas Revolution that some of the most important contributions of David J. Weber's *Mexican Frontier* may be seen. Having taken a fresh look at the revolt in Texas as a part of the broader story of the American Southwest under Mexican rule, Weber finds insufficient the previous explanations of the rebellion as an ethnic or cultural conflict. Granting Barker's point that racial distrust impeded communication and hardened positions between the Texans and the government, and sympathetic to Lowrie's notion of a conflict of political cultures, Weber nevertheless observes that "Mexicans fought Mexicans over the same political issues in other areas of the frontier where Anglo-Americans played a minor role."[62]

Weber's comparative overview of the north Mexican provinces reinforces the point that the Texan revolt did not center on the culturally sensitive issues of race, language, or religion. Instead, the struggle was prompted by questions that divided other frontier areas from the Mexican metropolis: disagreements over states' rights and local autonomy, exorbitant tariffs and the haphazard suppression of smuggling, inefficient and arbitrary administration of the laws, and the weakness and corruption of the army. Moreover, these complaints produced resentment and alienation toward the national government among *mexicanos* in California, New Mexico, and elsewhere. In these areas, just as with the Anglo-Texan colonists, there developed widespread separatist sentiment, a willingness to welcome American immigrants even against the wishes of Mexico City, and an opposition to centralism that sparked violent revolts against the conservative Mexican counterrevolution of the mid-1830s.

What are the implications of Weber's analysis for our understanding of the Texas Revolution and the republic it spawned? In the first place, it seems clear that Weber has moved even further away from an ethnic explanation of conflict in the Mexican Borderlands than when Arnoldo De

León criticized him in 1974 for largely ignoring the color prejudice of Anglo-Americans. Although he has not ignored Yankee bigotry, Weber's wider perspective has shown as never before the "Mexican-ness" of the Texas Revolution and has illuminated the frontier conditions that transcended or minimized ethnic divisions.

In the second place, although *The Mexican Frontier* takes us several steps toward a clearer understanding of the Revolution, it is not the comprehensive study of the revolt for which John Jenkins called in 1979. Its broader focus and self-imposed limitations, as well as its suggestive analysis, only highlight the historiographical vacuum that still exists. Forgivably, Weber ends his examination of the Texan situation with the Declaration of Independence, when the formal connection to the Mexican frontier was severed. Conversely, Arnoldo De León, from whom we can learn so much of the lives and struggles of the *tejanos* in the second half of the nineteenth century, has very little to say about their involvement in the revolution that created the Texas Republic.[63] Furthermore, De León's reluctance to acknowledge any significant change in Anglo attitudes over time prevents him from seeing in full the tragic drama of that transitional republic.

This tragedy may be glimpsed in "Tejanos and Texans," the fine unpublished dissertation of Andrew Tijerina, who provides in it the best narrative and analytical bridge from the pre-independence *tejano* world of Weber's book to the postannexation period that is De León's chief interest.[64] But Tijerina summarizes the traumatic after-effects of the Revolution for the *tejanos* in only sixteen typescript pages. He largely ignores the motivations and attitudes of the Anglos, whose own tragedy he captures in one terse sentence: "At first, men fought for political principle, but soon political principle became racial polarization as well."[65] The tale told by that sentence is worth a book!

Finally, the works of both Weber and Tijerina offer considerable evidence supporting the proposition that ethnic conflict in Texas was less a cause than a consequence of the Revolution. And given what we know about Anglo-Mexican relations there by the time of the Mexican War, the Texas Republic must be the cauldron in which much poison was brewed. Even if Weber is technically correct in downgrading the "grandiloquently"-termed "revolution" to the status of a mere frontier revolt,[66] the changes wrought in the lives of the *tejanos* in the decade following Texan independence were nothing short of revolutionary. Yet no historian has adequately charted the dark growth of ethnic enmity in the Texas Republic.[67] Perhaps because for so long it was assumed that racial polarization was a prerevolutionary phenomenon, few historians of Mexican Americans have looked closely at the drastic changes that occurred within the republic.[68] Likewise, the best histories of the republic give little indication that the *tejanos* even existed after the Revolution.[69]

After a century and a half of myth-making, it is easy to remember the Alamo but far too easy to forget that the man who offered the first official eulogy for its martyrs was Colonel Juan Nepomuceno Seguín of the Texas army.[70] A proud veteran of the remarkable victory at San Jacinto, Seguín won the war but eventually lost the peace. The Revolution was a turning point for Texas and for Seguín—not because it culminated a growing hostility between Anglos and *tejanos* but because it radically restructured political and ethnic alignments in Texas. At the same time, it vastly accelerated the pace of economic and demographic change. These transformations, as Seguín and other *tejano* supporters of the republic discovered to their chagrin, did not benefit equally all those who had helped to bring them about.[71] Juan Seguín's ultimately tragic fate may serve as a symbol for the profound social changes that took place under the flag of the Republic of Texas. It is also testimony that the Texas Revolution was less a consequence of racial friction than a precipitating cause of it.

So another challenge can be added to that of John Jenkins. As we rewrite the history of the Texas Revolution, let us follow the logic of our revisionism past San Jacinto. During and after the sesquicentennial decade, there will be a horde of taxidermists at work on the Republic of Texas, doing their best to portray that quaint and colorful nation in the most flattering of poses. Let us hope that the republic will also become the object of study of a few skilled pathologists, who should strive not merely to identify and curse the crippling infection of racism but also to understand the conditions that favored its growth. Perhaps in so doing, they will derive some lessons for the living from their examination of the dead. These historians may shed some light on what could be the ultimate irony of the sesquicentennial: our belated recognition that the greatest measure of oppression in Texas came not before 1836, but after.

"IN THIS WAY WE DID THE COUNTRY SOME SERVICE":

Ben McCulloch and the War with Mexico, 1846–47

Thomas W. Cutrer

AFTER THE UNITED STATES ANNEXED TEXAS, RELATIONS WITH Mexico quickly deteriorated and war seemed likely. Especially disputed was ownership of southern Texas between the Nueces River and the Rio Grande. To support the American claim, President James K. Polk sent the United States Army of Occupation under General Zachary Taylor to Corpus Christi in August, 1845. After waiting seven months while American and Mexican diplomats negotiated unsuccessfully, Taylor's army moved south to the Rio Grande.

One of Taylor's most pressing needs as he moved beyond the Nueces was a unit of horsemen to serve as scouts. In addition to volunteer cavalry regiments from Arkansas, Kentucky, Missouri, and Tennessee, Secretary of War William L. Marcy authorized Taylor to call for two regiments of mounted volunteers from the Texans—"by whom legs were valued chiefly as a means of sticking to a horse."[1] On April 26, 1846, Colonel John Coffee (Jack) Hays received orders from General Taylor to prepare the Ranger companies of his command, stationed at San Antonio, Austin, and Goliad, to join the American army on the Rio Grande.[2] By May 6 the *Telegraph and Texas Register* reported that "all the ranging companies on our western frontier . . . are on the march for the American camps." Hays's Rangers, designated the 1st Texas Mounted Riflemen, with a "company of volunteers from Gonzales under the command of Captain Ben McCulloch," were expected to "amount to 500 efficient troops . . . all well mounted" and eager "for a brush with the Mexicans. They will doubtless," said the newspaper editor, "hasten to the camp with all possible speed, and we doubt not that they will give a good account of themselves if they get within gunshot of their old enemies."[3]

The Texas mounted volunteers were, indeed, a formidable foe. Of Scottish, Scotch-Irish, English, French, and German descent, they were the product of generations of border warfare in Europe and North America. Always on the cutting edge of the frontier, representatives of this warrior people had fought and displaced the Indians of the Eastern Seaboard and trans-Appalachian states and were among the first to enter Anglo-Texas. In 1836 they wrested the province away from Mexico, and for the next decade carried on a sporadic border warfare with their former political rulers while at the same time subduing the Comanches, the de facto lords of Central and West Texas.[4]

Although some contemporaries believed that every Texan was his own soldier and police force, the most militant of them were impelled irresistibly into the Texas Rangers. The term *ranger* was first applied to Texas fighting men as early as 1823, when Stephen F. Austin commissioned ten officers to enforce the laws of the colony. For the next twenty years, the force grew in numbers and responsibilities. Especially during those years when the infant republic could not afford to maintain a regular army, the Rangers provided an inexpensive and efficient frontier defense force. Most effective in small, well-mounted squads, they were prepared to ride great distances on short notice to repel or destroy intruding enemies. At times these forces were given such titles as mounted gunmen, spies, and mounted riflemen, but customarily they were simply referred to as Texas Rangers.

During the period of the republic, the Rangers opposed Mexican incursions from the south and Comanches and Kiowas from the north and west. They fought at Council House in San Antonio in March, 1840; played a prominent role under Ben McCulloch in the victory over the Comanches at Plum Creek on August 12, 1840; and were largely responsible for the repulse of the two Mexican expeditions against San Antonio in 1842. To many Texans, the United States' war with Mexico was but a continuation of the war for independence.[5] It was the only conflict in which Texas Rangers have operated as a unit of the United States Army.[6]

In common with other American frontiersmen, Texas Rangers had little respect for formal authority and less for formal discipline. As one Mexican War veteran commented, "There was no discipline among them, and they wouldn't pay attention to any order or anything."[7] "A more reckless, devil-may-care looking set, it would be impossible to find this side of the Infernal Regions," observed a dragoon of the regular United States Army. "Take them altogether, with their uncouth costumes, bearded faces, lean and brawny forms, fierce wild eyes and swaggering manners, they were fit representatives of the outlaws which made up the population of the Lone Star State."[8]

Most professional military men were thoroughly perplexed by the

Rangers and had a difficult time finding a suitable place for them. "Them Texas troops are the damndest troops in the world," Zachary Taylor was quoted as saying. "We can't do without them in a fight, and we can't do anything with them out of a fight."[9] The Rangers, according to Colonel Albert G. Brackett, a leading mid–nineteenth-century authority on the mounted arm, "were good troops for reconnaissances and for scouting, but were not the best class for anything like regular movements."[10]

Although lacking the formal discipline and uniform of the regular soldier or militiaman from the older states, the Ranger did not lack the essentials of a soldier: namely, first-rate arms and equipment, excellent leadership, and extraordinary courage. Lieutenant Colonel Ethan Allen Hitchcock, an 1817 West Point graduate and inspector general of Winfield Scott's army in Mexico, observed that Hays's Rangers were "well mounted and doubly well armed: each man has one or two Colt's revolvers besides ordinary pistols, a sword, and every man a rifle.... The Mexicans," he added, "are terribly afraid of them."[11] As Walter Prescott Webb has pointed out, the Rangers were led by men who "possessed in a higher degree the qualities they admired in others and found necessary in themselves":[12] courage, endurance, and a canny if untutored tactical sense in border warfare.

Among the most extraordinary of the antebellum Ranger captains was Ben McCulloch, who was born in Rutherford County, Tennessee, on November 11, 1811. He was the son of Major Alexander McCulloch, a substantial farmer and surveyor and aide-de-camp to General John Coffee, who fought at the battle of Horseshoe Bend under Andrew Jackson in 1813. It was after Coffee that John Coffee Hays had been named. After moving to Dyer County, Tennessee, in 1830, the family's closest friend and neighbor was David Crockett, whom young Ben followed to Texas in 1835. Falling ill at Nashville, Texas, McCulloch was unable to accompany Crockett and the other members of his party to their rendezvous with immortality at the Alamo. He did, however, recover in time to join another old family friend, Sam Houston, and served as cannoneer for one of the Twin Sisters at the battle of San Jacinto. McCulloch thereby won a commission as first lieutenant in the army of the Republic of Texas.

Dividing his time for the next few years between surveying and Indian fighting, McCulloch earned a reputation "as one of the most useful and efficient officers in the Republic,"[13] demonstrating leadership and bravery in the battle of Plum Creek in 1840 and in the repulse of General Adrian Woll and the subsequent Mier Expedition in 1842. Houston characterized him as "a fine officer for cavalry or dragoons" and heartily recommended him for a commission in the regular army of the United States at the time of Texas's statehood.[14] At the beginning of the Mexican War, one editor wrote that "McCulloch with 200 rangers" can "cut through [the Mexicans'] ranks as easily as he would dash through a herd of deer."[15]

Samuel C. Reid, a Louisiana attorney who joined McCulloch's company at Matamoros, described the young officer in 1846 as a man "of rather delicate frame, of about five feet ten inches in height, with light hair and complexion. His features are regular and pleasing, though, from long exposure to the frontier, they have a weather-beaten cast. His quick and bright blue eye, with a mouth of thin compressed lips, indicate the cool, calculating, as well as the brave and daring energy of the man."[16]

According to Reid, McCulloch raised his Ranger company in a mere thirty-six hours after the call for volunteers reached the Guadalupe Valley and had it ready to ride by May 11. Upon first seeing his new comrades-in-arms, Reid wondered at these men "with long beards and moustaches, dressed in every variety of garment . . . and a belt of pistols around their waists. . . . A rougher looking set of men we never saw."[17] Although McCulloch's officers and men were orderly and well-mannered, their appearance belied their stations in life and their levels of education. Despite their "ferocious and outlaw look," the company boasted two future generals besides the commander, three lawyers, two doctors, and one newspaper editor. "I do not recall any ministers of the gospel in our party," said Ranger private J. D. Brown, but it did have six or seven former Mier prisoners, among them its first lieutenant, John McMullen.[18]

Although nominally Company A of Hays's 1st Texas Mounted Riflemen, McCulloch's command for the most part operated independently of Hays under the direct control of the commanding general, Zachary Taylor. It was assigned the important and hazardous task of a "spy company," and McCulloch was named Taylor's chief of scouts. This was a position for which his "intimate acquaintance with the Mexican character and language admirably qualified him," according to a contemporary newspaper account.[19]

Accustomed only to "light marching order," the Rangers quickly proceeded toward the rendezvous with their regiment and Taylor's army on the Rio Grande. Unencumbered by wagon train or other baggage, including tents, they rode from Gonzales to Corpus Christi in just two days. Their ability to travel light and live off the land was legendary. "I can't afford to pack lead and tire down my horse like they do in the old world," said one of McCulloch's men. Unlike the soldier of the Napoleonic wars, who expended an estimated one hundred rounds of ammunition for each

Ben McCulloch. Courtesy Thomas Cutrer Collection.

casualty, McCulloch's men carried but twenty rounds. "If I don't kill or cripple just twenty greasers," said one, "it will be because they are licked before I have had time to load and fire twenty times, or else because I have been 'sent under' early."[20]

From Corpus Christi, the company rode down Padre Island to Port Isabel, and from there to Matamoros by way of the battlefields of Palo Alto and Resaca de la Palma. Disappointed by their failure to arrive in time to fight the first battle of the war, they were nevertheless gratified that Samuel H. Walker's company of Rangers had acquitted itself well and contributed materially to the twin American victories.[21]

The company arrived at Matamoros to find most of Hays's regiment already there. J. D. Brown remembered the service there as "sometimes arduous." Even after their arrival on the Rio Grande, the Rangers were not supplied with tents. Their camp was downstream from the army's slaughter pens, and refuse thrown into the river often failed to clear the banks and was blown by immense swarms of flies. The Rangers used the river water for washing, drinking, and cooking and on some days had to wade fifty or more yards beyond the bank to be free of floating offal. This place McCulloch's men dubbed Camp Maggot. After two or three weeks in this dreadful location, the company was ordered back across the Rio Grande to Fort Brown.[22]

McCulloch's company remained encamped at Matamoros until June 12, when it received orders to harass the rear guard of General Mariano Arista's retreating columns as far as possible. They were also instructed to explore the country as far as Linares, 165 miles to the southwest.[23] After slight skirmishes with one or two groups of Mexican irregular cavalry, the Rangers pushed "over rough, barren country . . . nearly destitute of water" to within thirty miles of Linares before determining that the route "is almost impracticable for an army [with] large trains and heavy baggage wagons."[24] Having accomplished his reconnaissance, McCulloch cut across the desert in hopes of obtaining "a fight or a footrace" with the Mexican partisan general, Antonio Canales, who was greatly despised by the Texans. The Chaparral Fox was not in his den, however; so, finding only a cold trail, McCulloch turned back toward Reynosa, a town that the Rangers considered "the most rascally place in all Mexico."[25] There the Rangers celebrated the Fourth of July by consuming two horse buckets of whiskey and eating a feast of pigs and chickens "accidentally killed while firing in honor of the day."[26]

McCulloch's report of his company's expedition allowed General Taylor to report to the president on July 2 that "the direct land route from this point [Matamoros] to Monterrey is much longer than the line from Camargo; in wet weather, impassable for artillery or heavy wagons, and in dry scantily supplied with water."[27] Taylor had learned that when he required knowledge of the enemy or the country, the Rangers could get it for him. Although they had been unable either to reach Linares or to catch Canales, for ten days McCulloch's command had operated with impunity in the triangle formed by Matamoros, Linares, and Reynosa. They returned to the army with precise and timely intelligence reports. In recognition of this service, McCulloch was breveted to the rank of major and appointed regimental quartermaster, a duty that was never to interfere with his mission as Taylor's chief of scouts.[28] Although pleased with the Rangers' prowess as scouts, the general was a good deal less happy with their conduct as gentlemen. As he lamented to Colonel George T. Wood of Texas, "I fear they are a lawless set" and "too licentious to do much good."[29]

On July 5, Taylor sent his scouts out again from Matamoros, this time to reconnoiter the road along the south bank of the Rio Grande as far as Camargo. Constantly on the alert against attack, the Rangers rose shortly after midnight in order to travel under the cover of darkness and during the cooler hours. They rested during the hot part of the day, sprawling under the sun without shelter. New Orleans *Picayune* correspondent George Kendall, who often rode with McCulloch's company, expressed wonder that anyone could ever sleep as they did: fully dressed, "belted round with two pistols and a Bowie, boots on and spurs to boot."[30]

However uncomfortable, this scout was able to report more positive results. The road to Camargo was passable, with sufficient food and water along the route. General Taylor ordered his army down it. Fearful of ambush from mounted partisans in the chaparral, Taylor ordered the Texans to screen the advance of his infantry from Reynosa. Sharing the place with the dragoons at times, at least one company of Rangers—often McCulloch's—was always at the head of the American column until it reached Monterrey. McCulloch's mission as a scout often rankled his command, and escort duty was considered even worse. The men had come to Mexico to fight, and the rare excursion against roving bands of Comanches did not satisfy that need. "Captain McCulloch was ordered not to fight," recalled one of his Rangers, "but to survey various sections of the country and report. He was well known as a reckless fighter; but he knew how to obey orders, and he certainly did so. We begged him to give us a brush with the enemy, but he simply answered, 'orders.'"[31]

Perhaps unknown to his men, McCulloch, too, was chafing under the restraints imposed upon him by higher command and begging his superiors to be allowed to slip the leash and come to grips with the enemy. Juan N. Seguín was reported nearby with a force of irregular cavalry. Seguín—formerly a friend of Stephen F. Austin and an officer in the Texas revolutionary army but now a colonel in the Mexican army—was notorious among the Anglo-Texans as a traitor. Although Seguín in his memoirs argued compellingly of his innocence,[32] McCulloch, like most old Anglo-Texans, held him accountable for the murder of Captain Nicholas M. Dawson and his men after they had surrendered near Salado Creek in September, 1842. McCulloch wanted above all else to bring him to account. From Camargo on July 20 he wrote plaintively to Taylor, "I am quartered in the town, and without your permission to move until my term of service will expire" on August 18. McCulloch considered himself and his command to be "worthless here" and requested permission to make a reconnaissance in force in the direction of Monterrey. He was convinced that General Canales no longer posed a threat to Taylor's line of communication at Camargo but had been informed that "Seguín has forty men between this [place] and Monterrey; they are those cut throat fellows from San Antonio."³³

Three days later McCulloch again wrote to army headquarters from Camargo, this time to Taylor's adjutant, Captain William W. S. Bliss, requesting more active service. Captain Richard A. Gillespie had just arrived from San Antonio with "forty well mounted men." Eager for a scout, McCulloch suggested the mutually agreeable solution of the new company taking over his duties at Camargo, thus freeing McCulloch's men to ride off in search of Seguín. "I am extremely anxious to make one more trip into the country before my company is discharged," he wrote, "and wish you would be so kind as to mention this to the General." McCulloch reiterated his belief that his company was "of no use" where it was. He argued that it might render better service by scouting the road toward Monterrey or by visiting some of the villages and ranchos in the area in order to make "impressions that would be favorable to our cause."³⁴ Still smarting, perhaps, from a rebuke from Taylor regarding the company's behavior at Reynosa on the Fourth of July or from the more serious accusation that some of the Rangers had assassinated one or more Mexican civilians there, McCulloch pledged that Taylor's orders not to molest any unarmed Mexican would be strictly observed.³⁵

The regular officers of the United States Army had been justifiably proud of their troops' behavior after the victories at Palo Alto and Resaca de la Palma and the occupation of Matamoros. The army, they contended, did not interfere with either the civil or religious rights of the inhabitants. Matters of civil justice remained in the hands of Mexican authorities, and, according to one of the regulars, "the most perfect respect is paid to law and order, and every infraction of either is severely punished." Thus, Taylor and his officers believed, the friendship and respect of the Mexican people was being won. "Such conduct should make our country proud of their army," wrote Lieutenant William S. Henry, a 1835 graduate of the United States Military Academy.³⁶

Taylor, therefore, for reasons both humanitarian and political, severely disapproved of the harsh and ruthless conduct of some Texans against the Mexican civilian population and told his chief of scouts so in no uncertain terms. "Were it possible to rouse the Mexican people to resistance," Taylor wrote later in the war, "no more effectual plan could be devised than the one pursued by our volunteer regiments." The commanding general did not have every volunteer regiment in mind but wrote specifically of "the companies of Texas horse." Of the infantry, Taylor had "little or no complaints" but maintained that "the mounted men from Texas have scarcely made an expedition without unwarrantably killing a Mexican!"[37]

In response, perhaps, to a dressing-down from the commander, McCulloch wrote to Bliss, "I know very little about how the people are disposed towards us off in the country, but presume they are under wrong impressions, as we have always found them [to be] upon first arriving among them." McCulloch contended that the average Mexican peon regarded the Rangers first with suspicion and fear but later as liberators, once the generosity and fairness of his men came to be known. Only those who had committed crimes against Texas—such as the banditti, guerrillas, and certain army officers who had harassed South Texas for the past ten years—needed to fear the Rangers' retribution.[38]

The Rangers, however, seem to have viewed the execution of Mexican citizens who had committed crimes against Texas as just retribution for the Alamo, Goliad, the Dawson massacre, and the decimation of Mier prisoners. "The law of retaliation in war," wrote Ranger captain Tom Green on the eve of the war with Mexico, "the most salutary of all laws in preventing the excesses of an enemy—as yet has never been resorted to by the Texans; that law which should have been inflicted upon Santa Anna, and each and every one of his men at San Jacinto for his recent murder of Colonel Fannin and his four hundred, was permitted to sleep."[39] Those scores the Texans now began to repay.

Most eagerly sought was the man whom Ben McCulloch's brother once compared to Benedict Arnold and Judas Iscariot. "Seguín passed up the River San Juan a few days before we arrived here," McCulloch informed Bliss, "and might have been overtaken. He had forty thieves and murderers from about San Antonio, to kill which would be doing God a service. It would be ridding the world of those that are not fit to live in it. They will never come to terms, because they would be condemned by the Civil Laws and executed. Accordingly, they must do the frontier of Texas no little harm by robbing and stealing from its citizens. Any orders the General may give will be thankfully received and obeyed to the letter."[40]

Perhaps in response to McCulloch's pleas for action, Taylor ordered McCulloch's company back into the interior of Mexico to report on the condition of the roads and to eliminate Seguín if he could be found. On the morning of August 3, to the "great joy" of the company, McCulloch's men departed for the village of China, thought to be the partisans' headquarters, sixty miles to the southwest. Seguín, however, had received word of the Rangers' coming and disappeared into the chaparral. After leaving a bellicose challenge for the partisan chief with the village *alcalde*, the Rangers began their ride back to Camargo.[41] Not only had they been unable to force a fight with the *rancheros*, but, as McCulloch reported to Worth, Taylor's army would have to find another route to Monterrey, as well. The road to China was impassable for artillery because of its "narrow passages and deep ravines," and the crossing of the San Juan River, about two miles above the village, was flawed by high and precipitous banks.[42]

With the road to China unusable for the main army, McCulloch's Rangers were ordered to probe the one remaining route, the road running through the valley of the San Juan River. Through August and the first half of September, the Texans scouted the way and led Taylor's infantry deeper into the heart of Mexico. General Pedro de Ampudia, now in command of the forces on Taylor's front, sent one thousand cavalry under General Anastasio Torrejón to harass the advancing American column. McCulloch's men opened the fall campaign with a sharp skirmish against two hundred Mexican troopers at Tamos. Pushing on to Marin, they encountered a large body of regular Mexican cavalry drawn up in the streets and, according to Kendall, "evidently much flurried by our appearance." With only twenty-five men, McCulloch ordered a halt. The plaza was concealed by the church and adjoining buildings, making it impossible to tell whether infantry and artillery were in the town as well. The place offered every opportunity for concealing a force of thousands; and, as McCulloch "was not so particularly certain that the Mexicans might not send an 18 pound shot . . . up our way on a flying visit," he ordered his men to deploy in an open formation along the brow of the hill, extend their flanks to prevent a surprise turning movement, and settle in to await developments.[43]

Several of the poorer citizens of the town were either captured in the chaparral or simply came into the American lines to talk to the Rangers. Torrejón, they said, had driven them from their homes, which he threatened to burn before allowing them to fall into American hands. "They pointed out their *jacales* and *casas* to us and implored our assistance in saving them! Singular war," remarked Kendall, "and more singular the people." In about an hour the cavalry moved off in good order, joining the rest of Ampudia's forces at Monterrey to await the coming of the American army and the showdown battle of the campaign.[44]

Monterrey, a city of nearly fifteen thousand, was situated on the main highway to central Mexico and guarded the strategic Rinconada Pass. Recognizing its vital importance to the defense of the Mexican interior,

General Ampudia concentrated all available forces there. He fortified the already naturally strong position to the point that he, and many of his American adversaries, considered it impregnable. Taylor established his headquarters at San Domingo and prepared his army for an assault on the city. The 1st Texas Mounted Riflemen, composed of three months' volunteers, had served out its term of enlistment more than two weeks before the army arrived at Monterrey. But, according to Buck Barry, a private in Hays's regiment, "some of us had traveled six hundred miles to kill a Mexican and refused to accept a discharge until we got to Monterrey where a fight was awaiting our arrival."[45]

McCulloch's Texans spent the afternoon of September 19 escorting engineer officers on their reconnaissance of the city's defenses and playing a daring game of "dodge the ball" with the garrison's gunners. To the horror of the United States regulars, the Rangers would intentionally draw the fire of the Mexican artillery. Gauging the trajectory of each cannon ball, they would race their horses at the last moment from its path. The Mexicans might as well have attempted "to bring down skimming swallows as those racing daredevils," wrote an awed officer of Ohio volunteers.[46]

Following their report, and against all conventional military wisdom, Taylor divided his force in the face of a numerically superior enemy. He then dispatched William Jenkins Worth and his division around the city to sever the Saltillo road and provide the anvil against which Taylor's two remaining divisions would hammer the city's defenders. In fact, Worth's men would be the hammer. Hays's regiment was selected to accompany Worth around to the rear of the city. About noon on September 20, with McCulloch's and Gillespie's companies in the vanguard, Worth's column began its march toward the rear of the city. The Texans encountered remarkably light resistance through the day. Near the Saltillo road they bivouacked for the cold, rainy night with neither blankets nor provisions.[47] During the five days of fighting that followed in and around Monterrey, the Ranger regiment was too busily engaged by day and too certain of drawing artillery fire by night to cook even the bit of food they were issued. Nevertheless, said Private Barry, "It seemed that we did as well on raw green corn as if we had beefsteak and flour bread."[48]

At dawn, under a continuous but ineffective fire from the guns on Independence Hill, Worth's division, with McCulloch's company in the vanguard, set out once again to interdict the Saltillo road. When they had advanced a mile and a half, a turn in the road at the hacienda San Jeronimo brought them face to face with fifteen hundred of the enemy. Lancers were drawn up across their route, while the road to the city swarmed with more cavalry and foot soldiers.⁴⁹

Worth quickly deployed his division with Hays's regiment on the right. The enemy line moved forward, supported by the artillery on Independence Hill. Suddenly the *"adelante"* was heard from the Mexican line, and a squadron of lancers swept down upon the American right. "Each man had a Mexican flag waving from his lance, making the most beautiful spectacle of mounted men I ever expect to see," recalled Ranger Buck Barry. "Although everything was silent, these little flags told us in plain language they were after our blood."⁵⁰ Hays ordered his regiment to move up to the shelter of a fence and dismount. McCulloch's company, deployed in the chaparral at the extreme right of Worth's line, failed to receive the order to dismount and received the charge of the Mexican lancers in the saddle "with their unerring rifles and usual gallantry."⁵¹ As the distance between the two bodies of mounted men diminished, the Rangers fired a volley, "pouring in a perfect storm of lead from their rifles, double-barreled guns and pistols."⁵² The commander of the lancers, Colonel Juan Najera, "a tall, splendid-looking fellow, with a fierce mustache,"⁵³ fell at the front of his men. The charge was broken midway. "The lancers tumbled from their saddles by dozens' yet with uncommon daring the survivors dashed onward, engaging hand to hand with the rangers still mounted."⁵⁴ The latter used their Colt revolvers and bowie knives with murderous effect.

After absorbing appalling casualties, the Mexican cavalry retreated in disorder, carrying with them McCulloch and a portion of his men who had fought their way nearly to the enemy's center. Seeing their peril, the encircled Rangers began to fight their way back. McCulloch, in a desperate effort to rejoin his company, put spurs to his horse and, "running everything down in his way," escaped without a scratch.⁵⁵

This charge of the lancers was one of the most spectacular made by the Mexicans during the war. Although the engagement lasted but fifteen minutes, of the one hundred and eighty men who made the charge, Kendall estimated that no fewer than forty died, while nearly one hundred were wounded. Only one Texan was killed, although several of McCulloch's men suffered lance wounds.⁵⁶ Gunfire and shock—if not numbers—had favored the Rangers. The heavier horses ridden by the Americans gave them a decided advantage over the Mexicans, who were mounted on mustangs. The Texans' rifles emptied many saddles long before the lances could be brought to bear, and in cavalry melee, no other arm could match the six-shot Colt revolver, then the exclusive property of the Rangers. Mexican bravery on this field was nevertheless superb, and the Texans considered it the best fight put up by the enemy during the war. Even the rabidly anti-Mexican Clarksville *Northern Standard* reported that the lancers fought "with a fierce desperation almost unparalleled amongst the Mexicans."[57] "I have never called a Mexican a coward since," said Barry.[58]

As the few remaining lancers attempted to regain the safety of their lines, fire from American infantry and artillery sent the entire Mexican column—no doubt already demoralized by the slaughter of one of its finest cavalry units—reeling toward the defenses of Monterrey. The Saltillo road, Monterrey's last link with the rest of Mexico, was now in American hands. Having gained this foothold on the Mexican rear, Worth sent a detachment of four companies of United States Army regulars and six dismounted Rangers toward Federation Hill, south of the Santa Catarina River. This mesa was nearly one thousand feet high and very steep, defended by artillery and five hundred infantry, and crowned by El Soldado, an imposing Mexican fort. At noon Worth gave the word: "Men, you are to take that hill—and I know you will do it."[59]

The assault force of two hundred Rangers and four hundred regulars crossed the Santa Catarina River under fire from Mexican musketry and artillery and scrambled up Federation Hill. The assault "was handsomely done," according to Lieutenant George G. Meade.[60] The Rangers and regulars captured the Mexican guns and turned them upon El Soldado, soon disabling the last of the enemy artillery. A quick dash upon the fort sent its defenders fleeing back into Monterrey. The storming of the heights lasted about one hour and thirty minutes. Mexican losses were severe, while Worth's men suffered only some eighteen wounded, two fatally. "When the advantageous positions which the enemy occupied and the difficulties which had to be surmounted on our part are taken into consideration," wrote Reid, "the small loss seems almost incredible."[61]

In the fighting of September 21 the American army, spearheaded by McCulloch's Rangers, had interdicted the Saltillo road and seized the important works on Federation Hill, two of the main objectives of the battle. Despite having gained a foothold on the enemy's rear, however, the primary objective remained to be taken. The formidable Independence Hill, dominated by the Bishop's Palace, loomed large beyond the Santa Catarina, firmly athwart the final approach to Monterrey.

At 3:00 A.M. of the twenty-second, a storming party of some five hundred regulars and Texas volunteers was prepared to assault the Bishop's Palace. Independence Hill, which Reid judged to be "between seven and eight hundred feet in height" and an "almost perpendicular ascent," was heavily defended by well-entrenched infantry and artillery. The men who were ordered to take it held but a forlorn hope of either succeeding or surviving.[62]

The Americans moved forward with great elan, however, and by daylight were at the summit, driving the enemy from the rim of the hill and into the Bishop's Palace. When the United States' forces turned the guns of the captured outer works on the Bishop's Palace, the Mexicans counterattacked in a desperate attempt to retake their lost artillery. The attack was shattered by American rifle fire, however, and the routed Mexicans streamed from the hill and back into Monterrey, closely pressed by the pursuing Rangers. In his report on the storming of the hill and capture of the palace, General Worth specifically cited McCulloch for "distinguished bravery" and as one to whom his "thanks are especially due."[63]

On the morning of the twenty-third, McCulloch's company was again assigned to escort duty, accompanying Lieutenant Meade of the Topographical Engineers on a reconnaissance of the western approaches to the main plaza. They learned that the enemy had abandoned the city as far as the cemetery. The remainder of the day was spent with two other companies of Hays's regiment, guarding the pass on the Saltillo road west of Monterrey. From that direction, rumor held, Santa Anna was advancing in great force. While the Rangers were pulled from the fighting to watch for enemy reinforcement that never came, their comrades continued to push the Mexicans back toward the center of the city.

By noon Worth had occupied the plaza of La Purissima, from which he increased pressure on the already concentrated Mexican garrison. The Mexican army still occupied the main plaza and some two squares around it in each direction, which they had turned into a veritable fortress and defended with savage tenacity. Every street had been cut by a deep ditch behind which rose a solid masonry wall, each with its own embrasure from which artillery raked the approaches. Every house was garrisoned with infantry, and—as each had a flat cement roof above which loophole stone walls extended three to four feet on all sides—every house became a fortress. "Had we attempted to advance up the streets," said Meade, "all would have been cut to pieces; but we were more skillfully directed."[64]

Inch by inch, the Americans drove the Mexicans to the center of the city. Only the width of a street, and often only the width of a wall, separated the contenders. With "every street a plain road to death,"[65] the Texans advanced toward the plaza by the same tactic that they had employed in the capture of Béxar in 1835 and Mier in 1842, breaking holes in the adobe walls of the houses and fighting from room to room. As soon as the Rangers had punched a hole through a wall, the Mexicans would begin firing through it. "It was nothing strange for the muzzles of the Texans' and Mexicans' guns to clash together," recalled Barry, "both intending to shoot through the hole at the same time."[66] By nightfall this nightmare battle had reached to within one square of the plaza and guaranteed a fight to the finish the next day.

At daylight on the twenty-fourth McCulloch's company, relieved from picket duty, dashed into the city on their horses. Joining their comrades on the rooftops and looking down upon the regiments of Mexican soldiers massed in the main plaza, they felt that the enemy was now in their grasp, to be dispatched at leisure. The old score of the Mier Expedition was at last to be settled.

Much to their displeasure, however, an hour-and-a-half truce was declared. Both armies used the time to improve their positions, fully confident that the fighting would soon be renewed. The Texans were at work with axes and bowie knives, picking holes through the parapet walls so that they could fire from a prone position. At the same time, the Mexicans were busy piling sandbags across streets and doors.

At noon, however, the cease-fire was extended, and news of the armistice was announced at 5:00 P.M. The city with all its public property was to be surrendered to the Americans, but Ampudia's army was to be allowed safe conduct beyond Rinconada Pass. "The Texans," said Reid, "were maddened with disappointment."[67] "Old Rough and Ready," the Rangers believed, had "committed a great blunder, with no justifiable excuse." One of the general's guards remembered that for days afterward "Ben McCulloch's Texas Rangers were still loud in their expressions of indignation, threats were made against General Taylor, and the old hero deem'd it necessary to double the Dragoon guard around his Headquarters."[68] Ampudia requested and was granted an escort of regular United States Army officers to protect him from the Texans.[69]

Yet, in his congratulatory order to his army for their victory at Monterrey, Taylor was effusive in his praise of the Rangers. He declared that he was "assured that every individual in the command unites with him in admiration of the distinguished gallantry and conduct of Colonel Hays and his noble band of Texan volunteers—hereafter they and we are brothers, and we can desire no better guarantee of success than by their association."[70]

So complete was the American success that no probability of another fight existed for months. Most of the Rangers were content to go home, and on September 30, 1846, the Texans were mustered out of the service and two regiments disbanded.[71] Ben McCulloch requested and received furlough from General Taylor, with the understanding that if hostilities were renewed he would recruit a new spy company and return to the army.[72] Taylor breathed a sigh of relief as the last of the Rangers rode out of his camp. "With their departure we may look for a restoration of quiet and good order in Monterrey," he wrote to the adjutant general, "for I regret to report that some disgraceful atrocities have been perpetrated by them."[73]

Finding its terms too liberal, the Polk administration abrogated Taylor's armistice on November 2, and the army at Monterrey began preparing for further offensive operations. Although he had received instructions from the government not to attempt to hold territory beyond Monterrey, Taylor marched through Rinconada Pass and, on November 16, occupied the strategic city of Saltillo unopposed. On November 30, McCulloch wrote to his mother from Galveston, "I hope this war will not last long as I am compelled to go again." He was induced to return, he told her, not so much by "the love alone for a soldier's life" but by a sense of duty. "My hand is at the plough, and I will not look back."[74] Although Ben McCulloch's previous Mexican War service had been outstanding, his greatest achievement was to come after he had recruited a new company and returned to Taylor's army.

By the winter of 1846, ardor for the war had waned, even in Texas, and McCulloch found great difficulty in filling his new company. Not only were fewer recruits willing to fight in Mexico, but those who did rally to the colors were generally younger and less experienced than the men of his first company. Nevertheless, McCulloch raised twenty-seven men and by February 4, 1847, was at Monterrey.[75]

Because they had paid their own expenses, the men requested that McCulloch offer Taylor their services for six months as regularly enlisted soldiers or extract a promise of food for themselves and their horses only until the prospect of a fight was over. Taylor, at first, replied that he could legally receive the company for the duration of the war only. The Rangers held out, however, knowing, as McCulloch recounted, "that the General was in a tight place and the services very hazardous." Major Solon Borland, Major John P. Gaines, and Captain Cassius M. Clay, with scouting parties of eighty of Taylor's best cavalry, had been captured at the Hacienda de la Encarnación by three thousand Mexicans under General José Vincente Miñón on January 22. In a day or two, Major Bliss rode into town with the welcome news that the company would be mustered in for six months.[76] After spending two weeks in Saltillo, McCulloch's company pushed on to Taylor's forward position at Agua Nueva.

With almost all of northeastern Mexico in American hands and the Mexican government still reluctant to end the war, the Polk administration decided to invade central Mexico by launching an attack by sea upon Vera Cruz and marching directly upon Mexico City. In order to build an army for this purpose, Taylor's command had been stripped of many of its veteran regiments and reduced to a dangerously low level of manpower. Taylor was ordered to stand on the defensive at Monterrey, but, believing that any potential adversary had been withdrawn from northern Mexico to check the new invasion threat, he had extended his line twenty miles beyond Saltillo to Agua Nueva.

Justifiably nervous in this militarily and politically indefensible situation, Taylor ordered McCulloch to make a reconnaissance of Encarnación, some fifteen miles to the south. As McCulloch had suspected, he and his party encountered a sizable Mexican vedette within a mile of the rancho. In a brief midnight skirmish, the outnumbered Texans put the enemy pickets to rout. This was all that McCulloch desired, for he well knew that "if we could not make them run, we must ourselves, as both our *orders* and their *numbers* cautioned us against fighting." The Rangers pursued the Mexicans far enough to learn their probable strength: "about two companies with a bugle each." Having learned this much, the patrol returned to headquarters and reported that the picket guard it had met at Encarnación did not appear to belong to the screening force commanded by Miñón, the only organized Mexican force then thought to be in the area. Other intelligence, arriving simultaneously through Mexican informers, indicated that Miñón was nowhere in the region.[77]

On the morning of February 20, McCulloch was summoned to Taylor's marquee and told to accompany Lieutenant Colonel Charles A. May of the dragoons on a scout to La Hedionda, about twenty-five miles to the southeast. McCulloch asked the general if he intended sending anyone to Encarnación. When Taylor replied that he did not, McCulloch told him that he believed that the party with which he had skirmished at the rancho was the advance of Santa Anna's army and that if Taylor were to send anyone there, he would like to go. Having a great deal of faith in his chief of scout's instinct for enemy movement, Taylor changed his orders and dispatched McCulloch and six other scouts back to Encarnación. Indeed, McCulloch's instincts had been correct. After a series of debilitating and demoralizing Mexican defeats and faced with war on two fronts, Santa Anna knew that "if we did not move now we were dead. Victory was the only way out." Believing that San Luis Potosí "was a strategic point in the campaign," Santa Anna slipped away from the second front on the gulf and, by forced marches, traveled two hundred terrible miles to Taylor's weakened and unsuspecting army.[78]

McCulloch's mission, however, foiled Santa Anna's plans for a surprise attack. The Texans were within five miles of Encarnación when the lights of the general's campfires became visible. Working his way toward the Mexican camp on foot, McCulloch came close enough to see the Mexicans' lances by the "gleam of the light from their cigars." The Rangers surmised that Santa Anna was preparing to march, for his soldiers were up very late cooking the next days' rations. Satisfied that Santa Anna was indeed at Encarnación in force, McCulloch placed Lieutenant Fielding Alston in command of the little detachment with instructions to return to Agua Nueva to warn Taylor. McCulloch and a single volunteer, William I. Phillips, remained to "take a daylight view of the enemy." Thus began one of the great adventure stories of the Mexican War.

McCulloch's decision to remain "was thought by all the party to be extremely hazardous at the time," he later wrote to his old friend Richardson Scurry, "owing to the country being destitute of any timber sufficiently tall to conceal the movements of a man on horseback." In addition, the road back to the American camp passed through a narrow gorge between high mountains on both sides. Even McCulloch admitted it was "indeed a *risky* affair."

After Alston and the others left, McCulloch and Phillips examined the enemy's camp. Moving close enough to see the Mexicans playing cards by firelight, the scouts were sure that their enemies were "betting off their interest in the spoils of the American Army. If one was allowed to judge of their opinions of success by their hilarity," McCulloch wrote, "then they were *certain* of success, as a more jolly set of singers was never listened to by anyone." As McCulloch and Phillips prepared to leave the Mexican camp to report to Taylor, noise from their horses alerted the guards. The two Rangers placed a small hill between themselves and the Mexicans and began a game of cat and mouse. When the Mexicans rode, so did the Texans; when the Mexicans halted to listen, the Texans did the same. To avoid any unnecessary noise, the Rangers unslung their canteens, which held all the water they had or could get that side of Agua Nueva, and laid them on the ground "as tenderly as if they were babies." At last the guards went back to their camp, and the scouts "got off without a race for it." They were still trapped behind enemy lines, however, and the morning was becoming brighter with every minute.

After hours of waiting for a favorable opportunity to pass back through the enemy picket line, McCulloch and Phillips at last determined to give it a try. Hiding their rifles under their legs on the off side of their horses, they rode slowly toward the guards. "I don't think my feeling was ever wrought up to such a pitch," wrote McCulloch. Only the outer picket farther up the road restrained him from "giving them a fire, raising the war-whoop, and breaking it up with a race." Dressed a good deal like Mexicans, the two men were apparently taken for vaqueros and allowed to pass. "We felt like we had a new lease on life when we got fairly out from between these two pickets," McCulloch confided.

Four miles below Tank Lavaca, at a narrow pass through which ran the road to Agua Nueva, the Rangers encountered four pickets in the uniform of regular Mexican cavalry who had to be passed as well. To the south, clouds of dust clearly indicated that Santa Anna was on the march. McCulloch was painfully aware that Alston's party might have been killed or captured, and should Taylor's army be attacked at Agua Nueva, defeat was inevitable.

No option remained but to attempt to pass. Hugging the rugged mountain on the west side of the road, the two Rangers decided to take advantage of its rocky slope if discovered. "We could have baffled them a long time," McCulloch told Scurry, "and killed many of them with our rifles where we were captured, or should I say killed, surrendering being out of the question. To do so was to be hanged." Both men agreed to take death by shooting in preference. Providence, however, seemed to favor the Texans. The two Rangers traveled four long miles in full view of the Mexican pickets—seeing them all the time, yet going unseen, or at least unchallenged. After passing Tank Lavaca, they had nothing further to contend with but the distance to Taylor's army and the great thirst that seemed to beset them as soon as they were out of danger. Pushing their horses as hard as their heated condition would permit, McCulloch and Phillips reached Agua Nueva about 4:00 P.M.

No sooner had they dismounted at the water hole than an officer of Taylor's staff rode up, saying the general wished to see McCulloch. "He seemed right glad to see me, saying, 'Major, I feared the Mexicans had caught you.'" The chief of scouts gave the general an account of what he had seen and what had detained him. This satisfied Taylor, who said only, "You must be tired, Major. You had better repair to camp and take some rest and sleep." He and his staff mounted and rode for Buena Vista, where the army was now stationed on a ridge just behind a narrow pass through which Santa Anna's army must come. Alston's patrol had reported early that morning, and the American army had fallen back immediately to that superb defensive position.

"When night came on," said McCulloch, "those of us who were not out as pickets slept on our arms" in a cold, drizzling rain.[79] On the following morning, McCulloch sent Lieutenant William H. Kelly with fifteen men toward Agua Nueva to see what the Mexican generalissimo was up to. Kelly had not gone more than two miles before he met the enemy advancing in great haste. The exchange of fire between the Rangers and Santa Anna's vanguard notified the army of the Mexicans' approach. McCulloch galloped to Saltillo to inform Taylor, who mounted and rode for the army. Little else was done by the Rangers on the twenty-second; most of the day was devoted to reconnaissance and parley between the opposing lines. Wishing to save Taylor from "catastrophe," Santa Anna offered the American commander the opportunity to surrender with all of the "consideration belonging to the Mexican character."[80] Mindful, perhaps, of the Alamo, Goliad, and Mier, the Americans declined.

About 8:00 A.M. of the twenty-third, the "long roll" was beaten in both camps. Riding out with General John E. Wool, the second-ranking United States officer on the field, McCulloch thought the enemy line looked "like a great wounded serpent dragging its unwieldy length" toward the American army. "The sight," McCulloch recalled, "was grand." With the first shots of the day, McCulloch received instructions from Wool to attach his small company to the dragoons. But because May's horsemen had not yet arrived, he formed on a line with the other troops and awaited the Mexican attack. In a few moments the action became hot and general, and very early in the fighting McCulloch's horse was shot from under him.[81]

With the arrival of May's dragoons, the Texans fell into line just as a charge of Torrejón's lancers broke the American left wing. Mexican cavalry poured through the breach, threatening the American wagon train at Rancho Buena Vista, three miles to the rear. May ordered his squadrons after the Mexican horses. Before he could reach them, however, the enemy cavalry was shattered by fire from the wagoners and United States infan-try that had straggled in from the front. May's dragoons arrived just in time to meet the retreating Mexicans head on. In the ensuing melee, McCulloch wounded and captured a captain of Mexican horsemen. Then, inexplicably to the Rangers, May halted the pursuit. His reason: the dust was so thick that other American soldiers might mistake them for Mexican cavalry. To McCulloch, this was not reason enough; May had missed a splendid opportunity to inflict heavy casualties on a shattered and retreating enemy. The American horsemen did, however, force the Mexicans from the field and prevent most of them from rejoining their own army.

Eager for further action, McCulloch urged May to order an advance against the enemy's right wing. May agreed on the condition that the ground between the two lines first be thoroughly scouted, and McCulloch trotted forward to make the reconnaissance in person. While examining the field, McCulloch took a second prisoner, an officer of the lancers. Returning with him to his own line, McCulloch met Major Andrew Jackson Coffee, son of General John Coffee and acting aide-de-camp to Zachary Taylor. Together they returned to the front but found the fighting to be at a lull; the Mexicans had begun their retreat. "The victory is ours," McCulloch told Coffee. "Then," replied Coffee, "here is a bottle of champagne. We will drink to the success of the American armies." So saying, he took from his holsters the best wine he ever tasted, McCulloch later reported.[82]

In his official report of the battle of Buena Vista, Zachary Taylor acknowledged that he and his army were "greatly indebted to Colonel May and Captain McCulloch, who rendered us much good service as spies. The intelligence which they brought caused us to leave the plains of Agua Nueva for a very strong and advantageous position."[83] On June 18 he reported to the adjutant general that "the services rendered by Major McCulloch and his men, particularly in reconnoitering the enemy's camp at Encarnación, and advising us certainly of his presence there, were of the highest importance."[84] On March 5, McCulloch was granted leave to return to Texas on a recruiting trip. He left his company under Alston's command and did not return to the army but accepted discharge on September 6, 1847. With the discharge of McCulloch's company, Taylor was left with only five companies of Texas Rangers, which, with the fighting done, seemed to him five too many. Atrocities attributed to discharged Rangers moved him to request "that no more troops may be sent to this column from the State of Texas."[85]

Ben McCulloch's own attitude toward the Mexican people seems to have been somewhat equivocal. Before 1842, his letters made no mention of them except as enemy soldiers. As a cofounder of Guadalupe College in Gonzales, however, he stressed strongly the need for Texas youth to learn the Mexican culture and insisted that "the Spanish language shall be considered and treated as only second in importance and utility to the English" in the school's curriculum.[86] Having left the Mier Expedition before its surrender, decimation, and incarceration at Perote prison, he lacked the personal grievance against the Mexicans common to many of his fellow Rangers. Often he wrote with respect of the bravery of individual enemy soldiers, but in general he considered the Mexican soldiery inferior to the American. In 1849, on the road from Parras to Mazatlán en route to the California gold fields, he wrote that he had a "better opportunity of seeing the Mexican as he is than ever . . . before. A more indolent, worthless, and stupid race does not exist."[87] No evidence exists, however, to indicate that he personally ordered or participated in the killing of any Mexican civilian or prisoner of war.

Unquestionably, Zachary Taylor esteemed McCulloch very highly, both personally and as a soldier and scout. General Walter P. Lane, a veteran of the Monterrey and Buena Vista campaigns, recalled having "often seen the two sitting by the campfire, late at night, talking to each other for hours."[88] Yet on June 10, Taylor reported that many of the volunteers, on their return to Texas, "committed extensive depredations and outrages upon the peaceful inhabitants" of the lower Rio Grande. "There is scarcely a form of crime that has not been reported to me as committed by them," the general wrote, and he found them to be a "disgrace [to] their colors and their country."[89]

An outraged Sam Houston defended the Rangers on the floor of the United States Senate, declaring that the people of Texas "have been unwarrantably assailed, traduced, and defamed" by Taylor's criticism of the soldiers and pointing out that "when called upon, the Texans went into battle like chafed lions." He reminded Taylor and the Senate that "at Monterrey, it was Texans who first took the plaza, the key of the victory" and that "the Bishop's palace and heights, too, were taken by Texans." McCulloch, he reminded them, "reconnoitered the enemy's camp, and possessed himself of the first information of the advance of Santa Anna, and thus in time enabled our troops to fall back from Agua Nueva" to the superior defensive position at Buena Vista. "But even these deeds," Houston raged, "were not enough to rescue them from obloquy and defamation."[90]

Indeed, in battle and on scout, the Texans had been formidable. Hays's regiment of Rangers was surely the most valuable of any of Taylor's units; without it, Monterrey and Buena Vista might well have been American disasters. McCulloch characteristically understated his Mexican War experiences in a letter to Scurry. "In this way we did the country some service."[91] It is tragic, therefore, that the Texans repaid barbarity in its own coin, tarnishing a splendid military record with a campaign of terrorism, spawned by racism and ancient grudge. Ironically, too often the Rangers were but the mirror images of the Mexican soldiery whose ethnocentrism, indiscipline, and brutality they despised.

TEXAS IN THE SOUTHERN WAR FOR INDEPENDENCE

Ralph A. Wooster

TEXANS GREETED THE OUTBREAK OF THE AMERICAN CIVIL War in 1861 with mixed emotions. In his study of the secession movement in Texas, Walter Buenger has shown that before the election of Abraham Lincoln in November, 1860, a majority of Texans supported the Union that they had worked so hard to join fifteen years earlier.[1] Lincoln's election, however, was regarded by many Anglo-Texans as a threat to southern institutions, including slavery. Although only one in four white Texas families owned slaves, most Texans considered any interference with the practice detrimental to the continued growth of the state.

After Lincoln's election, many Texans requested that Governor Sam Houston call a convention of the people to consider secession from the Union. Houston was a Unionist, however, and resisted all demands for a convention. The demands grew louder with the secession of South Carolina in December and the meeting of conventions in Mississippi, Florida, Alabama, Georgia, and Louisiana in early January. A group of prominent Texas citizens issued its own call for a convention, and elections for delegates were held in early January. In a desperate effort to forestall action, Houston called a special session of the legislature to consider the issue. The governor recommended that the legislature refuse to approve the convention. To his disappointment, the legislature endorsed the convention with the stipulation that its final actions be subject to a vote of the people of Texas.[2]

The state convention that assembled on January 28, 1861, moved quickly to adopt an ordinance of secession by a vote of 166-8. Voters overwhelmingly approved this ordinance: 46,153 to 14,747. The convention reassembled in early March, declared Texas out of the Union, and adopted an ordinance uniting the state with the newly formed Confederate States of America. Governor Houston, who had reluctantly accepted the voters' endorsement of secession, refused to recognize the authority of the convention to take this action. When called upon to take the oath of allegiance to the Confederacy, he refused to do so. The convention thereupon declared the office vacant and elevated Lieutenant Governor Edward Clark to the position.[3]

Even before the voters approved secession, a Committee of Public Safety created by the secession convention had taken steps to seize Federal property throughout the state. The committee named a four-member commission to open negotiations with Major General David E. Twiggs, commander of United States troops stationed in Texas. Twiggs, an aging Georgian in poor health, was sympathetic to the Texas position but was awaiting orders from the War Department. On the night of February 15, Ben McCulloch, a veteran Texas Ranger and hero of the Mexican War, secretly assembled five hundred volunteers at Cíbolo Creek near Twiggs's headquarters in San Antonio. The next morning McCulloch, dressed in a handsome black velvet uniform, led his volunteers into San Antonio, where they surrounded Twiggs and his one hundred sixty headquarters troops. Reluctantly, Twiggs agreed to surrender all Federal property in Texas and evacuate the twenty-seven hundred Union troops scattered in frontier forts throughout the state. Without firing a shot, Texas acquired military supplies and other properties valued at $3 million.[4]

The Committee of Public Safety authorized the recruiting of volunteer troops during late February and March, 1861. Colonels Henry McCulloch, younger brother of Ben, and John S. "Rip" Ford each recruited a regiment of cavalry. McCulloch, working in Central Texas, signed up ten companies of mounted troops known as the 1st Texas Mounted Rifles, the first military unit from Texas to enter Confederate service.[5]

The colorful Rip Ford, already a legend for his exploits as a Ranger, soldier, and explorer, recruited five hundred volunteers in the Houston area. Under Ford's leadership these troops sailed to the mouth of the Rio Grande, where in late March they captured the Union outpost at Fort Brown. Ford was made commander of the lower Rio Grande district with headquarters in Brownsville. During 1861 and 1862 he constructed coastal defenses, negotiated trade agreements with Mexican authorities, and fought his old nemesis, Mexican outlaw Juan "Cheno" Cortina.[6]

The firing on Fort Sumter in April, 1861, and the subsequent call for volunteers by Confederate president Jefferson Davis spurred efforts of Texas authorities to recruit additional soldiers. Governor Clark divided the state into six military districts to recruit and organize troops requested by the Confederate government. In May, Clark appointed Ebenezer B.

Nichols, a wealthy Galveston merchant, as agent to purchase arms and ammunition for the troops recruited in Texas. Later in the summer others, including Samuel Maverick, Hamilton P. Bee, and Lemuel R. Evans, were also appointed purchasing agents by Governor Clark.[7]

As the demands of the Confederate army grew, Governor Clark devoted more attention to military matters. In June, 1861, the governor issued a proclamation revising the archaic militia system of the state. Camps of instruction were set up in each of eleven militia districts. Members of the militia mustered into volunteer companies and reported to the training camps. Soldiers were required to furnish their own weapons because the state had exhausted its own supplies.[8]

By the end of 1861, approximately twenty-five thousand Texans were enrolled in the Confederate army. Two-thirds of these were in the cavalry, for Texans preferred riding to walking. A British visitor, Lieutenant Colonel Arthur Fremantle of the Coldstream Guards, noted this fondness for cavalry service. "It was found very difficult to raise infantry in Texas, as no Texan walks a yard if he can help it."[9] Governor Clark also recognized the Texan preference for mounted service. In a message to the state legislature he observed "the predilection of Texans for cavalry service, found as it is upon their peerless horsemanship, is so powerful that they are unwilling in many instances to engage in service of any other description unless required by actual necessity."[10]

Sixteen regiments, three battalions, and three independent cavalry companies were raised in Texas the first year of the war. Four of the cavalry regiments recruited that year—the 2nd Mounted Rifles, the 4th Cavalry, the 5th Cavalry, and the 7th Cavalry—participated in Henry H. Sibley's ill-fated invasion of the New Mexico Territory. Benjamin F. Terry, a Brazoria sugar planter, raised the most famous of all the mounted Texas units, the 8th Cavalry—better known as Terry's Texas Rangers. Mustered into Confederate service on September 9, 1861, the Rangers left Houston for Virginia. The need for additional troops in Kentucky, however, forced the regiment to join General Albert Sidney Johnston's command in that state.[11]

Seven regiments and four infantry battalions were recruited in Texas in 1861. Three of these regiments—the 1st, 4th, and 5th—were ordered to Virginia in the fall of the year. There they became part of the Texas Infantry Brigade, commanded first by Louis T. Wigfall and later by John Bell Hood. As Hood's Texas Brigade, the unit distinguished itself in battles at Gaines' Mill, Second Manassas, Sharpsburg, Gettysburg, and Chickamauga. The Texas brigade received the highest praise from Robert E. Lee, the commanding general of the Army of Northern Virginia, who later in the war stated, "I never ordered the Brigade to hold a place, that they did not hold it."[12] The 2nd Infantry Regiment, organized at Galveston, was another regiment formed in 1861 that saw extensive military service. Commanded first by John C. Moore and later by William P. Rogers and Ashbel Smith, the 2nd Infantry fought at both Shiloh and Vicksburg.[13]

Recruitment of soldiers became more difficult as some of the early enthusiasm for combat waned. Governor Clark and his successors, Francis R. Lubbock and Pendleton Murrah, found meeting Richmond's calls for additional troops to be a more serious problem as the war continued. The passage of a general conscription law by the Confederate Congress in April, 1862, relieved state officials from having to institute a local draft and momentarily stimulated volunteering. The normal distaste for any form of discipline, the desire to remain at home with friends and loved ones, the possibility of obtaining occupational exemption or hiring a substitute, and the growing dissatisfaction with policies of the Confederate government all added to the difficulties in raising troops.[14]

Approximately ninety thousand Texans served in the Confederate army during the war. Because of duplications and errors in reporting, the exact number is not likely to be ascertained. The 1860 national census lists 92,145 white males between the ages of eighteen and forty-five living in the state. Allowing for a slight increase in population within the next four years and considering that some Texans both younger and older served, between one hundred thousand and one hundred ten thousand Texans were potential soldiers. Governor Lubbock reported to the legislature in November, 1863, that ninety thousand Texans were in the army, but this figure seems high for Texans in Confederate service at any one time.[15]

Most Texans enrolled in military service spent the war west of the Mississippi River, either defending the state from Indian attacks and Union invasion, fighting in Louisiana, or participating in expansionist movements to the West. The month after the firing upon Fort Sumter, Colonel William C. Young and the 11th Texas Cavalry, recruited in North Texas, crossed the Red River and captured Forts Arbuckle, Cobb, and Washita. Afterward they rode through Indian territory negotiating with the Comanches, Kiowas, and Chickasaws. A second unit, recruited originally as state troops and known as the Frontier Regiment, patrolled the area between the Red River and the Rio Grande. Commanded first by Colonel James M. Norris and later by Colonel James E. McCord, the regiment, which was later transferred to Confederate service as the 46th Texas Cavalry, fought several battles with the Comanches during the course of the war.[16]

"The Struggle for Devil's Den," drawing by A. R. Waud showing an attack by Hood's Texas Brigade, July 2, 1863, at the Battle of Gettysburg. Courtesy Confederate Research Center, Hillsboro, Texas.

Texans were keenly interested in Confederate expansion into New Mexico and Arizona. In June, 1861, Lieutenant Colonel John R. Baylor and four companies of Rip Ford's 2nd Cavalry were ordered to occupy the extreme western portion of Texas. In July Baylor captured Fort Bliss at El Paso, then moved north into New Mexico Territory. He occupied the small village of Mesilla, located on the left bank of the Rio Grande about forty miles north of El Paso. After a brief skirmish, Federal troops surrendered Fort Fillmore on the opposite bank of the Rio Grande. On August 1, 1861, Baylor declared most of the Territory of New Mexico to be the Confederate Territory of Arizona, with Mesilla as the capital and himself as military governor.[17]

Baylor's advance into southern New Mexico was the first step by Confederates to occupy the entire territory. Henry H. Sibley, a West Point graduate from Louisiana and formerly captain of the U.S. 2nd Dragoons stationed in New Mexico, convinced President Jefferson Davis of the importance of New Mexico and Arizona. Sibley, a veteran soldier who had seen extensive duty in the Southwest, was commissioned a brigadier general with instructions to raise and equip a brigade of cavalry to drive Federal forces out of New Mexico. In August Sibley established his headquarters in San Antonio, where he began recruiting men for the Army of New Mexico. The prospect of invading New Mexico had great appeal to Texans, whose interest in the Santa Fe area dated back to the days of the Texas Republic when the Lone Star government had claimed it. By late October thirty companies had been formed and organized into three regiments: the 4th, commanded by Colonel James Reily, a native of Ohio who had settled in Texas shortly after independence and was an experienced politician, diplomat, and soldier; the 5th, commanded by the highly popular Colonel Tom Green, a veteran of San Jacinto and the Mexican War; and the 7th, commanded by Colonel William Steele, a native of New York, graduate of West Point, veteran of the Mexican War and—like Sibley—a former officer in the 2nd Dragoons.[18]

In early November the brigade began the long and difficult march to El Paso, a journey of nearly seven hundred miles through rolling plains, bleak desert, and rugged mountains. Stephen Oates observed "it was a motley crowd that moved on the road to Fort Clark . . . some on horses and others on foot, armed with bowie knives, shotguns, and rifles that varied in make and caliber."[19] Uniforms were also of various colors and styles. Many troopers wore the civilian clothes they had brought with them. Sibley himself followed behind in a carriage. The commanding general was suffering from ill health and was also a heavy drinker. Already there were indications that his "efficiency as a commander was hindered both by lack of physical strength and by overindulgence."[20]

Sibley reached Fort Bliss on December 14. He issued orders proclaiming himself commander of all Confederate forces in the El Paso area, in New Mexico, and in Arizona. On January 11, 1862, Sibley marched to Mesilla, where he assumed command of forces formerly under John R. Baylor and now commanded by Major Charles L. Pryon. After sending out detachments to Tucson and isolated posts, Sibley moved northward along the west bank of the Rio Grande to Fort Craig, where he encountered Union troops commanded by Colonel E. R. S. Canby. Sibley had approximately 2,600 men, compared to 3,810 for Canby. Concluding that Fort Craig was too strong to assault from the south, the Confederates crossed to the east bank of the river and then swung back above the fort at Valverde ford. On February 21 the Confederates found Canby's main forces blocking the crossing at Valverde. In the fierce battle that followed, the Confederates—led by Tom Green and William R. Scurry, now commanding the 4th Cavalry—captured a Federal artillery battery and drove

Union forces back to Fort Craig.[21]

Because Canby still refused to surrender the fort, the Confederates decided to bypass Fort Craig and move northward up the valley to Albuquerque and Santa Fe. Morale among the Texans was low. Although they had won the battle at Valverde, commissary supplies were virtually exhausted, some of the soldiers no longer had horses, and the weather was bitterly cold. Accusations against Sibley, who had relinquished command to Tom Green during the battle, were mounting. "Among the soldiers I hear ridicule and curse heaped upon the head of our genl.," wrote one soldier. "They call him a coward, which appears plausible, too."[22] The capture of Albuquerque on March 8 and Santa Fe on March 18 momentarily improved the matter of supplies, but the logistical problems were proving much greater than Sibley had anticipated.[23]

While Sibley remained in Santa Fe, Colonel Green and much of the army moved to the east into the mountain valleys, where fresh water and wild game were available. Meanwhile, Union forces at Fort Union to the east were receiving reinforcements from the Colorado gold-mine fields. On March 26 Confederates fought a brisk skirmish with a regiment of the Pike Peakers in Apache Canyon. Two days later a larger battle between Federals led by Colonel John Chivington, a Colorado preacher, and Texans commanded by Colonel William R. Scurry took place at La Glorieta Pass. During the fierce fighting, each side suffered about one hundred casualties. The Texans drove the Federals from the field and thus won the battle, but later in the afternoon Scurry's wagon train, containing badly needed food, medicine, and ammunition, was captured by Union forces.[24]

The loss of Scurry's supply train was a major blow to Sibley's hopes. With the Federals receiving reinforcements from both Colorado and California, the Confederates faced the prospect of being trapped between enemy forces without adequate food or ammunition. The decision to retreat was made in early April. On April 12, the withdrawal toward El Paso and Fort Bliss began. The Confederates were demoralized, men and horses were exhausted, food and medicine were in short supply, confidence in Sibley had disappeared, and the hopes and dreams for a Confederate New Mexico had vanished. Fortunately, Union pursuit was poorly coordinated and lacking in vigor. By early May Sibley was back at Fort Bliss, where he issued a valedictory proclamation praising his men for their sacrifices. The Army of New Mexico, now reduced by a thousand casualties, headed for San Antonio in June. Confederate—and Texas—military operations in New Mexico, Arizona, and extreme West Texas had come to an end.[25]

Texans were more successful in defending their four-hundred-mile coastline from enemy invasion than they were in securing New Mexico for the Confederacy. Indeed, a widely used textbook for Texas history describes defense of the Texas coast as "one of the most brilliant chapters in the story of the Confederacy."[26] These efforts for coastal defense began in the late spring of 1861. Brigadier General Earl Van Dorn, the Mississippian who commanded the Texas district from April to September, 1861, organized volunteer defense companies, authorized the use of slave labor for building fortifications, and worked to secure heavy cannon for coastal defense. In Galveston the 3rd Battalion, Texas Artillery, consisting of seven companies, was organized under the command of Major Joseph J. Cook, a graduate of the United States Naval Academy. The 4th Texas Volunteers, commanded by Colonel Joseph Bates and including four artillery batteries, defended the coast from San Luis Pass to Caney Creek. Farther south, three additional artillery companies defended the Matagorda Bay–Corpus Christi area. In November an independent company, later part of the 1st Regiment, Texas Heavy Artillery, was formed to defend Sabine Pass on the Texas-Louisiana border.[27]

In September, Van Dorn was transferred from Texas to the East. His replacement as commander of the Texas district was Brigadier General Paul Octave Hébert of Louisiana. Hébert, who graduated at the top of his West Point class of 1840, had a reputation as a textbook general "of no military force or practical genius" who "preferred red-top boots, and a greased rat-tail moustache, with fine equipage, and a suit of waiters, to the use of good, practical common sense."[28] Such a reputation did little to endear Hébert to Texans, who admired military leaders not for their uniforms or administrative skills but for their fighting ability.

In the first month after his arrival in Texas Hébert pushed efforts to fortify Galveston and Houston, the two largest Texas cities on the coast. An attempt was made to improvise a harbor defense fleet, and coastal garrisons were increased in numerical strength. But Hébert could not overcome the lack of heavy ordnance. In a report to Secretary of War Judah P. Benjamin, Hébert confided that because "it will be impossible to prevent a landing at some point upon this extensive and unprotected coast, I have settled upon it as a military necessity that he must be fought on shore or in the interior."[29]

In November, 1861, Union naval vessels operating off the Texas coastline surprised and partially burned the Confederate patrol schooner *Royal Yacht*, increasing Hébert's concerns about the safety of Galveston. Fortunately for Texas, no serious Union attacks were made against the city in 1861. Union forces contented themselves with occasional naval bombardment of Confederate positions near Aransas Pass, Port Lavaca, and Indianola.[30]

The Union navy increased its pressure on the Texas coast during 1862. Although its main efforts during the spring and summer were directed toward Forts Henry and Donelson in Tennessee and New Orleans and Memphis on the Mississippi River, the navy established a blockade along the Gulf Coast and occasionally raided the Texas mainland. Lieutenant John W. Kittredge, commander of the bark *Arthur*, was especially active in the Aransas region in the early summer months, obstructing coastal trade and lobbing shells into coastal towns. In August Kittredge, then commanding a small flotilla, tried to capture Corpus Christi but was repulsed by Confederate troops commanded by Major Alfred M. Hobby. But another Union force, under Lieutenant Frederick Crocker, overwhelmed the Confederate defenders at Sabine Pass in October, destroyed the small fort, and burned the railroad bridge at Taylor's Bayou before withdrawing.[31]

The main Union thrust against the Texas coast in 1862 was reserved for Galveston. General Hébert, convinced that defense of the city was impossible, was constructing a Confederate fort across the bay on the mainland at Virginia Point. Consequently, all but one of the heavy guns were removed from Fort Point on the island and placed on the mainland. Galvestonians were bitterly opposed to the move and accused Hébert "of greater love for his cannon than for their city."[32]

On October 4, 1862, the Union gunboat *Harriet Lane* sailed into the Galveston harbor and demanded the surrender of the city. Shortly thereafter, she was followed by seven other warships that sailed past Fort Point on the tip of the island. The garrison at Fort Point opened fire with its ten-inch gun, the only remaining heavy artillery in the city, but this gun was quickly silenced by fire from eleven-inch guns on the Union gunboat *Owasco*. After two salvos from smaller guns proved ineffective, Confederate resistance on the island ceased. Texas's largest seaport was now in Union hands.[33]

The loss of Galveston in early October was followed by a change in Confederate command in Texas. General Hébert, who had never been popular in Texas, was replaced by General John Bankhead Magruder, a proud Virginian who had a reputation as a fighter. Although Magruder—popularly known as Prince John for his courtly bearing, suave manners, and regal dress—had been careless in the Seven Days Battle near Richmond and had incurred the displeasure of General Lee, no one in Texas doubted his aggressive spirit. Most agreed with Rip Ford that "the advent of General Magruder was equal to the addition of 50,000 men to the forces of Texas."[34]

When Magruder assumed command of the Texas district on November 29, 1862, he began planning the recapture of Galveston. In late December, he gathered his forces for the assault: the 26th Texas Cavalry under Colonel Xavier B. Debray, French-born graduate of Saint Cyr Military Academy; several other cavalry groups, detachments, and companies commanded by the popular Tom Green; and some volunteer infantry. Magruder also had several artillery batteries and two river steamers, the *Bayou City* and the *Neptune,* that had been converted into gunboats. Magruder's plan of attack called for his land forces to move across the railroad bridge from the mainland to the island during the night. Meanwhile the river steamers, commanded by Captain Leon Smith, would descend from the mouth of the Trinity River and sink the Federal warships anchored in the harbor.

The attack on Galveston was timed for the early morning hours of New Year's Day. At 1:00 A.M., while the Federal troops slept, Magruder led his land forces quietly across the old railroad bridge. Between 3:00 and 4:00 A.M., Confederate artillery opened fire on Federal ships and positions along the waterfront. The Federal troops drove back the first attack of the Confederate infantry, but the Texans charged again and again. Meanwhile, the two Confederate gunboats moved against the heavily armed Union warship *Harriet Lane.* Dismounted Texas cavalry, firing from behind cotton bales, picked off Union sailors from the *Harriet Lane*'s decks, but the Confederate *Neptune* was hit by a shell from the *Lane,* veered off into shallow water, and sank. The *Bayou City* continued to move toward the *Lane* with the Confederate riflemen still firing at the *Lane*'s sailors. When the *Bayou City* finally pulled alongside, the Texas horse marines stormed aboard, captured the *Lane,* and hauled down her colors.[35]

The other Union ships in the harbor were having troubles of their own. The *Westfield,* the Union flagship, ran aground on Pelican Spit just off Pelican Island, and efforts by a sister ship, the *Clifton,* to free her were unsuccessful. Three other small Union vessels, the *Sachem,* the *Owasco,* and the *Corpheus,* had been firing at the Confederates near the waterfront but in an uncoordinated effort. The *Owasco* moved in briefly to aid the *Harriet Lane* but pulled away to avoid hitting Federal prisoners. In the midst of the confusion the *Westfield* was rocked by an internal explosion caused by premature detonation as her commander, William S. Renshaw, prepared to destroy her rather than risk capture. The explosion killed Renshaw and several members of the crew. The Union naval forces, now leaderless, confused, and disorganized, pulled out of the harbor and abandoned the fight. More than two hundred men of the 42nd Massachusetts Infantry, who were still fighting on the waterfront, looked on as the Union vessels steamed out to open sea. Without naval support, the Union infantry soon surrendered to Magruder. Galveston was once again in Confederate hands.[36]

Magruder received great praise for the recapture of Galveston. The Texas press, state officials, and the Confederate Congress all lavished tributes upon the Virginian for his bold attack. Unfortunately, he had little time to enjoy the accolades as Union gunboats soon returned to resume the blockade and to bombard Confederate installations along the coast. Magruder worked diligently to prepare for a Union counterattack at Galveston but was hampered by a lack of heavy artillery. To make up for this deficiency his engineers, Colonel Valery Sulakowski and Major Getulius Kellersberg, improvised fake guns from wood. These "Quaker" guns appeared very formidable from a distance and fooled Union naval officers until an early spring storm blew away one of the cannon. By June, some real cannon, moved from Houston and also taken from the hulk of the *Westfield*, were in place.[37]

The main Union thrust along the Gulf Coast in 1863 came not at Galveston but at Sabine Pass. Major General Nathaniel P. Banks, the Union officer commanding the Department of the Gulf, determined to move a large army regiment onto the Texas coast, march overland to Houston, and then capture Galveston from the rear. For this effort Banks selected the XIX Army Corps, consisting of four thousand infantry and commanded by Major General William B. Franklin. Banks planned to ferry the troops by transport to the coast, land them on the sandy beaches several miles south of Sabine Pass, and move overland to the railroad running from Beaumont to Houston. The transport vessels ferrying the troops would be protected by four light draft gunboats, the *Clifton, Sachem, Arizona*, and *Granite City*, commanded by Lieutenant Frederick Crocker.[38]

The Union invasion force was delayed by poor navigation and false rumors that the Confederate sea raider *Alabama* was off the Texas coast at Sabine Pass. In early September, however, the Union fleet appeared off the Texas coast. General Franklin decided to abandon the original plan of landing on the beaches. Instead, he planned to move the gunboats up the narrow channel at Sabine Pass, knock out the guns of the small Confederate fort guarding the pass, and bring his transport ships up into Sabine Lake where landings could be made. Early on the morning of September 8, 1863, Union gunboats fired on the rough Confederate earthwork fortification guarding the entrance to the pass.[39]

Lieutenant Richard W. Dowling, an Irish barkeeper from Houston, was commanding the small Confederate garrison at Fort Griffin when the

Union attack began. Under his command were the Davis Guards, Company F, 1st Texas Heavy Artillery. This force consisted of forty-seven artillerymen, four thirty-two-pound howitzers, and two twenty-four-pound howitzers, as well as a converted river steamer, the *Uncle Ben*. When the four Union gunboats tried to force their way past the fort that afternoon, the cannon from Fort Griffin were leveled with deadly accuracy, firing 107 rounds in thirty-five minutes. The Union vessel *Sachem* was hit by one of Dowling's guns on the third or fourth round and, a helpless wreck, was driven up against the Louisiana side of the channel. The Confederate guns were then turned on the *Clifton,* closest of the three remaining vessels. A cannonball cut her tiller rope, throwing her out of control and soon aground. Many of her men, thinking the ship was about to explode, plunged overboard and swam to shore. They were then captured by the Confederates, who crowded down to the water's edge to repel the invaders. The two remaining Union ships, the *Arizona* and the *Granite City,* turned and withdrew from the pass. General Franklin, overestimating the size and nature of the Confederate defense, ordered a withdrawal of the expedition back to New Orleans.[40]

Repelled at Sabine Pass, Federal forces next tried to invade southern Texas. In November, 1863, about seven thousand Union troops under General Banks landed at the mouth of the Rio Grande and captured Brownsville, cutting the vital trade link between the Confederacy and Mexico. Banks then divided his forces, sending one wing up the river to capture Rio Grande City and the other along the coast to capture Corpus Christi, Aransas Pass, and the Matagorda peninsula. General Magruder took the field himself and gathered a force of home guards, old men, and anyone else who could fight. Then, suddenly, Federal forces fell back down the coast toward Brownsville. Unknown to Magruder, a massive Union offensive was being planned for Louisiana in the spring of 1864, and troops were needed in that area. This worked to the advantage of Confederates in Texas because Union forces in the state were weakened. This allowed Confederate troops under Rip Ford an opportunity to retake the area occupied by Union soldiers. After sharp fighting in the summer of 1864, Ford's Confederates recaptured Brownsville, thus reopening a vital trade link with Mexico. By the end of the year Brazos Island, along the lower coast, was the only territory along the Texas coast held by the Federals.[41]

While Rip Ford was regaining control of the Rio Grande Valley, other Texans were fighting in Arkansas and northern Louisiana. In March, 1864, General Nathaniel Banks moved an army of twenty-seven thousand men and a naval flotilla up the Red River toward Shreveport. He hoped to advance across northwest Louisiana, link up with the fifteen thousand men under General Frederick Steele moving southward from Little Rock, and extend Federal control over northeast Texas. In an effort to prevent this alliance, Texas troops in the Indian territory under Brigadier General Samuel Maxey were moved to Arkansas to support Sterling Price, who was retreating from Steele's advance. With Maxey's assistance, Price was able to halt the Union advance at the battle of Poison Spring, fourteen miles west of Camden.[42]

Banks, meanwhile, was repulsed in northern Louisiana. On April 8 about eight thousand of his troops reached Sabine Cross Roads near Mansfield, some fifty miles below Shreveport. Here they were defeated by Confederates commanded by General Richard Taylor. Texans played a key role in the Confederate victory. The veteran Tom Green led Texas cavalry in the opening attack against the Union forces in what turned out to be a great Confederate victory: twenty-five hundred prisoners, twenty-two cannon, and one hundred fifty loaded supply wagons were seized by the Confederates. The next day the rebel forces resumed the attack at Pleasant Hill, fourteen miles down the river, but here superior Federal numbers prevented a Confederate victory. Again Texans played a major role in the fighting; Walker's division, Green's cavalry, and Polignac's Texas brigade all saw heavy action. Texas losses in the battle were heavy, however: Colonel Augustus Buchel was killed, and Brigadier General Hamilton P. Bee, Colonel James Walker, and Colonel Xavier B. Debray were wounded.[43]

The Confederates continued to attack the retreating enemy. Tom Green, most popular of all the Texas commanders, was killed while leading the attack on the Union fleet at Blair's Landing. Bee, Polignac, and John A. Wharton, who succeeded Green as cavalry commander, hit Banks's army as it retreated southward. In mid-May the Federals crossed the Atchafalaya River, thus ending the Red River campaign. General Taylor and other Confederates were pleased that Banks had been repulsed but were disappointed that his army had not been destroyed.[44]

While many Texans were defending the boundaries of their state from enemy attack, others were fighting east of the Mississippi River. Thousands of Texans took part in the great battles in Virginia, Tennessee, Georgia, and the Carolinas. Albert Sidney Johnston, for example, commanded Confederates in the bloody battle of Shiloh in April, 1862. Some believe that had Johnston not been killed on the first afternoon at Shiloh, the outcome of the battle would have been different. Others, pointing to his earlier failures at Forts Henry and Donelson and noting the strength of the Union army, argue that the outcome would have been the same even if Johnston had lived.[45]

Troops from Texas figured prominently in the heavy fighting in the eastern theater of operations. In the savage battle at Sharpsburg, Maryland, in September, 1862, the 1st Texas, one of the regiments of Hood's brigade, sustained casualties of 82.3 percent—the highest of any regiment in a single day of the Civil War. John Bell Hood himself lost the use of an arm at Gettysburg and a leg at Chickamauga. Another Texas brigade, commanded by Lawrence Sullivan Ross, endured enemy fire for one hundred days as it fought against Sherman in northern Georgia in the summer of 1864. Granbury's brigade, commanded by a Waco lawyer, Colonel Hiram Granbury, also saw extensive combat in the Atlanta campaign. The brigade later joined the futile Confederate attack at Franklin, Tennessee, where Granbury was one of six Confederate general officers killed or mortally wounded.[46]

Although most Texans supported the Confederacy, Union sentiment was strong in some areas, especially the German counties of the Hill Country and in a group of counties north of Dallas. Some Texas Unionists, such as former governor Sam Houston, withdrew from public life and attempted to avoid controversy. Others, such as James W. Throckmorton, one of the eight delegates in the Texas convention who voted against secession, accepted and actively supported the Confederacy after Fort Sumter. Some Unionists left the state, many to join the Union army. Frank Smyrl, in an article in the *Southwestern Historical Quarterly*, points out that 2,132 whites and 47 blacks from Texas served in the Union army. Best known of these was Edmund Jackson Davis, a former state judge who organized and commanded the 1st Texas Cavalry Regiment, which served in Louisiana and the Rio Grande Valley. Andrew Jackson Hamilton, a former congressman, was another prominent Texan who left the state. Both Hamilton and Davis would later serve as governor of Texas during Reconstruction.[47]

Those attempting to aid the enemy were often harshly treated by Texas Confederates. Sixty-five German Unionists trying to flee to Mexico were overtaken by Confederates near the Nueces River in August, 1862. In the brief battle that followed, thirty Germans were killed and twenty wounded. Another fifty Unionists were hanged in the Hill Country several weeks later. The greatest roundup of suspected Unionists occurred in Cooke and Grayson counties in North Texas. A citizens' court in Gainesville tried one hundred fifty individuals for Unionist activities. Thirty-nine were executed in what contemporaries called "the great Gainesville hanging."[48]

Confederate military reversals in the fall of 1864 had their effect upon Texas. Hood's crushing defeat at Nashville in mid-December caused many to realize that the Confederacy's situation was desperate. Captain James P. Douglas from Tyler had earlier remained optimistic, even in the heavy fighting around Atlanta. Now, in a letter he cautioned not to be shown "out of our family," he wrote that "our country is in much the worse condition it has ever been. If a great deed is not done this winter, the Yanks will close the war in the spring."[49]

Some Texans remained defiant even after Lee's army surrendered in April, 1865. Captain Samuel T. Foster, with Granbury's brigade in North Carolina, admitted that Lee's surrender had "a very demoralizing affect on the army" but still believed "we will whip this fight yet." George Lee Robertson, serving in South Texas, vowed to fight on. "If I can't have a Confederacy I don't want anything else." W. W. Heartsill of the W. P. Lane Rangers believed if the Southern people would unite as one, "the Trans-Mississippi could defy the combined powers of all Yankeedom."[50]

Most Texans were not as optimistic or determined, however. Regiments and companies began melting away in late April and early May as soldiers headed for their homes. Colonel John Ford defeated Union troops at Palmito Ranch near Brownsville on May 13, 1865, in what proved to be the last battle of the war. But from captured prisoners he learned that Confederate forces were surrendering all over the South. Edmund Kirby Smith, commander of the Trans-Mississippi Department, urged his men to remain at their posts but found that many were deserting. There was little Smith could do. On June 2, 1865, with General Magruder at his side, Smith boarded a Union ship at Galveston and signed the formal terms of surrender. The Civil War was over.[51]

BLACK REGULARS ON THE TEXAS FRONTIER, 1866-85

William H. Leckie

BLACK MEN HAVE FOUGHT IN ALL THE WARS IN WHICH THE United States has engaged from the American Revolution to the present. For too long, their willingness—indeed eagerness—to serve in the armed forces went largely unheralded if not scorned and ignored. This is certainly true of their invaluable service on the Texas frontier for nearly a generation after the Civil War.

The Civil War provided the first need and opportunity for the large-scale use of blacks in the Union army. It also was the background for the employment of black regiments in Texas after the war. After a reluctant Lincoln administration finally approved enlistment of blacks, nearly two hundred thousand of them wore the Union blue. More than thirty-three thousand died in that bloody conflict.[1]

Blacks in both the eastern and western theaters of the war had fought well. Nevertheless many, in and out of the military, still believed that they would never be reliable soldiers and urged that their use be discontinued. Among these doubters were Generals William T. Sherman, Philip H. Sheridan, Nelson A. Miles, George A. Custer, and Eugene A. Carr.[2] A majority in Congress disagreed, however, and when the army was reorganized in the summer of 1866, legislation provided for six regiments of black regulars—four of infantry and two of cavalry—as an "experiment." All six—the 38th, 39th, 40th, and 41st Infantry regiments and the 9th and 10th Cavalry regiments—were to be staffed with white officers. Further reorganization in 1869 merged the four infantry regiments into two: the 24th and 25th.[3]

Because infantry personnel were drawn primarily from men already in service, organization of the regiments was accomplished with little difficulty. Soon thereafter a shift of these troops to the Texas frontier was underway; by 1869, all were stationed at posts along the Rio Grande and in West Texas. Headquarters for the 24th was established at Fort McKavett and for the 25th at Fort Davis. Eleven long years passed before these regiments were assigned to stations outside Texas.[4]

Organization of the cavalry units proved to be no easy matter. During the Civil War few black regiments had been designated as cavalry; recruitment and training, therefore, began from scratch. Fortunately two officers with outstanding records accepted appointment to command the 9th and 10th: Brevet Major Generals Edward Hatch and Benjamin Grierson. Both had distinguished themselves as cavalrymen but had observed black infantry in action during the war and had a high regard for their abilities as fighting men.[5]

Hatch organized the 9th at Greenville, Louisiana, though he encountered great difficulty in securing officers. Many eligible ones, including George A. Custer, refused to serve with black troops. By contrast, careless and indifferent recruiters quickly filled the enlisted ranks, though many of the men turned out to be unfit for military service and almost all were illiterate. When in March, 1867, the 9th was ordered to Texas, Hatch had little more than an ill-disciplined mob on his hands. Small wonder that when ten companies of the regiment reached San Antonio, the stage was set for serious trouble.[6]

The citizens of San Antonio were not prepared to welcome or accept black men in blue uniforms, and clashes soon occurred between troopers, civilians, and police. On April 9, as too few officers strove to control their men, mutiny broke out in three companies. Before order was restored, one officer and two enlisted men were killed. Hatch appealed for more officers, and these were soon forthcoming. In May, when the regiment was ordered west to Forts Stockton and Davis, both discipline and morale had improved significantly. Difficulties of this kind in newly created regiments were not peculiar to black units. In July, 1867, mass desertions from the new 7th Cavalry led to the shooting of three enlisted men.[7]

Grierson, headquartered at Fort Leavenworth, Kansas, did not experience the severe problems that had plagued Hatch. From the beginning he insisted on a high caliber of recruits. Where Hatch's ranks had been filled by men drawn largely from the Deep South, Grierson concentrated enlistment efforts in such cities as New York, Philadelphia, and Cincinnati. The result was a slow pace in organizing the companies of the regiment. It was midsummer of 1867 before the 10th was ready to take the field, and even then some of the companies were undermanned. Soon thereafter, most of the fledgling cavalrymen were stationed at posts along the line of the Kansas-Pacific Railroad. Then under construction in Kansas, the railroad was subject to constant attack by Indians.[8]

Early actions by troopers of the 10th against Cheyenne war parties earned them the title of "buffalo soldiers." By likening them to the noble buffalo, an animal vital to the Indians' way of life, this term marked the respect Indian warriors came to have for the courage and combat abilities of Grierson's 10th. The black troopers accepted the title and wore it proudly. It was not long before the most prominent feature of the regimental crest of the 10th Cavalry was a buffalo.[9]

While the 10th was earning its spurs on the plains of Kansas, the 9th was facing a formidable assignment on the Texas frontier. For hundreds of miles, the meandering Rio Grande was lined by a brush jungle that harbored as fine a collection of renegades as ever infested a border. It was a haven for outlaws, cattle thieves, and bandits. Vengeful Lipan and Kickapoo Indians from camps near the river in Mexico raided constantly and took a heavy toll of American lives and property. Nor was this all. Unstable conditions in Mexico produced nearly countless revolutionaries who crossed and recrossed the river as convenience or necessity required. From Indian Territory, marauding Comanches and Kiowas swarmed down the Great Comanche War Trail to strike the Texas frontier as well as ranches and small settlements south of the border.[10]

Hatch's 9th spent eight often frustrating years in near-constant action against these elusive enemies. It developed into a tough, hard-riding, campaign-wise regiment with a fair sprinkling of Medals of Honor awarded to its men. Their efforts were frequently supported by units of the 24th and 25th Infantry regiments, though unmounted troops were limited primarily to guard and escort duties. Even their combined numbers, however, were far too few for more than moderate success, given the array of opponents and the vast area in their charge. Indeed, conditions were so bad in 1871 that the entire 4th Cavalry was sent to West Texas. The 9th was then rotated counterclockwise southeast, in order to bring most of the companies into a thin line along the lower Rio Grande. In his annual report for 1872, General Christopher C. Augur, commanding the Department of Texas, wrote: "The labor and privations of troops in this Department are both severe. The cavalry particularly are constantly at work, and it is a kind of work too that disheartens as there is little to show for it. Yet their zeal is untiring and if they do not always achieve success they always deserve it."[11]

All too often, prejudice and discrimination hampered or compromised the 9th's searches, patrols, and pursuits. The capture of bandits, thieves, and outlaws did not necessarily mean swift punishment for offenders. Local judges and juries had a decided tendency to turn the rascals loose.[12] Hatch's appeals for permission to cross the Rio Grande in "hot pursuit" of raiding Indians or bandits were always denied, though permission was, at times, given to white units. For example, in May, 1873, Colonel Ranald S. Mackenzie, with the support of General Sheridan and the secretary of war, crossed the river and destroyed a Kickapoo village.[13]

After two more years on the Texas frontier, the 9th was ordered to stations in New Mexico and Arizona to gain some relief. Its relief was short, for the regiment was soon involved in a full-scale effort to round up recalcitrant Apaches. But the men faced that task with much less restraint on their operations than they had encountered in Texas.[14]

Grierson's 10th, meanwhile, had been concentrated in Indian Territory to serve as watchdogs over the tribes of the Southern Plains—the Comanches, Kiowas, Southern Cheyennes, and Arapahos—who had been driven onto reservations during the winter of 1868–69. For most of its tenure in Indian Territory, the 10th was headquartered at Fort Sill, a post built on a site Grierson had located. Much of the construction work was done by troopers of the 10th under their colonel's close supervision.[15]

Under then-existing policy, the buffalo soldiers were not permitted to attack hostile Indians unless called upon to do so by resident Indian agents. The agents, all Quakers, were opposed to the use of force, and the 10th could do little to halt Indian raiding into Texas. This policy was not generally understood by Texans, who came to regard Grierson, his officers, and the men as a collection of fumblers, misfits, and cowards who were a disgrace to the uniform.[16]

In the late summer of 1874, the buffalo soldiers of both the 9th and 10th were given an opportunity to remove doubts about their ability to fight when all barriers were withdrawn. Resentment by the Southern Plains tribes at restrictions imposed by reservation life resulted in a massive breakout that launched the Red River War of some five months' duration. Full control of the Indians was turned over to the military. Five strong columns, mostly cavalry, were thrown into the field in a continuing effort to defeat the "hostiles" and end forever their ability to make war.[17]

The campaign was fought in the western reaches of Indian Territory and the Texas Panhandle, and two of the five columns engaged were composed primarily of 9th and 10th Cavalry. Between them they forced the surrender of more Indians; destroyed more lodges, food, and equipment; and rounded up more ponies than any other regiments in the field. They received little credit for their efforts, however; most of the praise for an overwhelming victory was reserved for Colonel Mackenzie and his 4th

"Captain Dodge's Colored Troops to the Rescue," painting by Frederic Remington. Courtesy Frederic Remington Art Museum, Ogdensburg, New York.

Cavalry and for Colonel Nelson Miles and the 6th Cavalry. The most significant attention given the 10th was a charge that two companies of the regiment were guilty of cowardice in a skirmish near the Cheyenne Agency at the close of the war. The charge was made by a biased officer of the 6th Cavalry, but it compromised the achievements of the officers and men of the 10th.[18]

When the 9th was transferred from Texas in 1875, the 10th replaced it, headquartered at Fort Concho. From this outpost, Grierson and his troopers set out to thoroughly explore, map, and improve transportation and communication in what became in 1878 the huge District of the Pecos. In addition, the regiment conducted nearly ceaseless scouts and patrols and constructed subposts at strategic locations. By the end of 1879, Grierson believed he had cleared his district of any major sources of trouble and was delighted to receive a rare compliment from crusty old General E. O. C. Ord, who had replaced Augur as commanding general of the Department of Texas. Ord concluded: "Thirty-four thousand four hundred and twenty miles of marches; three hundred miles of roads opened; two hundred miles of telegraph constructed—all, except a portion of the telegraph, consummated in one year,—involving efforts which will lead to lasting results, of which, as tending greatly, to advance civilization, yourself and command may well be proud."[19]

In 1879, however, a threat of major trouble on the West Texas frontier did develop with the outbreak of the Victorio War in New Mexico. Victorio, one of the ablest of all Apache chiefs, feared and distrusted federal policy that forced the concentration of his Warm Springs people onto the Mescalero Reservation. In August he led his kinsmen and a few Mescaleros from the reservation, determined to fight to the death. He gave Hatch and the 9th a nightmarish year of campaigning before they succeeded in driving him into northern Mexico. After a brief respite, Victorio and his band entered Texas below Fort Quitman intent on reaching the Mescalero Reservation, where supplies could be gathered and additional warriors recruited. He found Grierson and the 10th prepared for the challenge.[20]

Possessing a knowledge of the region equal to that of the Indians, Grierson stationed his companies in mountain passes and near the sources of water. In what can only be described as a masterpiece of guerrilla warfare, the durable and swift-marching buffalo soldiers countered Victorio's every move, destroyed his supply camp in the Sierra Diablos, and administered a sound whipping at the battle of Rattlesnake Springs on August 6, 1880. Victorio and his dispirited people were driven pell-mell back into Mexico, where they fell victim to Mexican troops at Tres Castillos. Not a single Indian had penetrated the Texas settlements.[21]

Peace—which the 9th and 10th Cavalry and the 24th and 25th Infantry had done so much to bring about—came to the Texas frontier by the close of 1880. Three years later, headquarters of the 10th was moved to Fort Davis, a picturesque post that was a favorite of both officers and men. Grierson gave serious thought to making a permanent home there, and his reports on the future of Texas would have pleased any modern Chamber of Commerce. Two years later the regiment, once more replacing the 9th, was transferred to stations in New Mexico and Arizona, where it participated in the final roundup of Apache raiders. It was a company of the 10th that pursued and forced the surrender of the last Apache holdouts: Chief Mangus and his band.[22]

By 1885 black regulars had served longer on the Texas frontier than any other federal troops. In detachments, companies, and at times in battalion strength, they had operated out of every post along the Rio Grande from Fort Brown to Fort Bliss and across the length of Texas from Fort Clark to Fort Richardson. In addition to combat missions, black escorts had made mail and passenger service secure from San Antonio to El Paso.

Their labor, moreover, had provided roads and telegraph lines for civilian as well as military use. Detailed reports of these activities made essential information available concerning the sources of water and the nature of soil and vegetation. And, on occasion, they had been called upon to cope with civil disturbances that were beyond the control of local authorities.

One of the more valuable reports came in 1875 as a result of rumors that Comanche runaways from Indian Territory were infesting the Staked Plains, a largely uncharted region in the Texas Panhandle. It was believed troops could not operate successfully there. In July, Lieutenant Colonel William R. Shafter, 24th Infantry, left Fort Concho to sweep the plains clear of Indians, taking four companies of his regiment and six of the 10th Cavalry. In a four-month campaign—first in killing heat, dust, and thirst and then in bone-chilling cold—the dogged Shafter drove his troops to the limit of human endurance. Few Indians were found, but the expedition swept the mystery from the Staked Plains by thoroughly scouting and mapping hundreds of square miles. From Shafter's reports, widely circulated, the public learned that there were large areas with sufficient resources for successful cattle and sheep ranching. The tide of settlement thus began to flow into the Staked Plains.[23]

In the fall of 1877, quarrels over access to salt deposits around El Paso spawned large-scale violence. A company of Texas Rangers proved unequal to the task of restoring order, and Governor Richard B. Hubbard appealed for federal assistance. It came in the form of Colonel Hatch and two battalions of veteran buffalo soldiers on forced march from stations in New Mexico. Upon reaching San Elizario, center of the disturbance, Hatch issued an ultimatum to five hundred bloodthirsty rioters: he and his troops were there to "clean them out." The mob simply melted away, and the so-called Salt War was over.[24]

Black regulars performed well their assigned tasks, but they encountered two obstacles they were never able to overcome: prejudice and discrimination. Despite overwhelming evidence to the contrary, the belief persisted—and in some cases was promoted in military as well as civilian circles—that black troops could not or would not fight and were generally lazy, disobedient, and surly.

Charges of cowardice were not uncommon, and no better examples exist than those leveled at the 10th at the close of the Red River War and during the Victorio War. In the former case, over one hundred Cheyenne prisoners of war broke from their camps near the Cheyenne Agency. They then entrenched themselves in a nearby sand hill where they had buried arms and ammunition before their surrender. Lieutenant Colonel Thomas

H. Neill, 6th Cavalry, who was in command at the agency, had one company of his own regiment and two of the 10th on hand to corral the fugitives. He ordered an assault on the Indian positions, and a nearly daylong firefight developed. The Cheyennes managed to hold off the troopers and escaped after nightfall.

In Neill's official report, he charged that only his own company had done any fighting and that the buffalo soldiers had twice failed to advance when ordered to do so. In brief, he concluded, the Indians' escape was entirely attributable to the unwillingness of the blacks and their officers to do their duty. Neill's report was strange indeed if one consulted the medical report of casualties in the fight. Fifteen troopers had been wounded and one killed; of these, eleven were buffalo soldiers, including the only fatality. For troops that would not fight, they had certainly attracted a disproportionate amount of lead; yet Neill's report was unquestioned except by officers and men of the 10th. An outraged Grierson's demand for an official inquiry went unanswered.[25]

Colonel Grierson had earned a well-deserved reputation for unusual coolness and courage under fire during the Civil War and after. Even one as sparse with praise as General William T. Sherman had characterized Grierson as "one of the most willing, ardent, and dashing cavalry officers I ever had."[26] In August, 1880, Grierson and a few of his troopers faced Victorio and his warriors. Grierson had dispersed his command at strategic points to intercept Victorio. He was en route from Fort Quitman to a subpost at Eagle Springs with a small escort when he learned by courier that the Apaches were nearby and heading for Tinaja de las Palmas, the only source of water for many miles.

Instead of trying to avoid Victorio, Grierson, with only his sixteen-year-old son Robert and seven troopers, entrenched themselves on a rocky ridge beside the road and within easy rifle range of the water hole. He was squarely in Victorio's path and was prepared to deny the Apaches access to water and hold up their advance until troops arrived from Eagle Springs, some fifteen miles away. This he succeeded in doing, and when reinforcements arrived, the Indians were driven off in confusion. Grierson's actions and judgment were consistent with his entire career as a soldier as well as proof of his confidence in the fighting ability of his black troopers. Writing his wife about the battle, he related, "When it was understood that I was determined to stay and fight and that I felt no apprehension as to the result I did not observe any flinching upon the part of anyone."[27]

Grierson, Hatch, and other white officers of their regiments could survive the accusations cast at them and remain in the service, but this was not the case with Lieutenant Henry Flipper, the only black officer in either regiment. The first black graduate of West Point, Flipper joined the 10th Cavalry in 1878. Quiet and unassuming, he soon became a close friend of his company commander, Captain Nicholas Nolan, and won the respect of Colonel Grierson. He was cited for outstanding service during the Victorio War and was accepted as a gentleman and competent soldier by most if not all of the officers of the 10th.[28]

A promising future seemed in store for Flipper until he began riding, on occasion, with one of the few eligible young women at Fort Concho. At least one officer who had enjoyed the lady's undivided attention made clear his displeasure, and a few others soon followed his lead. One of these Captain Nolan acidly described as "an officer who never smelt powder except on his lady's face."[29] When Flipper's company was transferred to Fort Davis early in 1882, he was appointed post commissary. Shortly thereafter he was arrested, charged with embezzling about two thousand dollars, and confined to the post guardhouse.[30]

On June 30, 1882, a court-martial cleared Flipper of the embezzlement charge but nevertheless found him guilty of "conduct unbecoming an officer," and he was dismissed from the army. Pleas for leniency on the part of Captain Nolan and Colonel Grierson were ignored. For the rest of a long and constructive life, Flipper maintained he was the victim of a conspiracy by Colonel Shafter, who had proffered the charges, and two officers of the 10th. All efforts to clear his name before his death in 1944 failed. Not until 1976, after years of petitions by friends and supporters both black and white, was the blot removed from Flipper's record.[31]

Charges that black regulars were surly, lazy, and disobedient could only be supported by prejudice and ignorance. Given the challenges and conditions under which they operated—and an almost total lack of recognition for good and faithful service—one might conclude that morale was lacking, desertion rates high, and reenlistment rates low. The opposite was true. The men took great pride in their uniforms, their companies, and their regiments. The twin curses of the frontier army, desertion and alcoholism, were not serious problems in the black regiments. Their desertion rates were the lowest in the army, and chronic drunkenness was rare. In 1889 the Surgeon General reported: "The difference between the rate of white and colored troops in this case [alcoholism] is most noteworthy: admissions, whites 43.97; colored 4.55; non-effectiveness, [unfit for duty] white .44, colored, .03. This should be printed in italic to the credit of the colored soldiers."[32] Reenlistment rates were high, and no small part of their effectiveness on scout, patrol, or in combat was traceable to the large percentage of veterans in their ranks.³³

A constant refrain in official reports was the cheerfulness, obedience, and durability of the black cavalry and infantry. Many such reports came from officers of other regiments who temporarily commanded the blacks. Typical was the commendation of Lieutenant Colonel George Buell, 11th Infantry, who led a column of the 9th Cavalry in the Red River War. After weeks of relentless pursuit of fleeing Indians that ended in subzero cold and snow among the brakes of Red River, Buell wrote, "I cannot give them [the buffalo soldiers] too much credit for manly endurance without complaining."³⁴

It was not to be expected that citizens of Texas, a former slave state in the throes of Reconstruction and its bitter aftermath, would be free of prejudice toward black troops. Hatch and his 9th Cavalry had consistently encountered problems with civilians in the small towns along the lower Rio Grande. But nothing in their experience compared with the difficulties that Grierson and the 10th faced in tough little Saint Angela (later renamed San Angelo), adjacent to Fort Concho.

The town was the only source of recreation for the troopers, but their appearance to drink and dance in local saloons almost invariably led to trouble. Little of serious consequence occurred, though, until the spring of 1878. A group of cowboys and buffalo hunters insulted and then ripped the blouse and trousers of a sergeant from Company D. The soldier went back to the post, gathered up a party of his friends, and returned to the saloon. Armed with carbines, they entered the place. A blazing gunfight followed, in which one trooper and one hunter were killed and two other hunters and a soldier wounded. Nine men of Company D were indicted for murder, but the hunters and cowboys escaped without so much as a lecture.³⁵

In January, 1881, another saloon incident also had serious results. A sheep rancher shot and killed an unarmed and unoffending private from Company E. Though the killer was arrested, word reached the post that the man had been set free. A small party of the dead soldier's friends marched into town and fired some one hundred fifty shots into local buildings. No one was killed, and Grierson swiftly sealed off the post to prevent any further incidents. There were threats from the Department of Texas headquarters to disband the 10th, though only a handful of troopers had been involved in the affair. The rancher, tried for murder in Austin, was quickly acquitted.³⁶

Not all clashes between civilians and federal troops stationed in Texas involved blacks. Troopers of Colonel Mackenzie's 4th Cavalry threatened to burn down the town of Jacksboro after suffering what they regarded as consistent mistreatment by local citizens. No such furor as that raised over the trouble in Saint Angela occurred, however. Strangely, the racial clash in Saint Angela ended on a positive note. Tension between post and town eased, passions cooled, and at least some understanding prevailed. A grand jury returned no indictments, and Grierson was praised for his cooperation with local authorities. When the 10th left Fort Concho in 1883, general good feeling prevailed.[37]

By 1885, black regulars had served in Texas for nearly two decades and on one of the longest and most turbulent frontiers in the American West. By any objective standards they had, under the most trying conditions, made significant contributions to peace, security, and settlement in the Lone Star State. Texas has a rich military heritage, and these black soldiers earned an honored place in that legacy.

6

WOMEN AND THE TEXAS MILITARY EXPERIENCE:

The Nineteenth Century

Sandra L. Myres

THE TEXAS MILITARY EXPERIENCE ECHOES WITH THE names of familiar places: the Alamo and San Jacinto, Sabine Pass, Palmito Ranch, and Palo Duro Canyon. It is also reflected in the names of units: the Mounted Rifles, Hood's Texas Brigade, and the Texas Rangers. It includes heroes and villains, battles and blunders, courage and cowardice. It is studded with names like Sam Houston, William Worth, Robert E. Lee, Albert Sidney Johnston, John Bell Hood, Ranald Mackenzie, and George Armstrong Custer. In recent years, the tradition has been broadened to include other, less familiar names: Hispanics Juan Seguín and Santos Benavides; free blacks, such as Samuel McCullough and Greenbury Logan; Comanche chief Quanah Parker and Delaware scout Jim Shaw. But when one thinks of the Texas military experience few would respond with names like Angelina Eberly, Francisa Alvarez, Lydia Lane, Teresa Viele, Frances Boyd, or Elizabeth Custer. Yet I would submit that these women, too, were part of Texas military history. Along with other now nameless women, they contributed significantly to the state's growth and development as well. Their main contribution to its military experience came in the publication of their memoirs, which contained vivid descriptions of army life and the frontier.

Women have always been an adjunct to armies, whether as wives and daughters, nurses, laundresses, servants, or those euphemistically known as "camp followers." From time to time they have played a direct role in military campaigns by carrying ammunition, helping to load weapons, and even firing them. One has only to remember the warrior women of Visagothic Spain, the Ladies of the Light Brigade, Doña Eufemia Penalosa aiding in the defense of Santa Fe, or Barbara Fritchie and Molly Pitcher in the American Revolution.

But such military women were unusual. Far more important, both in numbers and in their contributions to military history, were the other women of the army: the women and children who "faced the same hardships, dared the same dangers, and experienced the same feelings of frustration and alienation as did the soldiers."[1] We sometimes forget that the military, especially in the American West, transcended the role of combat and patrol. The army also had political, economic, social, and cultural areas of responsibility.[2] It was in these areas that the women of the army played a major part in the Texas military experience and "actively participated in the thankless chore of making the frontier safe for farmers and townsmen."[3]

Although women accompanied the military throughout Texas history—from the early Spanish *entradas* to the late twentieth century—this essay concentrates on the nineteenth century and especially on the women of the Texas military frontiers between 1845 and 1890. It is based on diaries, letters, and reminiscences of women whose husbands served on the Texas military frontier during this period. Unfortunately, the sample is skewed by the fact that all of these women were white, middle-class officers' wives. The roles of enlisted men's wives and of laundresses, domestic servants, and prostitutes is largely undocumented except in an occasional soldier's memoir or military report.[4]

In retrospect, the literary production of the army wives was prodigious in relation to their numbers. The frontier army was never large, and the entire officer corps numbered no more than two thousand at any one time. Many of the officers were never stationed in the West, and many who were either did not marry or left their wives and families in the East. Yet, from the relatively small group of army wives who did accompany their husbands west, a surprising number of journals and reminiscences appeared in print either as articles or books before 1900. Many more have been discovered and published since that time.[5] These women were perceptive observers, and they offered comments and insights that give a vivid, detailed, and intimate view of western military and civilian life and add a great deal to our knowledge and understanding of the nineteenth-century military frontier.[6]

Understandably, most of the women's journals concentrated on household events and garrison life, the difficulties of making a home and raising a family on distant frontiers, and the rigors of being "on the march" from one post to another. Or, as Elizabeth Custer phrased it, the wives wrote about "the domestic life of an army family, . . . our occupations, amusements, and mode of housekeeping . . . and in some instances . . . the trifling perplexities and events which went to fill up the sum of our existence."[7]

Of course, some of the women "joined the army" with dreams of leading a romantic, even heroic, life in the Great West. They had all sorts of misconceptions about the glamour and excitement of military life, and most approached frontier service with a sense of adventure and a desire to see new places and explore new things. Teresa Griffin, who married Lieutenant Egbert Viele in 1850, recalled: "No recruit ever entered the service with more enthusiasm than I did or felt more eager to prove himself a soldier. . . . Mars would have gloried in the wonderful female that my imagination loved to paint, and to follow her heroic footsteps seemed a high ambition. . . . I saw her the witness of many a thrilling and gory scene, with the din of battle in her ear, and stern endurance on her brow. With this vision before my eyes, I enlisted to 'follow the drum!'"[8]

Such romantic nonsense quickly vanished during the first few years of frontier service. The women soon found that army regulations made no provision for wives, other than laundresses, and the army's "benign neglect" coupled with the many inconveniences of frontier life brought frequent complaints. "The book of army regulations," wrote Elizabeth Custer, "enters into such minute detail in its instructions giving the number of hours that bean soup should boil, that it would be natural to suppose that a paragraph or two might be wasted on an officer's wife."[9] Such was not the case. The army was as insensitive to wives as its regulations were neglectful, and the ladies were left to cope with the problems of everyday life with little assistance.

In fact, army convenience and custom added to women's burdens. Few posts provided schools or medical care for dependents; quarters, when available, were unfurnished; and the basic necessities for setting up housekeeping and raising a family were often lacking. Indeed, as Randolph B. Marcy warned his daughter when she announced her intention to marry a frontier officer, "You would have to go to a company where his pay could hardly give you a miserable living, with a house that a man in civilized society would actually be ashamed to keep a horse in."[10]

Feeding their families posed a major problem for army wives. Although venison, buffalo, and other game were available at most posts, they quickly grew tiresome as a steady diet. As Lydia Lane remarked, they "would have welcomed a good beef-steak as a luxury." But good beefsteak was scarce, and fresh fruits and vegetables were difficult if not impossible to obtain. Even when such supplies were obtainable, the prices were often exorbitant. Most of the women tried to plant gardens and keep a few chickens and a cow or goat to provide fresh milk, but local conditions and frequent moves often made this impossible. Women were forced to rely on what was available from the post commissary or could be purchased or traded from settler families. Lou Roberts noted that "the rations issued to the Rangers included only the substantials, but were of such generous quantity that we had a surplus to exchange for butter, milk, eggs, etc." Others were not so fortunate. At Fort Inge, Lydia Lane reported, the closest farms and ranches were twenty miles away and "the commissary furnished only necessary articles of food . . . such as coffee, flour, sugar, rice, ham and pork, which list of eatables did not offer much to tempt the appetite." The situation was even worse at Ringgold Barracks, where Teresa Viele complained about the "unpalatable liquid butter," the "mouldy flour and rancid pork," and food "flavored with red ants" that "tasted something like caraway seed."[11]

Frances Boyd had a similar experience at Fort Clark. "We nearly starved in Texas," she recalled. "The butter was simply oil, if procurable at all; the milk thin—not tasteless, but with a decidedly disagreeable flavor of wild garlic and onions; and the beef dry, and with so strange a flavor we could not eat it. Vegetables could not be procured; and potatoes shipped from a distance were a mass of decay when received."[12]

Under such conditions, army women quickly learned to make tempting dishes out of practically nothing. Many, like Alice Grierson, kept a book of useful recipes for the frontier such as Rice and Bacon Main Dish, Green Chili Stuffed with Macaroni, and Cake without Eggs. Ellen Biddle included two "army standbys" in her reminiscences: "Custard without eggs or milk" and "Apple-pie, without apples."[13]

Children presented additional difficulties. Miscarriages and stillbirths were frequent, infant mortality rates were high, and many women buried at least one child in some barren, windswept post cemetery. Those children who did survive enjoyed the open air, frontier games, and sports such as baseball but received little formal education. Few posts had schools, and where they did exist they were often taught by enlisted men who knew little more than their pupils. Most army children were tutored at home and then sent east to school.[14] When this happened, Ellen Biddle related, the women found themselves with divided loyalties and faced a difficult decision: whether to remain with their husbands or accompany their offspring.[15] The ladies also complained about the low pay, the economies necessary to make ends meet, the frequent and often untimely changes of station, the difficulties of western travel, and the isolation and monotony of frontier army life.

Despite these hardships and inconveniences, garrison life was relatively comfortable, at least compared to that of other frontierswomen.

Most officers' wives had household servants brought from the East or recruited from the enlisted men in their husbands' commands. Few had more than minimal household tasks to perform, and they spent their days riding, hunting, reading, or writing letters to relatives and friends. Thus, along with their complaints, the army women also documented the pleasanter aspects of garrison life: parties and dances, amateur theatricals, colorful parades and band concerts at the larger posts, fancy dinners for visiting dignitaries, and an occasional wedding or holiday celebration. Emily Andrews wrote that during a visit to Fort Stockton in 1874, "we went to a very funny entertainment given by a blind man aided by some of the soldiers . . . the singing and dancing were something wonderful." She also reported: "It is quite the fashion at the Post for the ladies to go to the billiard room, so one evening we all went by invitation to see them play. The room was in a long adobe building, with a fine table in it and everything very nice. A Mexican Band was playing at one end, and some of the ladies and gentlemen danced while the game was going on."[16]

Despite such entertainments, post life was generally dull and monotonous, and any occasion provided an excuse for a picnic, party, or dance. Frances Boyd recalled that when she arrived at Fort Clark, "a large ball was given on our arrival, and the different posts at which we had stopped *en route*—Forts Bliss, Davis, and Stockton—had all honored us in the same way." Women fortunate enough to be stationed in or near a frontier town or one of the larger cities such as Austin, San Antonio, or El Paso enjoyed visits and sightseeing trips to nearby communities. Teresa Viele described several visits to "Davis's Ranche" (Rio Grande City) and Camargo, and Frances Boyd wrote that while Lieutenant Boyd was stationed at Fort Duncan, she was "able to enjoy everything Piedras Negras afforded in the way of sight-seeing." Indeed, Eliza Johnston complained that so many of the "wives of the officers of the reg[iment] which is stationed near here" called on her in San Antonio that "I fear I shall weary of these numerous morning calls."[17]

At the smaller and more isolated posts, however, the women were often lonely and longed for feminine companionship. At some posts there were no other white women, and the solitary spouse often found it hard to find enough to do to keep herself occupied.[18]

The army wives were understandably most concerned with the difficulties of making a home and raising a family under trying circumstances, and their journals and reminiscences focused on these issues. But they were also educated, curious, and anxious to learn what they could of the Great American West. Thus, in addition to cataloging the problems and pleasures of frontier army life, most women also wrote about the land and the people they met. In so doing, they helped to familiarize eastern readers with the opportunities available in Texas and other parts of the West. They shrewdly assessed the possibilities and potential for economic and social development and described the coming of civilization to the frontier. Indeed, some became outspoken publicists and active western boosters.

Almost without exception, the ladies found reason to complain about the climate: searing desert heat; sudden, violent, bone-chilling northers; Gulf Coast hurricanes; unexpected rainstorms and flash floods followed by prolonged droughts. "Leaving the bright and bracing climate of New Mexico for a country where one hundred and ten degrees in the shade was only to be expected, and for six months of the year, was indeed a transition," wrote Frances Boyd. Eliza Johnston, on the other hand, had reason to complain of the cold. Traveling along the Clear Fork of the Brazos River in January, she noted that it had been "so cold for 3 days past that I could not write . . . I have never seen such prolonged cold weather . . . we have had but one temperate day since the 22nd of Dec." And Emily Andrews observed with surprise, and some anxiety, that the Concho was "but one of the most treacherous streams in the country. It has been known to rise *60 feet* in *an hour* this season. This may seem to you incredible but it is perfectly true. This is in a great measure owing to the severe rain storms. . . . An inch and a half of water often falls in these rain storms in two hours time."[19]

Most of these Texas military wives came from the East or the North, and, like many immigrants today, they were often less than pleased by their first glimpses of Texas and Texans. Of her first trip to Texas, Lydia Lane recalled: "We travelled from Corpus Christi to the western frontier through a dreary, desolate country, where nothing lived but Indians, snakes, and other enormous reptiles, and I expected to see some dreadful thing whichever way I turned." Moreover, she reported, Fort Duncan "was a wretched place to live in, and I am sure some of our companions who were to remain there looked on their future station with sinking hearts." Along the Texas coast, wrote Teresa Viele, there were "no rocks, nor the smallest traces of vegetation could be seen in the hot sand; there was nothing to vary the monotony of the scene but vestiges of wrecks."[20]

Indeed, all of the women found much of the Texas landscape monotonous and unattractive, but, to their surprise, they also saw much that was pleasing. Despite her complaints about the climate, Eliza Johnston noted that parts of the country were "beautiful" and dotted with "live oak groves fine scenery and good soil." Around Fredericksburg, Emily Andrews was delighted by a familiar landscape. "The country was very beautiful," she wrote, "and the farming land really had a New England look, thrifty and well cared for." As she traveled farther west, she observed with amazement, "I suppose you can hardly imagine a country without any trees having a beauty, but all day we saw no trees, and yet the country with its mountains and valleys is beyond my description." Others, however, never became reconciled to the new land and would have agreed with the young woman traveling to meet her husband at Fort Brown. "If I had a choice, I would *never* live in Texas!"[21]

If the women were ambivalent about the country, they were also undecided about its inhabitants. Indeed, some of the women's most interesting comments concern the various frontier populations they encountered, especially Indians and Mexicans. They wrote extensively, although often critically, about these different peoples: their appearance, culture, and customs. Most found something to admire in these unfamiliar folk, and many changed their preconceived negative opinions to somewhat more sympathetic and positive ones during their frontier service. And in describing and writing about Indians and Mexicans, the army wives helped to present eastern readers with a more realistic picture of these cultures.

Throughout most of the nineteenth century, the army's principal mission in Texas was directly related to the Indians, so it is not surprising that the women wrote about them. Before coming to Texas or other parts of the West, the women had read a good deal about the American natives. They journeyed into Indian land, therefore, with a number of preconceptions and prejudices based on books, novels, newspapers, and magazines that portrayed Indians as both "noble redmen" and "ignorant, bloodthirsty savages." Such contradictory views were often reinforced by contact with the native peoples. Army wives, like their husbands, viewed the Indians with "fear, distrust, loathing, contempt, and condescension, on the one hand; curiosity, admiration, sympathy, and even friendship on the other."[22]

Like other women coming to the frontier from "civilized" society, the army wives' initial reaction to the Indians was one of fear and loathing. Conditioned by reports of Indian atrocities and captivity narratives, they were terrified of Indian attacks. Such fears were not allayed by some husbands or kind friends who presented them with pistols or revolvers and orders to shoot themselves, if necessary, to escape torture and captivity. The words of one Arizona officer to his wife were evidently frequently repeated: "If I'm hit, you'll know what to do. You have your derringer. . . . Don't let them get . . . you alive."[23]

With such warnings ringing in their ears, it is not surprising that even in the midst of a heavily armed column, these women feared for their own safety and that of their children. As she traveled from Fort Bliss to Fort Clark, Lydia Lane wrote, "I was constantly on the lookout for Indians, and a number of bayonet-plants together had given me many a scare, assuming in the distance almost any shape,—men on horseback and on foot." Even the security of the post did not calm her fears. "Our little house was so far from the other quarters, I think the Indians could have crept in upon us, taken our scalps, and ridden away, without being molested." Emily Andrews expressed similar fears as her party traveled toward Fort Davis. As they neared Limpia Cañón, she recorded, "We passed several places which seemed to me just made for an attack, especially as we neared the canon, with its hills so close on either side completely hemming us in." Neither woman suffered any trouble at the hand of the Indians, either on the march or in camp, but their concerns were shared by many.[24]

Despite their fears, however, the women were fascinated by the "aborigines." They often visited Indian camps and villages and reported on the customs and life-styles of various native peoples. The women devoted long passages in their journals to descriptions of Indian dress, behavior, and habits. A few even attempted to learn some of the Indian languages and collected bows and arrows, moccasins, and other Indian artifacts.[25] Although Teresa Viele harbored the usual fears of Indian attack, she nonetheless took advantage of an army escort to visit an Indian encampment. She described the customs and behavior of its inhabitants in some detail and later entertained "one of the warriors of the Carese tribe" whom she "regaled" with French bonbons—which, she reported, he "devoured . . . most remorselessly and with evident gusto."[26]

Indeed, the longer army women lived in "Indian country" the less concerned they were about their safety. Frances Boyd had seen a good deal of frontier service before arriving in Texas, and, she reported, she "soon regarded red men as fearlessly as if I had been accustomed to them all my life." Even Lydia Lane eventually grew accustomed to their presence, although, as she recalled, "I never could become accustomed to the Indians staring at me through the window when I was sewing or reading."[27]

As they learned more about the Indians, some of the army wives expressed a good deal of understanding and sympathy for the Indians' plight. Even Viele, who thought the Comanches "bloody, brutal, [and] licentious," believed they had been "driven from their rightful possessions, and [one] can see, in their ignorance, many excuses for their tiger-like ferocity and bitter hatred of those who they feel have wronged them so sorely." But even women like Viele, who felt some sympathy for the Indians, believed they were a "vanishing race," doomed to cultural extinction. And once the Indians were gone, the army's main mission in Texas and the West would come to an end. The women could then return to the East to write—and profit—from their experiences and read of nobler, and less threatening, Indians in the tales of James Fenimore Cooper and the poems of Henry Wadsworth Longfellow.[28]

Women whose husbands were stationed near San Antonio or along the Mexican border were also curious about the Mexican people. They delighted in the old-style Spanish architecture, "quaint" local customs, and the Hispanic-American society in the larger towns and cities. They attended fiestas, *bailes*, and bullfights; went sightseeing; visited Mexican homes; and commented extensively on a culture so different from their own. Interestingly, their comments were frequently positive. This is somewhat surprising in view of the anti-Mexican tone of most nineteenth-century literature. The Mexicans had no novelist like Cooper to romanticize their culture, and few writers understood or defended their way of life.

Despite such literary prejudices and preconceptions, the army women found many Mexicans and Mexican-Americans a charming and pleasant people. Frances Boyd commented that the Mexican families with whom they stayed en route from one post to another "were most truly hospitable. They made us welcome, and yet exacted no reward for the time and attention bestowed." Teresa Viele declared the Mexicans an "amiable, smiling, innocent race of people," and she was particularly impressed by "the feeling of sympathy in misfortune which pervades all classes of Mexicans. So universal is this sentiment that the bitterest enemy, in the hour of trouble, will receive care and attention. The well-known devotion of the Mexican women to the sick and wounded of our army during the war [with Mexico] finds no parallel in history."[29]

It should be noted, however, that most of the complimentary remarks came from women whose associations were with the *ricos*, or upper classes. The women were less inclined to find virtue in the peon class, and their prejudices coupled with the influence of anti-Mexican literature became apparent when they described the smaller Mexican settlements and mestizo servants. "Even when near Mexican settlements," Frances Boyd complained, "we would find that a long line of idle ancestry, together with every tendency of climate, surroundings, and viciousness, had so developed indolence in the natives as to utterly incapacitate them for serious employment." Nonetheless, she found the women "made admirable nurses" and employed them to care for her children—although "heavier household tasks were left for more energetic hands."[30]

To some extent, all of the army wives retained some of their prejudices about the Mexican people. Despite their deserved reputation for "sympathy in misfortune" and their "mild and inoffensive" manner, Viele declared, "they have enough Spanish blood left in their veins to be occasionally raised to deeds of desperation and bloodshed." Moreover, she opined, the peons were "lazy," the priests "a dissolute, carnal, gambling jolly set of wine bibbers," and the better classes only a pale reflection of their former "Castilian grandeur."[31]

Despite their criticism of Indians and Mexicans, the army wives reserved their most caustic comments for their own people. They could romanticize and make allowances for Indians and Mexicans, and at least to some extent they were able to view these people objectively. The same was not true of other whites—both in and out of the army. Like many other eastern women who traveled the trans-Mississippi West in the nineteenth century, the military women found much of Texas frontier society uncouth, unclean, ill-mannered, violent, and profane.[32]

The ladies of Galveston, for example, reminded Viele of "the baboon's sister in nursery tales." Although she reported that the town had "some good stores, and quite an extensive hotel . . . [and] churches of several denominations" that promised a "fine and rapid development," she nonetheless noted that the port city had an air of "melancholy." She concluded that she was glad "'my lot has been cast in more pleasant places.'" As she traveled west, however, Viele discovered that Galveston had much in its favor compared to other parts of the state. "Vermin," she commented, "are the scourge of this country, and cleanliness certainly not one of its virtues." Moreover, she wondered what sort of being inhabited a country where the hotels posted signs that read, "'Gents requested not to spit on the walls!'" and "'Keep their boots off the bed clothes!'" Viele soon found out what kind of being inhabited Texas. "There never was a country more unfitted . . . to be the home of civilized man, than . . . the region of the lower Rio Grande in Texas," she wrote. "It seems to hate civilization [and] seems intended as a home for desperate men, escaped refugees from the law; men who live in the saddle, and on the prairie seek their subsistence; such as give to Texas any bad reputation its population may have."[33] Elizabeth Custer was equally unimpressed with the Texas population. The countryside, she reported, was filled with "small, low, log huts, consisting of one room each. . . . I determined to camp out until we came to more inviting habitations, which, I regret to say, we did not find on that march."[34]

Emily Andrews was somewhat more daring than Custer and entered "a real Texan house. It is made of logs," she observed, "with daylight peeping in at the many crevices. The chairs are covered with skins, while the rest of the furniture is primitive in the extreme. Hens and chickens are running in and out the doors, and the pigs in the yard would, I think, be quite friendly were it not for the old darkie who sits at the door and keeps away all such intruders." Nor was Andrews more impressed with the Texans she met who, she found, rarely "tell the truth" about anything.[35]

The women found society somewhat more refined in the larger towns, but even there they found much to criticize. Although Elizabeth Custer described Austin as a "pretty town of stuccoed houses that appeared summery in the midst of the live-oak's perennial green," she was less impressed by the civilian population who marked their horses with "disfiguring brands that were often upon the fore-shoulder, as well as the flank. They spoke volumes for the country where a man has to sear a thoroughbred with a hot iron, to ensure his keeping possession." She went on to describe the dress and manners of the citizens in a similarly critical vein and berated the "general shiftlessness" that seemed to "creep into one's veins." In summary, she reported that "Texas was in a state of ferment from one end to the other. . . . Lawless acts might be perpetrated, and the inciters cross the Rio Grande into Mexico, before news of the depredations came to either military or civil headquarters. . . . I had serious objections to traveling in Texas, unaccompanied by a Division of cavalry."[36]

Perhaps Lydia Lane best summarized the wives' attitudes toward Texas settlers when she concluded: "We are told to take in the stranger, as by doing so we 'may entertain an angel unawares.' I do not think that class of guests often travelled in Texas and New Mexico . . . and if they did . . . their disguise was complete."[37] Small wonder that most of the army wives preferred post society to that found in frontier towns and looked forward to furloughs in the East and the day when they could return permanently to "civilization."

The women's condemnation of western manners and morals is more understandable if one considers their background, which reveals a good deal about nineteenth-century American social values and attitudes. With few exceptions, the army wives came from "close-knit, staunchly religious, middle-class families"; most had a finishing school or ladies' seminary education; and several were members of prominent, and often influential, eastern families.[38] Brought up to believe in the Cult of True Womanhood, they considered it was a woman's duty to be "modest, submissive, educated in the genteel and domestic arts, supportive of her husband's

General George and Mrs. Elizabeth Custer and other officers of the 7th Cavalry, Austin, Texas. Courtesy Little Bighorn Battlefield National Monument.

efforts, uncomplaining, [and] a perfect wife and mother." Although they believed that their first duty was to their home and family, the women also felt an obligation to set an example for others and improve the moral tone and gen-eral level of society. Undoubtedly, their perceived responsibility as "gentle tamers" and moral guardians helps explain their harsh criticisms of frontier society. Apparently they expected more from "civilized" men and women than from "savage" Indians and "backward" Mexicans.[39]

Most army wives came to Texas with the admonition of Catherine Beecher ringing in their ears: to "civilize and Christianize" raw frontier communities.[40] Certainly they attempted to discharge this duty in regard to the men around them. All of the wives complained of the profanity and gambling common on most posts, and they made occasional veiled references to fights in the laundresses' quarters and the conditions at local "hog ranches" that catered to lonely men's needs. The women also worried about the effects of frontier "immorality" on their families and on other officers and enlisted men. "I used to dread the arrival of the young officers who came to the regiment from West Point," Elizabeth Custer wrote, "fearing that the sameness and inactivity of garrison life would be a beast to which their character would succumb. I kept up a running line of comments to myself... 'I wonder if you are likely to go bad under temptation... I hope you don't drink; I pray that you have stamina enough to resist evil.'"[41]

The men, of course, were not always grateful for these self-appointed guardians of their virtue. As one disgruntled young (and most certainly bachelor) officer commented: "It is claimed by a prominent faction of the day that the influence of woman would be beneficent in the affairs of government—would purify politics and elevate the standard of public morals.... [But] observation and experience have demonstrated... that the presence of ladies in the Army is prejudicial to good order and military discipline.... However agreeable may be the presence of ladies, it is a noticeable fact that the lack of discipline is most conspicuous at stations where the number of ladies is greatest."[42]

He went on for some ninety pages to castigate the "ladies" for their various activities that he believed "prejudicial to good order and military discipline." Another male observer was more charitable, however. Like the officers and men, he maintained, the women were a mixed lot, ranging from the "female C.O. [commanding officer]," who "organized her staff, openly criticized the position of officers at dress parade, received reports and marvelled at the magnanimity that allowed a soldier 'seven nights in bed,'" to the "picturesque little lady" with "plenty to wear but nothing to do." There were also the "late sergeant's wife," her husband now an officer, thanks to the war, "who displayed a better development of muscle than brain"; the "beauty in laces and jewels"; the "aristocratic dame"; and of course "the charming conversationalist and delightful hostess and 'good Army woman.'"[43]

The ladies, of course, had their own opinions. Eliza Johnston vehemently criticized an officer who had "taken a woman from her good decent husband in Missouri and brought her... to Texas. oh! you immoral men what should be your fate for all the sorrow you cause in this world. I never can talk to the man with pleasure or patience again and yet he is considered a gentleman and a fine officer."[44] Johnston blamed harsh army discipline for many of the men's shortcomings, especially among the enlisted personnel. In describing the whipping and drumming out of several soldiers, she wrote that "this experience rather disgusted me... surely-surely, some less degrading mode of punishment can be substituted." Teresa Viele, however, saw it differently. Army discipline was not harsh enough, she maintained, and declared that punishments such as the "barrel jacket" tended to aid discipline.[45]

Whatever their concerns about civilian and army virtue, and despite their training in the Cult of True Womanhood, the army women did not completely conform to the model of submissiveness and domesticity demanded of the "ideal woman." In spite of their traditional background and often conservative point of view, army wives exhibited few of the inhibitions commonly ascribed to nineteenth-century gentlewomen. They traveled unchaperoned throughout much of the trans-Mississippi West, explored remote areas, and observed life in Indian camps and villages. They learned to ride, hunt, and fish and engaged in other outdoor pursuits. They were frequently on the march or garrisoned at posts where there were no other women, they sometimes bore their children without female assistance, and they learned to rely on their own resources to cope with the problems of everyday life in a predominantly male world. Simply by publishing their memoirs, these women were much more public than most of their contemporaries, freed at least to some extent from the strictures of the Cult of Domesticity and "proper" female behavior.[46]

Moreover, no matter what they may have believed to be their mission in civilizing and taming the frontier, it can be argued that the army women did not have much influence in this regard. They went west, they saw and recorded what it was like, and they gratefully returned to a more "civilized" society in the East. Perhaps the social and economic status of the enlisted men's wives, the laundresses, and the camp followers brought them into closer and more influential contact with the frontier population, and probably more of them remained in the West as permanent settlers. Nonetheless, there is little evidence that army wives—whether of either enlisted men or of officers—made many long-lasting contributions to western life.[47]

If the army women had little direct impact on most aspects of western life, however, neither did the men. Richard Ellis, Jack Foner, and Roger Nichols all argue convincingly that "rarely did the army have more than a slight impact in most frontier regions."[48] They are probably correct in concluding that in the long run, other frontier institutions were more influential in western development than the army. As Foner points out, even General William Tecumseh Sherman listed the railroads and the influx of white civilians ahead of the army as factors aiding frontier development. All three historians maintain that the frontier probably had more influence on the army than vice-versa, and the same might be said of the army women.[49]

All that having been said, we are concerned not with the *influence* of the army or the army women on the frontier but with the women's *role* in the Texas military experience. Certainly the women did not participate directly in such military objectives as enforcing federal Indian policy; protecting the lives and property of western settlers; guarding mail routes, railroads, and telegraph lines; or mapping and road building. However, the women did provide support services for these activities, which were as important as those of cooks, food contractors, sutlers, and hired laborers. From the women's point of view, their most important duty, as Frances Boyd wrote, was "devotion to husbands and the cause they represented." But as military historian Robert Utley points out, they also "played a special role in the life of the military community." They helped care for the sick and wounded, aided the often illiterate or semiliterate soldiers in writing letters home, and offered a sympathetic ear for the frightened, discouraged, and lonely men. Moreover, as Utley explains: "Women introduced an element of grace, refinement, and comfort to garrison life conspicuously lacking at the few primitive posts to which none would go. They took the lead in planning, promoting, and staging entertainments. They brought to them the indispensable element of feminine participation."[50]

In addition, women were an important part of what might be described as the "hidden command system": an informal network of military academy classmates; fellow Civil War officers (for example, members of the same regiment or aides-de-camp to a particular commander); and relatives or close friends from prominent families with political, economic, or social influence. Army wives helped establish and maintain these networks through their own relationships, friendships, and social contacts. For example, Egbert Viele was a member of a wealthy Hudson Valley family, and Teresa came from a prominent and influential New York City family. Their contacts with eastern lawyers, bankers, and literary figures—as well as Egbert's West Point classmates—not only helped Viele's army career but also aided him in establishing his own very profitable engineering firm when he left the army.[51]

Although her husband did not serve in Texas, Eveline Alexander was the niece of a former Democratic New York governor and a close friend of the Preston Blair family of Missouri. She was the wife of Colonel Andrew Alexander, who held numerous important commands in New Mexico, Arizona, and the northern plains. One of her sisters was married to General Emory Upton, a protegé of General William T. Sherman, and another sister was reputedly engaged to the dashing cavalryman Miles Keogh. Alexander's sister was married to one of the Blair clan, and Alexander himself was distantly related to them.[52] Many other examples could be given. The nineteenth-century army officer corps was something like a large extended family, and both officers and their wives sometimes used their influence, or that of their family and friends, to help promote the needs of the army and the frontier as well as their own careers.[53]

The army women also participated directly in the frontier army's "role as publicists for the West."[54] Indeed, they ranked alongside their husbands as some of the most perceptive observers of the western scene. Historian Merrill Mattes has praised these "female journalists" as "superior observers and recorders," and Utley labeled many of their contributions to literature as "minor frontier classics."[55] Their books, articles, and letters home presented a far more realistic picture of the West and its inhabitants than the sensational accounts in the "penny dreadfuls" and the eastern press and helped familiarize eastern readers with the frontier and its inhabitants. Some of the women authors actively criticized official policy regarding Indians, Mexicans, and the army's role in the West. A few, such as Libbie Custer and Frances Boyd, also used their books as a means of justifying their husbands' actions and keeping their names before the public. But all of them stripped away much of the romance and mythology that colored nineteenth-century views of western life. They helped describe and interpret, or at least explain, the West and the frontier army for eastern readers first-hand. The army women also left a valuable historical record. A careful analysis of their books and other writings can add greatly to our knowledge and understanding of life on the nineteenth-century frontier, help dispel many of the myths about army life and the role of women, and provide a more balanced and accurate assessment of the role of the frontier army in Texas and in other parts of the West. In many ways, then, women played a previously underappreciated part of Texas military history.

"THE AMERICAN CONGO":

Captain John G. Bourke and the
Texas Military Experience

Joseph C. Porter

CAPTAIN JOHN GREGORY BOURKE IS REMEMBERED FOR HIS frontier service with General George Crook and as the author of three books that became classics in the literature of the Indian wars. Bourke was also famous as an ethnologist and a folklorist with an international reputation. Yet he spent his adult life in the army, and, indeed, his scholarly accomplishments were a direct result of his military career. Furthermore, Bourke represents a significant facet of nineteenth-century military history because the army was a primary tool of American expansion into the western frontiers. Army officers were frequently the first Americans with technical or scientific training to encounter little-known areas, and they often functioned as scientists or explorers: gathering information, specimens, and artifacts. Bourke's achievements in Texas from 1891 to 1893 demonstrate the military scientist at work in the waning years of the nineteenth century. His contribution to the Texas military experience is twofold: first, as a scholar and pioneer of folklore studies in South Texas; and second, as a key army officer in the fight against armed forces intent on toppling the government of Mexican president Porfirio Díaz.[1]

Bourke was born in Philadelphia on June 23, 1846, to upper-middle-class Irish immigrant parents with high aspirations for their children. Devoutly Roman Catholic and committed to learning, they hired a Jesuit to instruct their eight-year-old son in Greek, Latin, and Gaelic. Three years later, he began a four-year course at Saint Joseph's College in Philadelphia. Another year of study would have earned him the Bachelor of Arts degree, but the young man abruptly left Saint Joseph's in the autumn of 1859. He accused his French professor of protecting another student who was cheating. When the Jesuit struck Bourke across the face, he cursed the surprised priest and quit school.[2]

After attending grammar school and a commercial college, Bourke planned to enter high school; but, as he later recalled, "the outbreak of the Rebellion made all the boys in the city crazy."[3] Sixteen years old, he lied about his age and enlisted as a private in the 15th Pennsylvania Volunteer Cavalry. Bourke saw action in several battles, including Stones River, Tennessee; Chickamauga, Georgia; the siege of Chattanooga; and the Atlanta campaign. Two weeks after his nineteenth birthday, he honorably left the volunteer service. That autumn he entered the United States Military Academy at West Point, graduating in June, 1869, and ranking eleventh in a class of thirty-nine.[4] Excelling in French, Spanish, ethics, law, English, mineralogy, and geology, his academic success at the academy reflected his rigorous childhood education.

John Bourke was twenty-three years old when he received his commission as a second lieutenant in the 3rd Cavalry in 1869. His personality had been shaped by his middle-class upbringing, his Civil War experience, and his West Point education. "If there was ever a maxim of Life-Conduct ground into me," Bourke later wrote, "it was this: That a gentleman was ever noble; that his nobility was most surely proved by his quiet unostentatious kindness to the suffering, and that one of the first Christian duties was 'to visit the sick and bury the dead.'"[5] He had a strict sense of moral strength and rectitude. Never questioning his own values, he became disillusioned in a world where his personal code seemed increasingly quaint and archaic.

Fascinated with the land and peoples of the West and fighting the monotony of garrison life on the frontier, Bourke began to keep diaries as soon as he arrived in New Mexico in 1869. The portrait of Bourke that emerges from his diaries is of a highly literate young man living on a frontier that the army was incorporating into the rest of the nation. He saw himself as both a participant and a scholar, and he initially thought that his diaries would record the development of "civilization" on the frontier. He did not realize these hopes, and his diaries revealed his disillusionment with the American West that came to be. His sense of disappointment was especially sharp by 1891 when he arrived in Texas. This mood certainly colored his experiences along the lower Rio Grande.

Reporting to Fort Craig in New Mexico in 1869, Bourke spent the next five years in the Southwest. Between 1869 and 1873, he actively fought various Apache groups. Searching for a solution to the Apache wars, the army ordered the eccentric George Crook to assume command of the Military Department of Arizona. Crook wanted officers of combat experience as his aides, and Bourke joined his staff in September of 1871. For the next fifteen years Bourke served with Crook, acting as adviser, confidant, amanuensis, and henchman to him. Bourke's expertise in the nineteenth-century science of ethnology formed the rationale of Crook's Indian policies.[6]

Convinced that only Apaches were capable of subduing their hostile brethren, Crook realized that the diffuse social organization of the Apaches made it possible to enlist the warriors of one band to fight against those of another. He recruited Apaches as auxiliaries, then sent mixed units of soldiers and warriors after the hostile natives.

Serving with these columns, Bourke found himself not only at war against hostile Apaches but also living with and fighting alongside other natives who were allies. Led by Apache scouts, the soldiers struck deep into Apachería and desperate battles ensued. By early April of 1873 the major military offensive was over, and Bourke noted that this "terminated the first and only successful campaign against the Apaches since the acquisition of the Gadsden Purchase."[7]

In 1875, when Crook became commander of the Military Department of the Platte with headquarters in Omaha, Nebraska, Bourke moved to the Great Plains. For the next two years he was at the center of military operations that destroyed the nomadic cultures of the Lakotas and the Northern Cheyennes. Bourke participated in the Bighorn Expedition, commanded by Colonel Joseph J. Reynolds, and the battle on Powder River of March, 1876. That summer, Bourke fought at the battles of the Rosebud, in Montana, and Slim Buttes, in South Dakota. The campaign was hard, trying, frustrating, and dangerous duty that could break the health or sanity of a soldier, and Bourke fought against some of the most formidable warriors in North America.[8]

Subsequently, Bourke would participate in the Northern Cheyenne flight from the Indian Territory in 1878, the Ute War in Colorado in 1879, and the Apache campaigns of the 1880s—but as an observer, not a combatant. Already his interest in ethnology was competing with his soldierly aspirations. After 1876 he approached Indians as an anthropologist, not as an enemy soldier.[9]

When the situation in Apachería deteriorated the army ordered Crook back to Arizona, where he and Bourke returned in 1882. Although still an officer on Crook's staff, Bourke returned to the Southwest as an anthropologist. Ethnology remained his primary concern, even during a frustrating war against the Chiricahua Apaches led by Geronimo. Between 1882 and 1886, books and articles from Bourke's pen won him an international reputation as an ethnologist and convinced powerful and important people to support his scientific efforts.

During both stints in the Southwest, Bourke was a keen observer of the Hispanic population. His experience among the Spanish-speaking people of New Mexico, Arizona, Sonora, and Chihuahua definitely sharpened his later interest in the residents of South Texas. From the outset of his first tour in 1869 he was fascinated with the land, history, and peoples of the Southwest. The Hispanic presence spurred him to master the Spanish language and to study Spanish and Mexican history, and his own religious background heightened his concern with the role of the Roman Catholic church in Spanish North America.

Bourke insisted that it was only common sense for Anglo-Americans to become well acquainted with their Mexican fellow citizens. He remarked that the United States might claim the Southwest, but "ethnographically" the region had "never ceased to belong to Mexico." If Anglos were to govern the region, Bourke believed, they must first attempt to understand the Hispanic and Indian people who lived there. Personal contact with the Mexican population sharpened his linguistic skills and prompted his concern about their culture. He attended mass at the churches in Rio Grande villages and in Tucson. On the banks of the Rio Grande, he noted the agricultural oases that Mexican farmers had coaxed from the arid landscape.[10]

Bourke liked the Mexican theater, circuses, and cuisine of Tucson, a veritable metropolis compared to the villages of the Rio Grande. At *bailes* he danced with señoritas under the withering stares of the *dueñas*, who remained impervious to his charm. "If ever there was created a disagreeable feature upon the fair face of nature," Bourke insisted, "it was the Spanish *dueña* . . . no flattery would put them in good humor, no cajolery would blind them, intimidation was thrown away."[11] Though never free of prejudice toward the Mexicans, he condemned other Anglos who did not appreciate the Hispanic heritage.

From 1886 until 1891 Bourke lived in Washington, D.C., under orders from the secretary of war to pursue his ethnological studies. Bourke was active among the Washington intelligentsia, joining numerous scientific societies and social clubs. He published in anthropological and folklore journals, and he earned a solid reputation as a folklorist as well as an ethnologist. Certainly his years in Washington were his most prolific as a writer.

In addition to his scholarly duties, Bourke worked to secure freedom for the Chiricahua Apache tribe. In 1886, during the aftermath of the last Geronimo outbreak, the army sent the entire Chiricahua tribe to Florida as prisoners of war. Chiricahua scouts who had actively helped the army pursue Geronimo were now prisoners.

Outraged by this treatment of the Indians, Bourke (and several other army officers) sought their release. Hoping to ignore the Chiricahua question, the War Department was irritated by Bourke's efforts on behalf of the Apaches. Several times he suspected that his concern over the Chiricahua cost him promotion to the rank of major. After his former patron George Crook died in 1890, Bourke was in a very vulnerable position in Washington. Almost at once the secretary of war sought to order Bourke away. Despite entreaties from the Smithsonian Institution and the Bureau of Ethnology, the pleading of politicians, and statements of military and civilian physicians attesting to Bourke's declining health, the War Department ordered him to join his 3rd Cavalry unit in Texas.[12]

The Rio Grande began and ended Bourke's western military career. Fort Craig, New Mexico, was his first post after West Point, and the lower Rio Grande Valley of Texas was the theater of his last field action. If it was true, as Bourke suspected, that the War Department wanted him out of the limelight, this tactic utterly failed by sending him to Texas. In November of 1891 his *On the Border with Crook* appeared, quickly becoming a popular success. Bourke's behavior in Texas also captured national newspaper headlines.

Bourke arrived in San Antonio on April 7, 1891, where he reported to Fort Sam Houston, headquarters of the Military Department of Texas. He proceeded to Fort McIntosh at Laredo and then to Fort Ringgold at Rio Grande City on May 15. Bourke praised Fort Ringgold, a four-company post, as "the best equipped" of its size that he had ever seen. Of Rio Grande City "the less said the better," he commented. It "has a population of 2,500 souls—is the seat of Star County (which is about as big as all New England) and has a County Court House and several other creditable buildings but the stores are poorly stocked and the life of the people generally squalid." He was familiar with General Philip Sheridan's remark that if the general owned both hell and Texas, he would rent Texas and live in hell. The heat often reached 110 degrees in the shade, which aggravated Bourke's poor health, and by July he was suffering from insomnia and diarrhea.[13]

At Fort Ringgold he commanded the garrison, which consisted of C Troop, of the 3rd Cavalry and A Company, of the 5th Infantry. During the summer of 1891 Bourke performed the usual chores of post commander. Fluent in Spanish, he traveled widely up and down both sides of the Rio Grande, visiting hamlets and ranches and conducting research into the folklore of the area.

Bourke mentioned Catarino Garza by name in the summer of 1891, but his diary first referred to Garza's "party of revolutionists" or "band" in September. He learned that Garza had raised an armed force to topple the government of President Porfirio Díaz in Mexico. The revolutionary leader indicted the Díaz regime in his newspaper, *El Libre Pensador*, which he had published in Eagle Pass, Texas, in the 1880s and in Palito Blanco, Texas, in the early 1890s. Bourke observed that "the sympathy of the population of the Rio Grande with Garza is scarcely disguised."[14]

The Mexican government demanded that the United States enforce its neutrality laws because Garza based his organization, including his army, in Texas. In turn the United States government ordered the state of Texas, the federal marshals in Texas, and the United States Army to stop the *Garzistas* from operating on Texas soil. Bourke appreciated the diplomatic rationale behind the U.S. government's decision, but he thought it impractical. He knew that the population of South Texas was largely Hispanic and that Garza moved through this vast geographic area with impunity. Also, he pointed out, many South Texans—Mexican Americans and Anglos—openly supported Garza. Forts McIntosh and Ringgold mustered only two troops of cavalry and two companies of infantry to patrol an area of five hundred square miles. Indeed, in October, 1891, Bourke asked to withdraw his units from the field, insisting that he was only wearing out men and animals in a futile task.[15]

Initially Bourke and other army officers were content to let federal marshals deal with Garza; however, severe dissension among civilian officials compelled the army to become more active. Sheriff W. W. Sheely of Star County alleged that three deputy federal marshals in South Texas and U.S. collector of customs F. D. Jodon in Rio Grande City actually assisted Garza.[16] Some county sheriffs, deputies, and other officials also helped the *Garzistas*. Fantastic rumors flourished, and informants sold American officials and Mexican consuls false and greatly exaggerated details.

Bourke, other officers, and their units had to respond to each rumor, no matter how wildly improbable, or risk being accused of laxness by the Mexican government. Bourke's patrol to Una de Gato Ranch is merely one example of many such fruitless ventures. On October 8, 1891, the Mexican consul in Rio Grande City sent Bourke information that *insurrectos* were hiding at Una de Gato Ranch about seven leagues north of Roma, Texas. At four o'clock the next morning Bourke, a sergeant, three privates, and a teamster set out for Una de Gato, where they found seven families. Bourke delivered a threatening speech in Spanish telling the "assembled . . . that I intended to come out and burn their huts to the ground if I learned that they were harboring or aiding any of the Mexican revolutionists in their attempt upon the integrity of the Mexican Republic with which we were at peace."¹⁷

Bourke's soldiers inspected "carefully for signs of fires, bedding in the chaparal, wheel tracks, horse tracks, fresh horse manure, human excrement, unusual amount of cooking or anything else to indicate the presence of strangers, but found nothing." Bourke and his exhausted men returned to Fort Ringgold that evening. Before sunlight the next morning the Mexican consul again aroused Bourke with newly purchased information that the *Garzistas* were "quite close to" Una de Gato Ranch.¹⁸

Frustrated and weary, Bourke complained in November of 1891 that "so many miserable lies and 'fake' rumors had reached me in regard to the Garza business that I felt I ought not to trust anybody, but seek knowledge for myself." Because of his fluency in Spanish, Bourke often gathered his own intelligence, visiting Hispanic festivals, parties, theaters, and circuses. Dressed in nondescript civilian clothes, he eavesdropped on conversations in saloons and restaurants on both sides of the border. Bourke was disdainful of Garza and his *pronunciados*, believing that they should not launch their struggle from Texas, but he was also critical of the Díaz regime in Mexico. Based upon what he had overheard, Bourke claimed that President Díaz had ordered the summary executions of three Mexican generals and thirteen colonels in northern Mexico in the past plus dozens of rivals or opponents, including many *Garzistas*.¹⁹

Bourke concluded that only the presence of the Mexican army prevented a majority of citizens in northeastern Mexico from openly supporting Garza. Although some federal marshals were pro-Garza, Bourke discovered that the Mexican government bribed other marshals to kidnap American citizens thought to be *Garzistas*. These marshals took their victims to Mexico, where they were interrogated and murdered. Bourke claimed that Mexican authorities had killed no fewer than one thousand persons along the Rio Grande in the past thirty years. "Díaz was an arbitrary despot and let nothing stand in his way, but the country was certainly advancing under him," Bourke concluded. "There were no longer any elections in Mexico. Only one state had a Governor supposed to be elected by popular suffrage—all the others were military satraps appointed by Díaz." By December, 1891, Bourke had established his own network of undercover Mexican-American and Mexican informants, some of whom were well acquainted with Catarino Garza.²⁰

One person that Bourke trusted was U.S. deputy marshal Manuel Banado of Edinburgh, Texas. Disguised as an *insurrecto* bearer of dispatches, Banado discovered that Garza and at least one hundred men were at La

Grulla Ranch. He also learned the identity of another deputy marshal who openly worked with Garza. Bourke, Banado, and nineteen soldiers went to La Grulla on December 21, 1891. En route they arrested U.S. deputy marshal Tomás Garza for supporting the *Garzistas*. "Tomás Garza agreed to place my men in ambuscade or conduct them to the place where the revolutionists were in camp at Retamal," Bourke wrote, "but he told me that if I went into that place, I should have to fight as I had only 19 men and the Mexicans 100." It was already dark, and Bourke was dubious, admitting that night attacks "rarely ever amount to anything." Guided by Tomás Garza, Bourke and his men quietly approached the *Garzista* camp. After a heated exchange of gunfire, the *pronunciados* scattered into the dense chaparral along with Tomás Garza, who escaped during the bedlam. The soldiers suffered no casualties and inflicted none, but they did capture some equipment.[21]

The next day Bourke sent patrols into the chaparral, where there was a vicious skirmish that included hand-to-hand combat between the soldiers and the *insurrectos*. According to Bourke, the *Garzistas* rallied with the cry "Kill the d____d Gringoes." They killed Corporal Charles H. Edstrom and in the confusion captured Deputy Marshal Pérez and an army private. Pérez escaped his captors, who later released the private. These brutal fights in the chaparral prompted some soldiers to carry shotguns loaded with buckshot instead of army-issue carbines or rifles. Some individuals in C Troop—fearful of close ambush and night fighting in the dense chaparral, which made their carbines relatively ineffective—used ten-gauge double-barreled shotguns, an act directly contrary to War Department regulations.[22]

The fight at Retamal and the death of Corporal Edstrom forced army officers in San Antonio and Washington to realize that a serious situation existed in South Texas. Brigadier General David S. Stanley, commanding officer of the Military Department of Texas, ordered Bourke to swear out federal warrants against Catarino Garza, Cayetano Garza, Sisto Longoria, Julian Flores, and Eustorgio Ramón, all charged with treason for firing upon federal soldiers at Retamal.[23] The Retamal skirmish and the subsequent warrants placed Bourke in the limelight, both in Texas and across the nation, and he quickly became one of the most popularly known field officers against Garza. Only Captain Francis H. Hardie, 3rd Cavalry, operating from Fort McIntosh, gained as much notoriety as Bourke.

The action at Retamal, the death of Corporal Edstrom, and other casualties blamed on the *pronunciados* destroyed Bourke's lackadaisical tolerance of the *Garzistas*. He now considered himself and his men at war with a military force, and he ordered his soldiers to kill any armed *Garzistas* they encountered. Still responding to rumors and false reports, Bourke, Hardie, and other officers patrolled the countryside, going from ranch to ranch. Captain J. A. Brooks and fifteen Texas Rangers joined Bourke and his soldiers on December 28, 1891. The next day, the Rangers and the soldiers found a camp with evidence that as many as two hundred *pronunciados* had been in the bivouac. On December 31, the soldiers wounded and captured Sisto Longoria, who had been named in one of Bourke's warrants.[24]

At this juncture, late December of 1891, Paul Fricke, the U.S. marshal for South Texas, instructed his deputies to cease helping the army. In February, 1892, strife between Marshal Fricke and the army officers broke into the open. Some deputy marshals continued to assist the army while others, with Fricke's blessing, openly cooperated with the *Garzistas*. Deputy marshals informed Bourke that Fricke coerced and threatened those deputies who aided the army, and Bourke suspected that Sisto Longoria, a top Garza lieutenant, had once been a deputy of Fricke.[25]

Newspapers outside of Texas discovered that the feud between federal marshals and army officers along the Rio Grande made excellent copy. In February, 1892, Sheriff W. W. Sheely of Star County told Bourke that Fricke had secretly appointed F. D. Jodon, U.S. customs collector at Rio Grande City, as a deputy marshal. Another deputy informed Bourke that Jodon was Garza's financial agent in Star County. Bourke also discovered that *Garzistas* who fought the soldiers at Retamal were hiding in Jodon's house in Rio Grande City within twenty-four hours of the battle. Jodon reportedly told the inhabitants of Rio Grande City that Bourke had murdered Catarino Garza at Retamal. Bourke instructed his men at Fort Ringgold not to recognize either Jodon or his son as marshals.[26]

Throughout early 1892, the Texas Rangers and army units from Forts Ringgold and McIntosh patrolled the back country. In February, Bourke's spies reported that Catarino Garza was at Palito Blanco, the ranch of his father-in-law, Alejandro Gonzalez. Bourke then ordered the detention of Gonzalez. Garza fled as the army approached and found sanctuary in the home of the sheriff of Duval County.[27]

The *Garzistas* and their supporters started to use the county and state courts and the press against Bourke. He learned that charges would be filed against him for kicking down a door during the raid at Palito Blanco, and Texas newspapers began to carry derogatory articles about him. In March of 1892, political pressure from South Texas convinced the governor to refer charges of unlawful arrest brought against Bourke to General Stanley.

People whom Bourke had accused of supporting Garza now signed complaints against the captain. That same month, a court in Star County indicted Bourke and a lieutenant for an unlawful arrest made in October, 1891. In January, 1892, a federal court convicted the defendant arrested by Bourke. Curiously, the defense attorney in that case was the Star County judge who now indicted Bourke.[28] Between April and June, Bourke spent most of his time appearing before a grand jury in San Antonio.

Bourke believed that some state and county officials in South Texas were exploiting all sides of the Garza conflict in order to develop political machines. By the spring of 1892, Bourke suspected that bandits with no political motivation were also taking advantage of the uproar. He complained bitterly about the abuse heaped upon him in the press and by certain "Texas shysters." Responding to one newspaper article, Bourke sent this letter to Sheriff Robert Haynes of Zapata County: "I enclose clipping from the 'Tribune' of Chicago, Illinois. If the quotation represents you correctly, you are a liar, scoundrel, and coward." Sheriff Haynes never responded.[29]

Captain George A. Drew reported to Fort Ringgold in the summer of 1892, and Bourke told his new commanding officer that he, Bourke, would decline to obey any further orders to go after the *Garzistas* until the exact line of his duties was defined by the highest military authority.[30] There was much unrest in July and August, but Bourke decided that some of it was from bandits not connected with the *pronunciados*. He maintained his network of spies, noting their information in his diary, which became a running account of his perspective on the Garza movement.

Bourke and other army officers remained convinced of the truth of their accusations against Marshal Paul Fricke. Bourke claimed that Fricke was systematically removing deputies who cooperated with the troops, replacing them with "school boys or old bums." "All those [marshals] now here not equal to one good yaller dog," Bourke informed a United States attorney in July.[31] In November, 1892, a federal grand jury in San Antonio asked Bourke to testify against Fricke. The date set for Bourke's testimony was November 14; that same day the press reported that Marshal Fricke had assassinated Bourke in the courtroom! Newspapers in Texas, Boston, Philadelphia, and Washington, D.C., ran stories about Bourke's murder, and, because of his reputation as a writer and Indian fighter, they carried fulsome obituaries. Mark Twain was bemused by premature reports of his own death. Bourke was furious, but he never determined the origin of the story, which had first appeared in the *Caller* of Corpus Christi.[32]

In December, the secretary of war ordered Bourke to Washington to report about conditions along the lower Rio Grande. Bourke insisted upon aggressively pursuing the *Garzistas*. He wanted to use Apache scouts as trackers, and he argued that once government forces had picked up a hot trail, they should stay on it until the *Garzistas* were run into the ground. Bourke advocated raising a battalion of Mexican Americans to deal with affairs such as the Garza movement. Demonstrating a view well ahead of his time, he believed that more Spanish-speaking people should be employed by the federal government as customs collectors, marshals, inspectors, and in other offices. He insisted that the government should try to attract Mexican Americans toward its own interests and away from those of local Texas politicians or Mexican groups.

Bourke testified before grand juries in Brownsville and San Antonio in January, 1893. By early 1893 army officers had become embroiled in the feuding between other federal officials. The officers were now bickering among themselves and siding with factions among the federal marshals and the local sheriffs. Bourke and his superior, Captain Drew, reached the point where they would hardly speak to one another.

On February 18, James O. Luby, an attorney in San Diego, Texas, warned Bourke that the *Garzistas* "would now put charges of some kind or another against every officer, state or federal, and every guide, scout, or witness concerned in the suppression of the '*pronunciadios.*'"[33] Later that month Star County officials charged Bourke with false imprisonment and assault during the raid on La Grulla. Stung by these charges, Bourke maintained his innocence for the rest of his life. He was outraged at newspaper stories reporting that he struck defenseless men and threatened women and children. One rumor held that Bourke had sacked Roman Catholic churches; one South Texas editor would label Bourke the "New Attila, the Scourge of God."[34] On February 24, 1893, Bourke was formally indicted and was to be tried in Star County Court. Evidence in Bourke's diary and in the National Archives does not substantiate the charges against him; however, the newspaper stories left their mark, and some Texans still believed the accusations against Bourke.

Bourke's departure from Texas came suddenly, and it was his scholarly credentials that rescued him. Despite his work against the *pronunciados* and his acrimonious relations with many South Texans, he had remained intellectually active. He studied the folklore of the lower Rio Grande, reviewed books, wrote articles, and basked in the success of *On the Border with Crook*.

An influential friend, William E. Curtis, arranged his escape from Texas. On February 20, 1893, Curtis wired, asking Bourke if he would consider a detail with the Latin American Department of the World's Columbian Exposition in Chicago, effective immediately. Bourke accepted that day. On March 1 he received his orders, and he arrived in Chicago nine days later. On March 14, the commanding officer at Fort Ringgold notified Bourke that officials in Star County would drop all charges against him if he did not return to South Texas.[35]

South Texas and northern Mexico had challenged Bourke's intellectual preconceptions because he thought that it was an ideal locale to study cultural survival. Despite some ethnocentric bias toward Mexicans, Bourke was still considerably more open-minded than many of his Anglo contemporaries. "The Mexican is tenacious of old usages; this is because he is the descendent of five different races, each in its way conservative of all that had been handed down from its ancestors," Bourke contended. "These races, it needs no words to show, were the Roman, the Teuton, the Arab, the Celt, and the Aztec." He argued that the lower Rio Grande was a good place to search through "the lore and custom of the folk for vestiges and tattered remnants, which, when patched together bring to light their original purpose and design."[36]

Bourke studied the popular uses of animals and plants in local *materia medica*. In a ledger he recorded the local names, descriptions, uses, and specimens of plants. He planned to write a book on the subject, but after the Smithsonian Institution sent him a herbarium, he sent his specimens to Washington. He learned which plant and animal substances supposedly cured dandruff, smallpox, asthma, and venereal disease. Other remedies promised to energize a diffident lover or spouse, ease menstrual pains, cause conception, expedite delivery, induce abortion, and cure melancholia.[37]

Bourke's most valued informant was Maria Antonia Cavazo de Garza. Señora Cavazo de Garza insisted that she was a *curandera*, but others around Rio Grande City maintained that she was *una bruja*, or a witch. Declaring that she was empowered *con el favor de Dios*, she effected wonderful cures. She met with Bourke regularly to "unfold her stock of mystic lore." Bourke claimed that she had been married four times and borne seventeen children, and he guessed her age as between sixty-five and seventy-five.[38] Her conversations ranged from folk *materia medica* to *brujería*, or witchcraft. She described the *Gente de Chuzas*, who had sold their souls to the devil and then must never think of God. After death their lost souls roamed about seeking sanctuary; however, they would not enter a house where there was mustard. A person who made a cross of mustard on the wall near their bed was protected from the wandering ones. This was highly significant to folklorist Bourke, who had also read

Captain John G. Bourke in the 1890s. Courtesy Nebraska State Historical Society.

that Italian peasants used mustard as a shield against witches.[39]

Bourke was also a pioneer student of Mexican plays of the Nativity as enacted along the lower Rio Grande. In November of 1891 he watched a rehearsal of *Los Pastores*, or the Miracle Play of the Shepherds, commemorating the birth of Jesus Christ in Bethlehem. Committing the lengthy stanzas to memory, local inhabitants performed the various roles. Francisco Collazo, a cobbler in Rio Grande City and leader of the play, gave Bourke a written copy of the libretto, which filled fifty-six pages in his diary. Bourke saw a full-dress performance of *Los Pastores* in December, 1891, and a year later he witnessed another cast present the play in San Antonio. After leaving Texas he procured photographs of the scenes and Edison cylinders of the accompanying music. In the spring of 1893 the *Journal of American Folk-Lore* carried Bourke's analysis of *Los Pastores*. Because of its length, the entire text that Bourke received from Señor Collazo did not appear until 1907, when the American Folk-Lore Society published *Los Pastores: A Mexican Play of the Nativity*.[40]

Bourke's research in Texas secured his reputation as a folklorist, and it confirmed to him the validity of such studies. "At first glance, the ceremonial observances of the humble *'curanderas'* of the Southwestern border would seem to be mummery pure and simple," he wrote, "but a more careful examination may perhaps discover a distinguished ancestry for all these practices which at least cannot have been the invention of those who are yet addicted to them." Despite his folklore research, Bourke's time in Texas was unhappy because of the controversy and acrimony that followed his Texas tour of duty from beginning to end.[41]

His public denunciation of Garza and his followers earned Bourke the undying enmity of many South Texans. His most searing comments appeared in an article, "The American Congo," which appeared in *Scribner's Magazine* one year after he left Fort Ringgold. In the piece Bourke described South Texas as the land of "Garza, the wife beater, defaulting sewing-machine agent, blackmailing editor, and hater of the Gringoes." "The American Congo" was a combination of description of the physical appearance and climate of South Texas and caricature of the Mexican-American population, which Bourke depicted as lazy, ignorant, lawless, and irresistibly attracted to individuals like Garza. He admitted "the existence within this Dark Belt of thriving communities, such as Brownsville, Matamoros, Corpus Christi, Laredo, San Diego, and others in which are to be found people of as much refinement and good breeding as anywhere else in the world, but exerting about as much influence upon the indigenes around them as did the Saxon or Danish invaders upon the Celts of Ireland."[42]

South Texans did not let Bourke's bitter comments pass unchallenged. In 1895, publishers of *El Bien Público* responded in kind when they issued *War against Peace; or, A New Attila*, which insisted that Bourke's "vandal deeds along the border call to mind that 'Scourge of God' beneath whose horses hoofs [*sic*] no grass ever grow."[43] *A New Attila* reviewed the accusations made against Bourke and other army officers during the Garza affair. Bourke saw the article, but it probably did not bother him much. The charges made by the state courts had stung, and he smoldered about the Garza affair after he left Texas. He began to study the neutrality laws in order to defend his actions against Garza, and for the rest of his life he kept a wary eye on affairs in South Texas. From a military standpoint, the army did issue a commendation for Bourke's "specially meritorious acts or conduct in service" for his role in "suppressing armed violation of the neutrality laws of the United States on the Southwestern border of Texas."[44]

John Bourke made two contributions to the Texas military tradition: his diary and correspondence. They are essential to any study of the *Garzista* movement, a specific event in the social and military history of Texas. He provides names, ample details, and his own perspective about this significant moment in South Texas and northern Mexico.

Some United States Army officers made substantial contributions to the intellectual knowledge of the North American continent, and in the nineteenth century they formed a definite tradition of the soldier-scientist within the military. Bourke represents this achievement in Texas military history. A pioneer of folklore studies in Texas, Bourke ranks with such notable folklorists as John A. Lomax, Alan Lomax, and J. Frank Dobie.

THE 36TH INFANTRY DIVISION IN WORLD WAR II

Martin Blumenson

MOST AMERICANS HAVE TWO LOYALTIES: ONE TO THEIR country, the other to their locality. Before the American Civil War, there was some question about which was more important. That conflict resolved the issue. The national takes precedence over the regional. Today, regardless of the different ways of speaking or the kinds of clothing worn, and no matter what the diversity of local customs, Americans are Americans first—southerners, Texans, Californians, or New Englanders second.

For Americans, World War II started at Pearl Harbor. They reacted to the attack not because it struck Hawaii but because it assaulted American soil. The 36th Infantry Division, rooted in the traditions of Texas, started the war as a regional organization, a National Guard or state formation. It soon grew into an all-American outfit and became a standard infantry division like all others. It had its distinctive patch—a block T for Texas imposed on an arrowhead, point down—and its special memories and customs. Although the comradeship developed by its soldiers during the war transcended the ties to the state, the 36th Division, unlike most other divisions, retained a local or regional identity and a special Texas flavor.

The 36th Division was a great division in World War I. No division fought harder, and very few divisions fought longer. Everyone who served in it was proud of belonging to it and of having contributed to its success, no matter where he came from—Texas, Ohio, or Alabama.

The 36th Division came into being on August 23, 1917, as a Texas National Guard unit at Camp Bowie. Almost a year later, on July 5, 1918, the division went overseas. As part of the Fourth French Army, it fought in the difficult Meuse-Argonne offensive, the climactic campaign of World War II. In the battle, its soldiers advanced twenty-one kilometers, captured 813 prisoners of war, and suffered twenty-six hundred casualties. Returning home in 1919, the division was deactivated on June 18. The people of Texas were proud of the division's achievements. Their wish to preserve the glory of the division's record was part of a desire to bring the 36th to life again. Four years later, on May 2, 1923, the 36th National Guard Division was reorganized in San Antonio.[1]

The history of the 36th Division was typical of many such organizations between World War I and World War II. The individual and subordinate headquarters and units met in hometown armories and school gymnasiums once a week to march, drill, and fire weapons. Members of the regular army made annual inspections. Once a year all the units came together, formed the division, and spent two weeks in summer training. Each man received a dollar for every day spent training, and the pay was important during the depression as an incentive for service. In addition to military duties, National Guard organizations were also social centers. Balls, dances, banquets, and patriotic celebrations supplemented the division's activities. All of these events kept alive the memories and traditions of the Great War of 1917–18.[2]

As war clouds loomed in the late 1930s, many men joined the National Guard. If war came to the United States, they wanted to be with their friends and neighbors, in whom they had confidence and trusted. Unit pride and cohesion increased.[3]

The United States began preparing seriously for war only in 1940—after the defeat of France in the spring. In the fall of that year, the Selective Service Act brought half a million draftees into the army. All eighteen National Guard divisions, totaling two hundred twenty-five thousand men; and one hundred thousand officers of the Organized Reserve were called to active duty for a year.[4]

The 36th Division entered federal service at San Antonio on November 25, 1940, and moved to Camp Bowie on December 14.[5] Soon afterward, draftees from all over the country flowed into the division to bring it up to authorized strength. These new recruits diluted the Texas character of the outfit, but the old timers took steps to imbue them with the Texas identity and tradition.

Under Major General Claude V. Birkhead, who commanded the division, the 36th took part in exercises around Brownwood, Texas, in June, 1941, then participated in the important Louisiana maneuvers of August and September. General Lesley J. McNair, who was then chief of staff of General Headquarters, U.S. Army, and the trainer of combat troops, judged Birkhead's performance in these exercises inadequate for combat.[6] Some National Guard officers owed their positions to political preference and appointment or were elderly or below standards in military education and professionalism. Like McNair, General George C. Marshall, the U.S. Army chief of staff, recalled the inability of several senior commanders in World War I. These men were too old to withstand the rigors of battle or lacked stamina and endurance. Accordingly, in 1941 Marshall searched for young and vigorous officers to place in positions of responsibility—men like Dwight D. Eisenhower, Omar N. Bradley, and Mark W. Clark. At the suggestion of Clark, McNair's principal assistant, McNair replaced Birkhead with Fred L. Walker, who had served with Clark at Fort Lewis, Washington. They were good friends.[7]

In September, 1941, Walker assumed command and soon thereafter was promoted to major general. Instead of carrying out Marshall's instructions transmitted by McNair to make sweeping changes among the division's senior officers, Walker made very few changes.[8] Consequently, many Texans remained in positions of command and staff leadership. This, no doubt, helped preserve the division's Texas identity and heritage.[9]

Continuing to train at Camp Bowie, the division was renamed the 36th Infantry Division on February 1, 1942, and then was triangularized to give it the same shape of the other army divisions. From a square division with two brigade headquarters, each with two regiments of four battalions, the division became one containing three infantry regiments—the 141st, 142nd, and 143rd—directly under the division headquarters. Each regiment had three infantry battalions. This was the standard U.S. infantry division organization in World War II.[10]

Transferred to Camp Blanding, Florida, in February, 1942, the division participated in the Carolina maneuvers of July and August. After a stay at Camp Edwards, Massachusetts, the soldiers left the New York port of embarkation in April, 1943, for North Africa.[11] The 36th then resembled all the others. "By the time it went overseas," an officer wrote of his own outfit, "the Ninth Division, like most so-called regular Army divisions, was no different in organization, equipment and quality of personnel than the National Guard divisions . . . or those units formed later from scratch."[12]

In North Africa, the 36th came under the VI Corps headquarters. Together with the veteran 3rd Division and the combat-inexperienced 45th, the 36th was scheduled to invade Sicily. Lieutenant General George S. Patton, Jr., who was about to activate and command the Seventh Army in the Sicilian campaign, preferred to attack with blooded organizations. He replaced the VI Corps headquarters with the II Corps, commanded by Bradley, which had fought in Tunisia. He also substituted the experienced 1st Division, which had done well in Tunisia, for the 36th.[13]

As a consequence, the 36th Division took part in the invasion of the Italian mainland.[14] Under Clark's Fifth Army headquarters and General Ernest Dawley's VI Corps headquarters, the 36th Division came ashore around Salerno early in September, 1943. It was the only American component in the initial waves. On the left, the X British Corps was to send two divisions ashore.

All amphibious landings are difficult and precarious. The operation in the bay of Salerno was particularly so for two major reasons. First, the surrender of Italy was announced on the evening before the landing. Although officers warned their men to expect German instead of Italian defenders, there was an inevitable let-down: many troops expected to walk ashore and pick up tickets for the Naples opera. Second, the terrain favored defense. A ring of hills around the beaches of Paestum where the 36th landed gave the Germans excellent observation of the incoming Americans. Accurate German artillery fires accentuated the normal chaos of an amphibious landing. Nevertheless, by nightfall of September 9, 1943, the first day of the invasion, the entire division was ashore and in possession of its initial objectives. The troops had done very well.

During the next few days, as the Germans concentrated against the British around Salerno, the 36th met relatively little opposition. The men advanced into the hills and took the villages of Altavilla, Agropoli, and Albanella. To help the British, Clark broadened the VI Corps zone. He sent his floating reserve, two regiments of the 45th Division, into the gap between the 36th and the British. Clark also extended the length of the 36th Division front so that Walker was responsible for thirty-five miles—a rather large area.

When the Germans counterattacked on September 13, they overran two battalions of the 36th Division. The 1st Battalion, 142nd Infantry, was reduced to sixty men. The 2nd Battalion, 143rd Infantry, ceased to exist. Other battalions, particularly the 3rd Battalions of the 142nd and 143rd Infantry regiments, suffered heavy losses. Despite these losses, the division hung on and the tide turned. On September 15, General Clark judged the battle to be won. The Germans soon began to retire slowly up the boot of Italy. On September 20, after eleven days of fighting, the invasion was termed complete, and a new phase of operations opened. The 36th Division came out of the line, passed into Fifth Army reserve, rested, received replacements, and trained again.

The division remained in the rear for two months. The casualties and the shock of the invasion had temporarily disrupted the division's efficiency. After six weeks, at the end of October, it was judged to be 75

The 36th Infantry Division occupying Schweigen, Germany, 1945. Courtesy U.S. Army Signal Corps.

percent combat effective. While in reserve, the 36th was earmarked for a variety of amphibious operations planned and then abandoned.[15] But two months of combat inactivity in a theater where resources were consistently inadequate was a long time for the recovery of proficiency and morale.

In mid-November, the division entered the line and held static positions during two weeks of miserable weather. On December 2, it attacked the rugged hill masses of Monte Sammucro, Monte la Difensa, Monte Maggiore, and Monte Lungo. On execrable ground and in bitter fighting, the 36th showed grit and determination and conquered the heights, wresting them from the Germans. Then came the village of San Pietro Infine, a virtually impregnable fortress. Taking San Pietro cost the 36th Division twelve hundred casualties, of whom one hundred fifty were killed.[16] Toward the end of December, after grueling combat in the worst kind of weather and terrain, the division came out of the line. The men were exhausted. They had acquitted themselves in strenuous mountain warfare with distinction and honor.

General Walker paid tribute to his men. In his diary, he wrote: "I regret the hardships they must suffer . . . wet, cold, muddy, hungry, going into camp in the mud and rain, no sleep, no rest. . . . How they endure their hardships I do not understand . . . they are still cheerful. . . . I do not understand how the men continue to keep going under their existing conditions of hardship."[17]

The 36th Division almost made the Anzio landings, but chance sent it instead to the Rapido River. The attempted crossings remain controversial. The circumstances perhaps made the operation a no-win situation. The mountains, the river, the flood plain, the strong German positions in the Gustav Line, the failure of the British on the immediate left flank to cross and thereby protect the 36th Division were some of the factors involved. Motivating the Rapido River assault was the need to support the Anzio landing, planned to take place two days later. The Fifth Army had to get troops across the Rapido and into the Liri River valley for three reasons: (1) to tie down the Germans in the Gustav Line and prevent them from sending units to interfere with the Anzio operation; (2) to attract additional German troops away from Anzio and Rome; and (3) to start the push to link up with the Anzio beachhead. That the 36th Division was selected for this extremely difficult task was a compliment. That the Fifth Army and II Corps commanders, Clark and Major General Geoffrey Keyes, had every expectation of success is another.

It is always extremely difficult to ascertain the exact number of casualties in any operation. According to the official records, the division at the Rapido sustained 1,661 losses during the month of January, 1944: 143 killed, 663 wounded, and 875 missing, most of the latter presumably captured.[18] The majority of these losses occurred at the Rapido River in forty-eight hours. Whether the 36th Division was by this time a Texas unit in its composition is a moot question. The division contained as many soldiers from New Jersey and New York as from Texas.

The most damaging evidence on the failure to cross the river was the German reaction. To the 15th Panzer Grenadier Division, which turned back the effort, the battle was hardly serious. The Germans took negligible losses and had no need to commit even local reserves. They thought the attack was a reconnaissance in force.[19]

Many years later, General J. Lawton Collins, a former U.S. Army chief of staff and the VII Corps commander during the war, speculated on the Rapido action. According to him, General Keyes, the II Corps commander and General Walker's immediate superior, was to blame for failing to supervise Walker. Collins was no doubt sensitive to the roles and responsibilities of corps commanders.[20]

After bloody engagements on the slopes of the Monte Cassino massif, the division was withdrawn in mid-March for rehabilitation. In mid-May, the men were shipped to the Anzio beachhead. There the division masterfully executed one of the great operations of the war, the capture of Monte Artemisio, which broke open the battle for Rome.

The II Corps, driving up the coast of Italy, had made contact with the VI Corps around Anzio. Both corps then attacked the German Caesar Line, hoping to secure access to Highways 6 and 7, the two major roads leading to the Italian capital. The 36th invested the town of Velletri, where a German garrison blocked Highway 7. For five days the Fifth Army made little progress, and the beginnings of a stalemate seemed at hand.

Then patrols from the 36th discovered no signs of Germans on the steep slopes of Monte Artemisio, which rises like a wall behind Velletri. Believing that a gap existed in the German defenses, General Walker drew up a plan and obtained approval from Major General Lucian Truscott, Jr., the VI Corps commander. What resulted was a spectacular success.

While the 141st Infantry engaged the Velletri garrison, the 142nd, followed by the 143rd, scaled Monte Artemisio during the night of May 30. Climbing stealthily by the light of a new moon, 36th Division soldiers reached the crest of the mountain at 6:30 A.M. They found and captured three German artillery forward observers, one of whom was taking a bath. Without a shot being fired, the troops swarmed over the top of the hill and moved quickly to take the key features while engineers improved a cart trail to permit passsage of vehicles and heavy equipment. By darkness on May 31, the entire four-mile ridge was in American hands. American artillery observers looked down on Velletri, which was now surrounded, and had a good view of the Anzio plain. The 36th Division, by capturing Monte Artemisio, dissolved the stalemate and opened Highway 7 into Rome, which fell five days later. The division's exploit ranks with the magnificent feats of military history.[21]

Passing through Rome, the 36th joined the pursuit of the Germans north of the city, and took Magliana and Piombino. There General Walker departed, returned to the United States, and took command of the Infantry School at Fort Benning, Georgia. He had commanded the division for three years, and he believed it right to share the honor of commanding a division in combat. He also wanted to pass on to infantry officers the lessons he had learned in the war. Had he known that the 36th Division would soon be chosen to invade southern France, General Walker would have continued in command.[22]

Under Major General John Dahlquist, the 36th, together with the 3rd and 45th, formed the VI Corps and began to prepare for ANVIL, code name for the invasion of southern France. The 36th, coincidentally, trained at Paestum, where their campaigning had begun. ANVIL was an on-and-off assault finally scheduled for August 15, 1944, more than two months after the Normandy campaign had opened. From the onset of the fighting in Normandy, the Germans in southern France had contributed a whole succession of units and equipment to reinforce the troops in the north. Thus, when the VI Corps landed on the Riviera, few German troops remained in the south of France to contest the invasion. The operation proceeded swiftly.[23]

Two days after ANVIL, Hitler ordered his troops in Normandy and in southern France to fall back and unite in Lorraine. With the "Ultra Secret" intercepts of German radio messages informing the Allies of German plans, Lieutenant General Alexander Patch, commanding the Seventh Army, looked for a place to cut off the German withdrawal. At Montelimar, eighty-five miles up the Rhone River from the coast, the main highway and the railroad to the north pass through a narrow corridor dominated by high ground. The mission to block the Germans at Montelimar fell to the 36th Division.

Reaching the designated high ground, the division disrupted the German movement, destroyed many vehicles and much equipment, and took many prisoners, but it was unable to prevent the Germans from escaping the trap. Hampering the 36th Division were the long distances involved, as well as shortages of transportation, fuel, and ammunition, and, most peculiarly, a host of misunderstandings between Generals Truscott and Dahlquist.

Early in September, the 36th Division halted to permit French forces to enter and liberate the city of Lyon. The division then forded the Doubs River and captured Vesoul. Pursuing the Germans to the Moselle River, the soldiers crossed the stream and took Remiremont in the foothills of the Vosges Mountains. There, deteriorating weather and extremely difficult terrain turned the campaign into a nightmare.

The division reached and crossed the Meurthe River late in November, then continued driving to the Colmar Pocket, where the Germans offered a strong defense. After a short rest, the soldiers took part in stiff fighting in mountainous and snow-covered terrain, cleared pillboxes west of the Rhine, and reached the river on March 24, 1945. In April the division moved to and crossed the Danube River. They had advanced to Bad Teel by May 1. The troops were in the Kufstein region of Austria when the war ended.

The 36th Division returned to the United States, debarked at Hampton Roads on December 15. It was inactivated at Camp Patrick Henry, Virginia, and returned to National Guard status on the same date.[24]

Few divisions in World War II can match the record of the 36th, which fought in difficult terrain and weather. The winters in Italy and in France, and the mountains, both the Apennines and the Vosges, provided a mighty test of unit morale, spirit, and determination. The 36th Division's achievements are admirable. It spearheaded the Salerno invasion, reduced mountain strongholds, and captured San Pietro Infine. After stumbling at the Rapido River, the division gained glory at Monte Artemisio and opened the way to Rome. At Montelimar, the division seriously interfered with the massive German withdrawal.

The 36th Division kept alive its Texas origins and traditions. Although the men from Texas dwindled in numbers and in proportion as soldiers from all over the country joined the organization as draftees and replacements, the Texans perpetuated the Texas spirit and connections to the state. As Americans and Texans both, they showed courage, devotion to duty, and the willingness to sacrifice for their country. Although the first man in the division to receive the Medal of Honor was Corporal Charles E. Kelly, from Pittsburgh, Pennsylvania, the division retained its Texas identity throughout the war. Soldiers in the 36th from other states proudly became honorary Texans.

The 36th Division Association, its local chapters, and newsletters like *Le T. Bone,* continue to preserve the warm memories and the shared experiences of the war. Americans all, many of whom happened to come from Texas, the veterans remind Texans that they have reason to be proud of the 36th Infantry Division.[25]

MAN AGAINST FIRE:

Audie Murphy and His War

Roger J. Spiller

THE WOODS WERE INFESTED WITH GERMAN SOLDIERS. THE men of Company B, 15th Infantry Regiment, 3rd Infantry Division, knew it. On the day before they entered the Alsatian forest called the *Bois de Riedwihr*, the 30th Infantry Regiment had been torn apart by the defenders of the *bois*. The 30th had gone too far too fast, outrunning their artillery supports as they pushed beyond the River L'Ill toward the town of Holtzwihr. The Germans had waited until the companies of American infantry entered the defense zones they had prepared. Then, the veteran regiment had been shelled to pieces and expertly machine-gunned. Those who could withdrew behind the safety of the L'Ill, and afterward the regiment could do no more.[1] That was why, on January 24, 1945, the 15th Infantry took up the approach march to the *Bois de Riedwihr*.

As B Company entered the forest the next day, they "encountered extremely heavy resistance," as the military historians would say. The resistance took the form of clouds of snipers, artillery bursts fused for treetop detonation, zones of mines and booby traps, mortars, and machine guns well sited for cross fire. The company had to fight its way virtually from tree to tree, and by the end of the day there was no more ammunition. During a pause in fighting, the company commander was seriously wounded by a mortar round. A fresh-faced second lieutenant who looked like one of Norman Rockwell's newspaper boys was ordered to take over the company and resume the advance at first light.[2]

The life of a second lieutenant in command of an infantry company during the Second World War was usually very short. His chances of surviving to become a first lieutenant were slim enough; of surviving the war, slimmer still; and of emerging physically unhurt, almost nil. In one fifty-day period, as this particular division fought its way through the hills of Italy, line units reported a 152 percent loss in second lieutenants.[3] Most of the battle casualties in the infantry were sustained during the first ten days of combat. That, of course, did not mean a combat infantryman who kept whole bones for ten days on the line would not be killed or wounded on the eleventh, or even that his experience would somehow shield him from what lay ahead. The longer one stayed in the line, the smaller the chances of survival.[4]

The new commander of Company B was, as Bill Mauldin's Willie and Joe and even he would later say, "a fugitive from the law of averages." He had joined the 3rd Infantry Division while it was still in North Africa. After serving for a time as a battalion runner because he was considered too frail for line duty—his friends called him "Baby"—he was permitted to join the line as a combat rifleman with Company B in July, 1943, during the campaign in Sicily. For nineteen months he had been pushing his luck, a quality that he appeared to possess in abundance. Only the day before the lieutenant assumed command, his right leg had been sprayed with fragments from a mortar burst. But compared to the mayhem he had witnessed, his wound seemed so slight that he simply pulled out what pieces he could, applied his own field dressing, and continued with his duties. Two officers who had been commissioned with him had been killed in the same barrage.[5]

Now, on January 26, 1945, the lieutenant moved his company through the *Bois de Riedwihr*, and the fighting was just as intense as the day before. By the early afternoon, the company had made its way to the edge of an open field. As the men emerged into the clearing, the Germans began firing from the opposite side with small arms, mortars, and artillery. As usual, the Germans placed their fire with murderous precision. In the barrage, an American tank destroyer supporting the company was set afire and abandoned by its crew. The lieutenant and his men had gone to ground with the opening shot, and he now called for artillery counter fire. In the meantime, large numbers of German infantrymen and six tanks advanced across the open ground, heading straight for the Americans. The lieutenant ordered his men to withdraw to the relative safety of the woods while he remained behind to direct artillery fire. The Germans were not dissuaded, however, and pressed their advance. Despairing of any more help from his artillery, the lieutenant crossed ground swept by enemy fire, leaped aboard the burning tank destroyer, and turned its .50-caliber machine gun against the advancing troops. As he worked this fearsome weapon, those of his comrades who could see him from the woods were sure that the commander would soon be blown to bits by exploding ammunition in the tank destroyer. By this time, six enemy tanks were actually abreast of the lieutenant. He was now enclosed on three sides by the enemy.

For almost an hour, an estimated two hundred fifty German infantrymen—two reinforced rifle companies—devoted themselves to killing this lieutenant, the only American then in their sights. As many as fifty of the enemy, perhaps more, paid for that devotion with their lives that afternoon. Finally, the enemy broke off the attack. Unscathed, the lieutenant left the still-burning tank destroyer and returned to his men, some of whom had seen this suicidal act of bravery.[6]

Four months later, in Salzburg, Austria, First Lieutenant Audie Leon Murphy of Hunt County, Texas, stood nervously as Lieutenant General Alexander Patch draped the Congressional Medal of Honor, the nation's highest award for valor in action, around his neck. On that day, Audie Murphy very likely became the most highly decorated American soldier not only in World War II but in all of American military history. The Medal of Honor was Murphy's twenty-eighth decoration.[7] He held every award for valor in battle the army had to offer, and several he had won twice. He was alive, more or less in one piece, and he was not yet old enough to vote.

The Medal of Honor is not an imposing piece of art. Held in the hand, it is rather unprepossessing. The object suspends from a pale blue ribbon, bedecked with white stars. The medal itself is silver, electroplated in gold, shaped like a five-pointed star. A relief of the head of Minerva, the Greek goddess of wisdom and defensive war, is enclosed within the star. As with its British counterpart, the Victoria Cross, it is a relatively recent invention. Any sort of regular official recognition of military heroism dates only from the nineteenth century.[8]

Extraordinary valor in mortal combat, of course, has been celebrated in verse and rhetoric since Achilles slew Hector. But the rise of the soldierly hero as a public institution originated in those days when individual action in battle acquired a greater significance than in times past when soldiers worked in unison as massive groups. Throughout the nineteenth century, battlefields were still full of clearly visible groups of men, maneuvering against one another in line and column. But the advent of rifled weaponry had two main effects: it dispersed these large bodies of soldiers into smaller and more furtive groups, and it forced commanders to rely more and more upon the discipline, aggressiveness, initiative, resourcefulness, and courage of the single soldier. As the commander's control over combat events dissipated, tactical decisions that had been the exclusive province of the military aristocracy were grudgingly passed to the ordinary soldier. These new military sensibilities coincided with, and perhaps were encouraged

Audie Murphy. Courtesy Confederate Research Center, Hillsboro, Texas.

by, a corresponding change in sentiment that emphasized the value of the individual human being.[9]

For all that, commanders who have led men into battle are not at all certain that heroes are militarily useful. Customarily, heroes are employed for inspirational purposes in military organizations. But if officers are given a choice between commanding a battalion full of heroes and one of ordinary soldiers, they will choose the latter.[10] Today, no less than in the past, successful military action depends upon the commander's success in imposing his order upon the chaos of battle—of turning his tactical ambitions into reality. That depends in the first instance upon discipline and regularity of behavior, and neither quality is widely found among heroes.

As to whether the prospect of a medal will propel a soldier headlong into combat, veterans would agree that this soup is so thin it will not begin to sustain a man faced with the prospect of his own death or dismemberment. Deeper motivations are required for that. The great puzzle is that most soldiers possess those motivations and have retained them over centuries of hard campaigning. The famous Private Henry Hook, who won the Victoria Cross at the Battle of Rorke's Drift against the Zulus, recalled, "It was curious, but until [the award] I had scarcely ever thought about the Victoria Cross; in fact we did not know or trouble much about it, although we had a VC man in the regiment."[11]

Inevitably, the medal winner is a dubious as well as an inspirational figure among ordinary soldiers. "The men know who deserve the medals and who don't," observed S. L. A. Marshall. Writing in *Collier's* magazine during the Korean War, Marshall cited several instances in which soldiers had performed acts well above and beyond the call of duty. In one case, a sergeant single-handedly fought off a battalion of German infantry and tanks at Normandy, a feat for which he was awarded "only" the Bronze Star. Marshall remembered one commander from the North African campaign who stopped recommending his men for decorations altogether, because invariably those least deserving received the medals while the true heroes went unrewarded. It hurt his unit's morale. After the sergeant's stand at Normandy, one of his comrades asked Marshall, "What do you have to do to get a Medal of Honor—capture Hitler?" Marshall claimed that during the Second World War, it was an unwritten rule that combat medics—the one class of soldier whose life expectancy was actually *less* than that of the combat rifleman—would receive no award higher than the Silver Star.[12]

Thus, despite an official injunction that "no act or deed of especially meritorious conduct should take place in any units without the immediate initiation of a letter recommending that proper award be made," the awarding of medals was too erratic to be just.[13] There could be little assurance among the men that the ribbons over a man's pocket told the real tale. Most servicemen were a little bashful about wearing them at all.

Among those who were not his immediate comrades and who did know the truth of the matter, perhaps it was inevitable that soldiers who fought the sort of valorous war Murphy did were somehow suspect.[14] An officer who served with Murphy's division during the war averred that "he [Murphy] was not the most admired guy in the world." There are good and practical reasons for combat soldiers to be wary of the consistent hero in their midst. Even though his act must be a public one, quite often the hero plays a solitary role that depends chiefly upon his individual passions, his skills, and his luck. It is his aloneness that singles out the hero. Yet heroes may get killed, and the people with them may die as well. Worse still, it has often happened that heroes survive while others do not. The bullet or shell may just not have the hero's name on it that day. One can easily sympathize with the ordinary soldier, whose first ambition is to survive the day, the next day, and perhaps even the war.[15]

Yet the bond among the men in the smallest fighting units was extremely strong. The great wartime cartoonist Bill Mauldin, an extremely perceptive observer of men in combat, believed that "you will seldom find a misfit who has been in an outfit more than a few months." And as for those occasions when one of their number is a candidate for an award, Mauldin added, "his friends are so willing to be witnesses that sometimes they have to be cross-examined to make sure they are not crediting him with three knocked-out machine guns instead of one."[16]

After his action in the *Bois de Riedwihr*, Murphy was pulled out of the line. Witnesses provided affidavits, and within a month the division had begun processing the award claim. By taking Murphy away from his unit—infantrymen were in very short supply in those days—the division signaled that the Medal of Honor was a foregone conclusion. The prospect of no other medal was sufficient to warrant relief from the line. He was, after all, a rare commodity: a living and relatively undamaged Medal of Honor candidate. The authorities, therefore, very likely did not want to risk any possibility of Murphy's death or injury. Captain Maurice Britt, also of the 3rd, had been recommended for the medal, but he had remained in the line—only to lose an arm in a later battle. Murphy was promoted to first lieutenant and given a leave to Paris; upon his return, he was assigned as a liaison officer with his regiment.[17] This assignment greatly improved Murphy's chances of surviving the war. There is no evidence that he complained.

In his letters home to family and friends about this time, Murphy frequently mentioned his medals, particularly the Purple Hearts. But he regarded them rather like war souvenirs: booty to be sent home, not badges of soldierly acclaim. He seemed to have understood that winning a Medal of Honor would get him out of the line: that was the basis of his enthusiasm when he learned he might get it. On April 11, 1945, he wrote to friends that he had been given the Distinguished Service Cross, a Silver Star, and a Bronze Star. He then was waiting at regimental headquarters for the Medal of Honor to be awarded "so I can come home." That, along with the Legion of Merit he was about to get, meant that "since that is all the Medals they have to offer I'll have to take it easy for a while."[18]

Eight days after receiving the medal, Murphy flew home to Texas. Only three days after leaving Salzburg, Murphy stepped off a plane at San Antonio with other Texas military notables; began a round of parades, toasts, speeches, and interviews; and slowly worked his way north to Hunt County. To the crowds that gathered around him that summer, Murphy was no doubt befuddling and endearing. He was anything but the iron-eyed, athletic, and self-contained warrior Americans seem to expect of their military heroes. He was still extremely slight, not very tall, and he did not swagger. He was polite, self-effacing, and clearly uncomfortable with all the attention. He spoke quietly. But for the tan officer's uniform, bristling with ribbons, he could have been the kid next door. The actor James Cagney, who was soon to help Murphy get his start in motion pictures, said that what appealed to him about Murphy was the young man's "assurance and poise without aggressiveness."[19]

He certainly did not appear to be a young man who had fought his way through the worst kind of infantry combat for nearly two years, from the hills of Sicily to the German frontier. Perhaps the crowds sensed the incongruity. In the story that accompanied Murphy's cover photo in *Life* magazine on July 16, there is a picture of Murphy getting a haircut at Mrs. Greer's barbershop in Farmersville. Outside the big plate-glass window stands a crowd of more than a dozen men, simply staring at him. There is an air of expectancy within the crowd, as if Murphy might suddenly bolt from the chair and do something herolike. His head is bowed and the barber's bib nearly covers his feet. He looks very young and mortally tired.[20]

What Murphy was on the verge of discovering was that the hero's deed is only the down payment of the price he must pay for his acclaim. Frequently the medal becomes a curse for the man who wears it. One hundred and eleven men won the Victoria Cross during Britain's campaigns in the nineteenth century. Seven of these took their own lives, a horrendous rate for a time when there were only eight suicides per one hundred thousand in the general population. Still more led utterly disastrous postwar lives, finding that they were unequal to the more pacific rhythms of life beyond the battlefield. We know of the sad fate of Ira Hayes, the Marine hero who helped raise the flag on Iwo Jima's Mount Suribachi, but no complete study of the postwar fates of Medal of Honor winners has ever been done. Of course, as studies of Vietnam veterans have made clear, one need not be a duly certified military hero to suffer problems after a war. The hero may carry a heavier burden still, however. As Captain Ian Fraser of the Royal Navy—a winner of the Victoria Cross in the Second World War—put it, "A man is trained for the task that might win him the VC. He is not trained to cope with what follows."[21]

Four hundred and thirty-three Congressional Medals of Honor were awarded during the Second World War. Of these, soldiers won two hundred ninety-three. But of all the fighting organizations in that war, Murphy's own 3rd Infantry Division was the most remarkable. Thirty-four men in that division won Medals of Honor—a startling 11.6 percent of all those medals won in the army—during campaigns from North Africa to Germany. In Murphy's regiment alone, fourteen soldiers won it.[22] By the time of Murphy's stand in the *Bois de Riedwihr*, he had already witnessed one of his sergeants win it. Later, on a notable day during bitter fighting in Nürnberg, three men from Murphy's regiment won the Medal of Honor.[23] In the other two regiments of the division, the 30th and the 7th, the incidence of medals was also unusually high.[24] These, in addition to its lesser awards, made the 3rd Infantry Division the most highly decorated American division in World War II.

The 3rd Infantry Division's record of awards naturally poses questions. Compared to other divisions, was the 3rd somehow different—better as a fighting organization? Were these awards somehow indicative of a more difficult, longer war? Were the division's leaders especially sensitive to the benefits of these awards to soldierly morale? And did Murphy's membership in this particular division encourage him to repeatedly perform brave deeds?

Unquestionably, the 3rd Infantry Division was a fine fighting group. It was a "heavy" infantry division as it entered the war during the North Africa campaign, carrying more than fifteen thousand soldiers on its rolls. During the war, this division participated in four amphibious landings (Casablanca, Sicily, Anzio, and southern France), fought ten separate campaigns, and was in battle more than five hundred days with very few opportunities to rest and refit. By the testimony of one of its early wartime commanders, Lucian K. Truscott, Jr., "few divisions have ever entered action in a higher state of combat efficiency." Truscott, a plain-spoken cavalryman not given to hyperbole, was one of the very best division commanders in that war. But the appraisal of one's enemies always carries a good deal more weight. After Albert Kesselring, field marshal and German theater commander in Italy, was captured, he was asked to assess the quality of the units his armies had fought. Kesselring replied that the 3rd "was the best division we faced and never gave us a rest."[25]

And then there are the numbers. Recently, an officer who served with the division early in the war was asked about its official view of awards. He agreed that the 3rd had had more than its share; then added, "Have you looked at the casualty figures?" The division's membership turned over five times during the course of its campaigns: battle and "nonbattle" casualties amounted to a staggering 74,044 soldiers by the division's own count. And of these losses, General Truscott reported during the fighting in Italy, 86 percent were in the infantry battalions. After the first thirty days of fighting, the infantry companies were at half strength, "although," recalled Truscott, "it had not seemed from day to day that losses were excessive."[26]

Truscott was a gifted commander. He did not wantonly spend the lives of his soldiers, but neither did he husband his units when the time came to give battle. He was aggressive, and he trained his division with an eye toward Stonewall Jackson's famous Foot Cavalry of the Civil War. At Anzio, Truscott was promoted and given command of the VI Corps; he was succeeded by John W. O'Daniel, also a fine commander. The soldiers admired both men, though neither was particularly soft with his troops. Both men understood well what happened in the battle lines and commanded their division accordingly.

If these division commanders were solicitous of their men and proud of what they accomplished, they could hardly be blamed. Early in the North African campaign, Truscott was among those who argued for the creation of some special insignia for the combat infantryman. "The prestige of the infantryman must be enhanced in proportion to the hazard, exposure, and hardship required of him."[27] A veteran writing years after the war put it differently: "For the infantryman it was a grim, colorless, almost hopeless existence . . . that the airman got extra pay for 'hazardous duty,' while the infantryman, whose casualties were infinitely greater, got none, was particularly galling."[28] Eventually, the "poor bloody infantry" got its recognition with the Combat Infantry Badge (CIB): a badge of blue with a rifle on it, surrounded by a silver wreath. The CIB signified membership in a very exclusive club, and to this day the man who wears one is accorded a certain deference among soldiers.

Military heroism cannot be understood without some appreciation of what a "normal" combat rifleman experiences in war. Cartoonist Bill Mauldin spent the war using his art to convey to the public the "doggies'" life. In a memorable passage from *Up Front* Mauldin tries to explain:

Dig a hole in your back yard while it is raining. Sit in the hole until the water climbs up around your ankles. Pour cold mud down your shirt collar. Sit there for forty-eight hours, and, so there is no danger of your dozing off, imagine that a guy is sneaking around waiting for a chance to club you on the head or set your house on fire.

Get out of the hole, fill a suitcase full of rocks, pick it up, put a shotgun in your other hand, and walk on the muddiest road you can find. Fall flat on your face every few minutes as you imagine big meteors streaking down to sock you.

After ten or twelve miles (remember—you are still carrying your shotgun and suitcase) start sneaking through the wet brush. Imagine that somebody has booby-trapped your route with rattlesnakes which will bite you if you step on them. Give some friend a rifle and have him blast in your direction once in a while. . . . If you repeat this performance every three days for several months you may begin to understand why an infantryman sometimes gets out of breath. But you still won't understand how he feels when things get tough.[29]

Mauldin's belief that combat must be experienced to be understood is widely shared among veterans and military writers alike. "Do you know what it's like?" challenged Captain Athol Stewart of the British army. "Of course you don't."[30] John Steinbeck, working as a war correspondent in Italy during some of Murphy's campaigns, believed that combat was beyond the powers of memory. "When you wake up and think back to the things that happened," Steinbeck wrote, "they are already becoming dreamlike. Then it is not unusual that you are frightened or ill. You try to remember what it was like, and you can't quite manage it. The outlines in your memory are vague. The next day the memory slips farther, until very little is left at all. . . . Men in prolonged battle are not normal men. And when afterwards they seem to be reticent, perhaps they don't remember very well."[31]

Lewis Millett, a captain with an infantry company during the Korean War, led one of the last bayonet charges in American military history and won a Medal of Honor for it. He recalls deploying his riflemen in a line, much as Pickett's men were deployed before their fatal charge at Gettysburg, but very few of the details. He felt as though he were in a trance, "floating" across the battlefield.[32]

Except for these "emergencies" of combat, occurring with frightening suddenness and sometimes overwhelming frequency, the rhythms of battle had a fatal sameness to them. Paul Fussell, author of the acclaimed

The Great War and Modern Memory, also served in an infantry company in the 45th Division in the spring of 1945. He remembers that after his baptism of fire, "one day was much like another: attack at dawn, run and fall and sweat and worry and shoot and be shot at and cover from mortar shells, always keeping up a jaunty carriage in front of one's platoon."[33]

Although the combat rifleman stands at the farthest and most dangerous end of grand military enterprise, elegant strategies and refined tactics mean little to him. The commonest infantryman is daily required to perform acts that no human being would attempt in civilian life. While experience in ordinary life is critical, it seems not to matter much in combat. The violence of battle is whimsically random at times. Murphy and his radiotelephone operator were once at the point of a small column, moving through some woods. An enemy sniper chose to kill the radio operator first, even though Murphy was at his side and clearly in command. The sniper had made a clever tactical decision, but it did him no good in the end: he showed himself, and Murphy killed him.[34]

If the combat infantryman has time, he may learn the finer points of fire and maneuver, he may learn the different tunes artillery shells make during their trajectories, and he may learn how to avoid mines. But there will come a point when he must stand up and move forward against the enemy and register his resistance with fire of his own. There will come a point, as in Murphy's own case, when, as he stands in a place removed from the line, an artillery round does not follow the rules of sound he has learned. There may come a time when, knowing a mine field is in front, he must run across it for the promise of greater safety. All this is why one captain returning from the fighting in North Africa wrote in an official report in 1943, "To one who has been 'up there' it is obvious that there is no such thing as 'getting used to it.'"[35] And it is why veterans of combat shake their heads knowingly when they see how James Jones remembered his war service with the 25th Infantry in the Pacific: "I went where I was told to go, and did what I was told to do, but no more. I was scared shitless just about all the time."[36]

For Murphy and his comrades in Company B, the authors of all these miseries were, of course, the Germans. Much has been made of the supposed inferiority of the American fighting man in comparison to his German counterpart. From the time Murphy entered the line in Sicily until his last day in combat, however, the German army was on the strategic defensive. It was largely on the tactical defensive as well.[37] In the terrain Murphy had to cross, the advantage naturally rested with the defense—and at this, the German troops were very, very good. Mauldin stayed alongside the

American fighting units throughout much of the Italian campaigns. "The doggies," Mauldin wrote, "have a deep respect for the German's ability to wage war. You may hear a doggie call a German a skunk, but he'll never say he's not good."[38] After fighting around Mount Fratello, Murphy wrote later, "I acquired a healthy respect for the Germans as fighters; an insight into the furies of mass combat." But, he added, "the Sicilian campaign has taken the vinegar out of my spirit."[39]

The Italian campaign was the worst yet for the 3rd Division. Casualties between the Allied landings at Salerno and Anzio amounted to more than the authorized strength of the division; as usual, the line units suffered the most.[40] Because of the atrocious weather and the limitations it imposed on moving vehicles through monotonously hilly terrain, troops were often stranded in the lines for several days without food or water. Mules were pressed into service to carry needed supplies when enemy fire subsided. The enemy gave ground grudgingly. Murphy participated in several attacks during this period, which succeeded less because of the power of assault than because of shrewd maneuvering. Often the enemy seemed impervious to anything the Americans tried. "If the suffering of men could do the job, the German line would be split wide open. But not one real dent do we make," Murphy wrote later of the fighting around Monte Lungo.[41]

When the enemy did give ground and the Americans occupied it, the Germans routinely shelled their old positions. The official history of the division recounted what came to be the all too familiar rhythms of combat in Italy: "deliberate withdrawal, covered by mining and demolition. He [the enemy] had consistently infiltrated our forward positions with night combat patrols; he came back to reoccupy positions which our patrols previously penetrated; he ambushed our supply trains and booby-trapped trails and bivouac areas; he employed armor frequently but sparingly, using tanks in twos and threes to work with groups of infantry; he sited self-propelled guns in defiled positions and towns where they were difficult to find. And he took full advantage of the rugged terrain, the greatest asset of defensive warfare."[42]

Murphy survived the Italian campaigns as a staff sergeant with two Bronze Stars for valor in command of a platoon, a position normally held by a second lieutenant. He had not been wounded, although he had been one of his division's twelve thousand nonbattle casualties. Meanwhile, he had come to the attention of his commanders as a canny soldier who possessed extraordinary combat sense. Insofar as a soldier could be "battle wise," Murphy was.[43]

On the morning of August 15, 1944, Allied troops invaded southern France, coming ashore south of Saint Tropez. Military historians would later dilate upon how relatively light the German defenses were compared to those at Normandy and how easily the VI Army Group moved northward along the Rhone against a rapidly disintegrating German army. But invasion day was a very bad one for Murphy: near the town of Amantuelle, Murphy's best friend was killed when enemy troops played a false surrender. After his friend died in his arms, Murphy launched a frenzied, single-handed attack, eventually killing or wounding thirteen German soldiers. "I remember the experience as I do a nightmare," Murphy wrote later. "The men . . . tell me that I shout pleas and curses at them, because they do not come up and join me." As a consequence of his spree at Ramantuelle, Murphy was given the Distinguished Service Cross, an award second only to the Medal of Honor itself.[44]

The army's advance along the Rhone cheered everyone by its speed—and then they were greeted by the Vosges Mountains. All of a sudden, it seemed like Italy again. Enemy resistance grew stronger and the weather more miserable. By now, nearly all of the original members of Company B, once 257 strong, were gone. Murphy began to withdraw, wrapping himself in a kind of fatalistic alienation. The comradeship that had sustained him had disappeared, and though surrounded by his fellow riflemen, he was essentially alone. Recalling this bleak time, Murphy wrote in *To Hell and Back:* "So many men have come and gone that I can no longer keep track of them. Since Kerrigan got his, I have isolated myself as much as possible, desiring only to do my work and be left alone. I feel burnt out, emotionally and physically exhausted. Let the hill be strewn with corpses as long as I do not have to turn over the bodies and find the familiar face of a friend. It is with the living that I must concern myself, juggling them as numbers to fit the mathematics of battle."[45]

After the fact of his survival, it was most remarkable that Murphy had not long ago succumbed to combat fatigue. At least one study of combat stress written after this war argued flatly that "practically all infantry soldiers suffer from a neurotic reaction if they are subjected to the stress of modern combat continuously and long enough." Originally, the authors of the study believed there might be a small percentage of men who were impervious to battle stress, but they later changed their views. After about the thirtieth day in combat, the soldier "began to lose the finer points of discrimination in which he had prided himself."[46]

Nor did respite from battle, such as Murphy had taken while training for the landing in southern France, help much in warding off combat fatigue. Often it only made things worse. Paul Fussell recalled that after he returned from the hospital to the line, the convalescence "helped me survive for four weeks more but it broke the rhythm and, never badly scared before . . . I found for the first time that I was terrified, unwilling to take the chances that before had seemed rather sporting."[47]

By October, 1944, both of the opposing armies were wearing down. *Generalmajor* Wolf Ewert, commander of the 338th Infantry Division, reported losses as high as 60 percent in the battles for Alsace. The casualties among the officers and noncommissioned officers were also very high.[48] On the American side infantrymen were at a premium, and as the winter approached, the shortages became severe. Murphy had earlier refused a battlefield commission because it would separate him from his men: newly commissioned officers were routinely transferred to another unit. But he accepted his commission on October 15 with the understanding that he could stay with Company B. The regimental commander, Colonel Hallett D. Edson, pinned on the gold bars and told Murphy to get a shave, take a bath, "and get the hell back to the front lines."[49]

Twelve days later, Murphy was seriously wounded by a sniper. Getting to the field hospital took too long; Murphy's wound became infected and gangrenous. He was hospitalized for the rest of the year.[50] When finally he returned to Company B, it was preparing to penetrate the Colmar Pocket in the direction of Holtwihr. But the *Bois de Riedwihr* lay across the line of march, and within the wood Murphy's fame awaited.

During the Second World War, battles of encirclement and annihilation were known to the Germans as *der Kessel*, or "the cauldron." The term evokes the stuff of close combat in confined spaces: the abiding and numbing fear of the next step that grinds down the swift movement of armies. To a degree perhaps not appreciated by modern military historians, the Second World War was one of places and lines. The rapier's thrust typified by Patton's "dash across France" was an exception in the war, not the rule.[51] Eventually, men who did Murphy's kind of work had to take the ground away from their counterparts on the other side of the main line of resistance. For the better part of two years, Audie Murphy lived inside the *Kessel*. He went to some lengths to get there, believing, as many do, that within war were mysteries of self to be discovered and intimations of worlds beyond the life of a Texas sharecropper.

In *The Red Badge of Courage*, Stephen Crane's classic story of the soldier's rite of passage, main character Henry Fleming is overtaken by a desire to see war. He frets that the war might be too modern to permit the attainment of glory. He wonders if "he might be a man heretofore doomed to peace and obscurity, but, in reality, made to shine in war." Remarkably—and all the more remarkable because Murphy later played Henry Fleming in the movie version of Crane's book—Murphy seems to have been "made to shine in war."[52]

No one tried harder than Murphy to see, as Henry Fleming did, "the great Red God of War." Whether Murphy had a predisposition for war is problematical, but there is little doubt that Murphy saw the war, as innocents often do, as a way of rising above the grinding poverty that had so dominated his young life. He was drawn to the elite units: the Marines were first on his list. Rejected twice, he tried to enlist for duty with the new airborne units, but standing only 5'6" and weighing just 112 pounds, he weighed less than the battle gear paratroopers were often obliged to carry.[53] Finally, he was made to settle for the infantry. "The infantry was too commonplace for my ambitions," he wrote unhappily late in his autobiography. Caught up in the great mobilization, Murphy was shifted from one place to another; at each place, well-meaning superiors tried to protect him from a combat assignment. "Fuming," he recalled, "I stuck to my guns." He was still just a child, really, when "finally the great news came. We were to go into action."[54]

So adept did Audie Murphy prove to be in infantry combat that one wonders whether he possessed some special predisposition for battle. He was a rural boy, of course, accustomed to hunting in the hills and dales of North Texas. The countryside and its forms held no mysteries for him. Despite his small size, he had the stamina born of years of hard farm work, but it cannot be said that he was any better prepared for the rigors of combat than anyone else. After a few weeks on the battle lines, infantrymen are usually in terrible physical shape, anyway.[55] Long before he was wounded, Murphy spent several days in the hospitals suffering from respiratory ailments. He had plenty of company.

Murphy appears to have believed—and his home state was quick to claim—that having been born and reared in Texas somehow affected his military success.[56] But pride in origins should not be mistaken as predestination. That Murphy was from Texas was rather incidental to what he did in the war. Most Americans who fought in the war and fought well were not from Texas, and many had been no closer to the countryside than the city park before they enlisted. How they performed in combat had more to do with what German military historian Hans Delbruck would have called "the material possibilities of the moment." Despite a great deal of official interest by the American army since World War II, a psycho-physical profile of "the natural fighter" has yet to be determined.[57]

Whether Murphy had a predisposition for valor is another question entirely, of course. During his war, Murphy developed certain habits that automatically brought him the approving notice of his superiors. Before the war he had been pugnacious, and this temperament stood him in good stead during his campaigns. And although he was as comfortable with his comrades as any combat soldier might be, he was given to independent action. He often volunteered for patrols to gather information or to take prisoners. Enemy snipers were in danger when Murphy was about: he would frequently take it upon himself to "go hunting." As he gradually acquired command responsibilities, he frequently would see his men safely placed and go forward alone or with a couple of others to reconnoiter the ground ahead. For Murphy, then, the sequence of events during the *Bois de Riedwihr* campaign, which won him a Medal of Honor, was not unusual. He ordered his men to withdraw, but he remained behind to face the enemy alone, hoping to prepare the way for his company's eventual advance. Even the most ordinary combat rifleman took terrifying risks day after day, but Murphy's practices were not at all typical.

Nor was Murphy's endurance in the face of stresses notorious for overcoming men who, superficially, were both physically and mentally stronger. One officer of the 1st Scots Guards who fought in Tunisia recalled seeing "strong, courageous men reduced to whimpering wrecks, crying like children." Murphy seems never to have had such a breakdown, although he had more than his share of reasons to do so.[58]

All of which is not to say that Murphy escaped suffering, either during the war or after it. After the sniper's bullet in Alsace proved he was not, after all, invulnerable, he adopted the fatalistic air of soldiers long at war. From his hospital bed, he wrote home: "These Krauts are getting to be better shots than they used to be or else my lucks [*sic*] playing out on me. I guess some day they will tag me for keeps."[59]

After he was recommended for the Medal of Honor and relegated to a regimental assignment, Murphy's luck was not tested quite so often. But there was plenty of war left, and on several occasions Murphy lapsed again into combat situations. And then, finally, the nation's war ended. But Murphy's war may not have.

In ages past, once the colors were furled, soldiers gratefully went home. The signing of the peace was a signal for nation and individual alike that the war could be left behind and normal life resumed. Modern war has changed this comfortable illusion. During the First World War, frequent concussions from exploding artillery shells were believed responsible for a condition known as "shell shock," a lassitude of spirit well documented by war memoirists Robert Graves, Siegfried Sassoon, and Edmund Blunden, among others. By the end of the war, shell shock had become "war neurosis," a diagnosis based more on the prewar personality of the soldier than on what happened to him during combat.

There were vast differences between World War II and the Vietnam War. Researchers, however, claim that a certain commonality exists between victims of shell shock, war neurosis, neuropsychiatric casualties, and post-traumatic stress disorders. Students of the Vietnam veterans' experience, for example, have noted that Vietnam vets did not have the advantage of returning home in troop ships, as did soldiers after World War II. The flight from Saigon to San Francisco took only about eighteen hours, after which they were discharged and left to their own devices. This more nearly matches Murphy's experience. Other World War II veterans were sometimes allowed several weeks as the ships made their way home, but after that, as Murphy told an interviewer in 1960, "they took army dogs and rehabilitated them for civilian life. But they turned soldiers into civilians immediately and let 'em sink or swim."[60] Too, Murphy experienced postwar stresses that Vietnam vets did not have to contend with. Few, if any, became public institutions. As his fame grew, a Dallas newspaper sought to tell the public "what Murphy is like—a swell kid, absolutely modest, sincere and genuine and unaltered by terrible experiences."[61] Well, not quite.

He could not relax, had an upset stomach and nightmares, and he was very sensitive to noises. Murphy began keeping the lights on while he slept, or attempted to sleep. Twenty-two years later the lights were still on, and a loaded pistol lay by his bed. Sometimes he carried the pistol.[62]

While other veterans were able to contend with their demons in private, every decision Murphy made after the war was played out in public. His skills did not easily translate into civilian life, and he was clearly unsure about what to do next. Fortunately, before too long he was "collected" by Hollywood, much as sports heroes are today. His cover photo in *Life* had inspired James Cagney to invite him west. Originally intending to put Murphy up in a hotel, the young man's fatigued appearance prompted Cagney to offer him the use of his pool house instead. He stayed with Cagney briefly, went home for a visit, and then returned to spend nearly a year at the actor's home.[63]

Murphy's career in motion pictures was modest. No histories of great films mention any of his work, perhaps wrongly, for he was perfectly cast in the film versions of *The Red Badge of Courage* and Graham Greene's *The Quiet American*. Murphy himself took a dim view of his acting abilities, and he did not seem to think of his movie career as more than a way to make a decent living. "I didn't want to be an actor. It was simply the best offer that came along," he recalled long after the war.[64]

The two years Audie Murphy spent in the cauldron of war dominated his life and—to an extent that could only be known by Murphy himself—determined its progress. Kept in the public eye by his wartime deeds, his heroism overshadowed everything he did. His identity as a hero was too vivid to permit any intrusion by postwar accomplishments, although by most standards he made a greater success of himself than his prewar history would have suggested. Without that vital identity as a military hero, Murphy might well have returned to a private life in Hunt County, never to venture near the public eye. And, perhaps, it was his fame that kept the war too much alive for him long after peace was declared. Asked once how people get over a war, Murphy replied reflectively, "I don't think they ever do."[65]

Audie Murphy has been called "the quintessential war hero of our time."[66] Yet there was always a difference between what the public thought and Audie Murphy knew. Remarkable for his own extraordinary prowess in war, he would have said that every man in combat deserves to wear the Medal of Honor.

10

THE TEXAS MILITARY EXPERIENCE IN FILMS

Don Graham

MOTION PICTURES, IN COMPLEX WAYS, REFLECT WHAT IS happening "out there" in the culture. The military experience of Texas and Texans has been portrayed in films in mostly favorable or even glowing ways, considering the state's checkered past. But more specifics about history are necessary before moving to the treatment of this topic in Texas films.

If one uses the number of battles that Texans have actually won as the means of measuring the state's military history—and it is possible to have a tradition, very vividly so, without the victories (witness Argentina)—then Texas has a very poor record indeed. In the Texas Revolution Texans lost two of the three major battles. They lost at the Alamo, although popular culture has converted that defeat into a kind of victory—so much so that Mexicans sometimes have to remind themselves that, after all, they won that one. Goliad was an even greater disaster than the Alamo. Fannin's command was a monument to inept leadership: all he succeeded in doing was turning his army of lambs over to that very able shearer, Santa Anna.

But Texans did win the one that counted the most—at San Jacinto—and won it in a characteristic, nonmilitary way, by backing into it. The Runaway Scrape can be viewed as the master plan of that wily old fox Sam Houston, or it can be seen as a piece of erratically developing good luck that succeeded largely because Houston caught Santa Anna napping. Santa Anna's view is instructive. He regarded the Texas army with scorn: "They fled disconcerted to hide behind the Trinity and the Sabine."[1] He also considered the Texan victory the work of "fate and fate alone."[2] Santa Anna's chief purpose, of course, was to justify his failure, but history has paid little attention to the Mexican side of the Texas Revolution. History is written mainly by the winners, and Anglo-Americans have managed to make themselves look good ever since.

The next round of military ventures in Texas that were not deserving of state pride concerns the Indian wars and the various episodes, fiascos all, directed against Mexico and New Mexico in the 1840s. Mirabeau B. Lamar, noted Indian fighter, ordered a campaign against the peaceful and loyal Cherokees of East Texas. In 1839, at the battle of the Neches, Chief Bowles was consequently killed and his tribe routed. It was nothing to be proud of, and Texans have spent very little time memorializing this tragic episode in song, verse, fiction, or film.[3]

Texas's record of achievement in the various "expeditions," as they were called, against Mexico and New Mexico is so poor that one wonders how the state ever achieved its status as a "braggart." First there was the Texan Santa Fe Expedition, launched in 1841 with Lamar's full support and doomed to the humiliation of surrender and capture without ever having fired a shot. This expedition got off to a bad start when the party mistook the Wichita River for Red River and spent a great deal of time headed in the wrong direction. Then there was the Somervell Expedition of 1842, which also ended in abject failure. Many of its participants immediately joined forces in what would turn out to be an even greater disaster—the Mier Expedition. In this infamous episode, Texans were captured by Mexican forces and marched to Mexico where, at Perote prison, a number of them remained until their release in 1844. The infamous black bean episode was perhaps the deepest humiliation that the Texas captives had to bear.[4]

Two other ill-planned and poorly executed expeditions into New Mexico round out this period of martial ineptitude. The Warfield Expedition of 1842–43 was intended as a retaliatory mission to invade New Mexico. The Texans captured one little town, Mora, but were routed when Mexican troops stampeded their horses. The Warfield contingent then joined up with Jacob Snively's expedition, said to have had the support of Sam Houston himself. Styling themselves the Battalion of Invincibles, they proved anything but invincible. In Kansas, where they sought to capture lucrative caravans on the Santa Fe Trail, Texas troopers ran afoul of the U.S. Army, which sent them packing.[5] The history of ill-fated Texan efforts to obtain the ski slopes of New Mexico is almost farcical in its total repudiation of their grand dreams. Many Texans perished, and those that did not had to suffer the humiliation of a forced march to Mexico, imprisonment, privation, and the sheer misery of being held captive by hated enemies.

The Mexican War deserves special attention, because here Texan successes were notable. They were not, however, representative of a military tradition so much as of the characteristic Texan point of view in such matters. This point of view can be described as amateurish, leaning more toward outlawry than formal military action. In Mexico, American objectives were pursued by the regular U.S. Army under Zachary Taylor and by companies of Texas Rangers attached to Taylor's command. The Rangers' mission was to act as scouts for Taylor's army and to provide firepower when necessary. The Rangers fought like demons, everybody testified, but they also behaved in a most unmilitary manner. General Taylor said of them, "I fear they are a lawless set."[6]

The Rangers were uncontrollable. Nothing about them bespoke a military tradition in any conventional sense. They hated the discipline necessary to military command, and they ran roughshod over civilians who got in their way. They were free-lancers bent on killing the enemy, whether man, woman, or child. To the Rangers, the war was a crusade against Mexicans. To the regular army, it was a military task to be performed for the nation's interests as defined by the commander-in-chief and the Congress of the United States. Indeed, the very concept of a formal military tradition is foreign to the Texas spirit. In Texas the martial spirit has been predominantly defined by frontier conditions. There is a preference for amateurish, free-lance operations: from the beginning, with pre-Republic filibusters, through the Revolution, the ventures into New Mexico, the Mexican War, and finally the Civil War.

In the Indian wars following the Civil War, the greatest success was achieved not by Texas free-lancing but by the brilliant military tactics employed by Colonel Ranald S. Mackenzie on the high plains. Pursuing a policy of constant attack and willing to carry the fight into the heart of Comanche encampments, Mackenzie vanquished the Comanches with considerable dispatch. By 1877 the Indian threat on the high plains was largely extinct, thanks to Mackenzie. Rangers such as Rip Ford and Jack Hays had earlier done their part in chasing and killing Indians, but these actions were largely retaliatory instead of being well-planned campaigns. The Texas free-lance military spirit seemed to work best in Mexico or along the border, against unarmed, ill-equipped citizens.

When the nascent motion picture industry turned to Texas for material, as it did very early in the twentieth century, certain subjects seemed especially suitable for the new medium. Texas's unique, colorful history afforded a ready source of plots and characters. The generic Texas cowboy inspired the first Texas film in 1908, called *Texas Tex*. The Texas Revolution was exploited very early, too. By 1917 the Alamo, Davy Crockett, and Sam Houston had each inspired motion pictures of varying merit.

The Alamo was easily the most significant subject. The first Alamo film, *The Immortal Alamo*, was made in San Antonio in 1911. Because neither a copy of it nor any review or plot summary is extant, one can comment only on some of the stills that have survived. They reveal a predictable iconography: Davy Crockett in stylish skins, striking heroic poses; Mexican troopers in matching uniforms; Susannah Dickinson shielding her baby from a Mexican bayonet; and Davy, not so heroically, with a knife in his gut.

The next Alamo film defined the Texas military experience in unmistakable fashion. In 1915, *Martyrs of the Alamo* was released under the supervision of the great D. W. Griffith. It presented the Alamo story as a racist episode in which noble Anglo-Saxons were pitted against inferior Mexicans led by a general qua dictator, characterized as a dope fiend and satyr. The Texans in this film affect the coonskin as their favorite headdress, but the rest of their clothing can only be described as motley. The Mexicans, on the other hand, clearly belong to a complex military organization and dress in standard-issue military uniforms. They march in orderly squadrons; they are adept at mass formations and maneuvers; they have overwhelming numbers and express a trained sense of precision. But of course they are also portrayed as rank cowards whose officers have to spur them on to do battle with the motley Texans by means of drawn swords, imprecations, and the threat of execution.

Here, as in all the Alamo movies, the battle reenacts that iconography cherished by the American soul: Americans are not fond of wars (though they have fought many, many of them); Americans are not like Europeans, enamored of large standing armies; and, above all, Americans are pragmatic warriors. The chief emblem of this in American history is the plucky, smart, and victorious Americans fighting from cover and in small bands against the ranked, priggish, and exposed armies of King George III. The Alamo movies carry forward this idealization of the amateur. The idea of a military tradition is therefore repugnant to both the American and Texan soul—this is what the movies seem to be saying.[7]

In this respect the movies may be fairly accurate, for as a military operation the Alamo stands as a model of improvisation. The commander-in-chief, after all, ordered Travis to abandon the mission and not engage the Mexican army. Travis, for reasons unknown, chose to ignore that order. The rest, as they say, is history—or myth. And it is myth that the movies about the Alamo have been best at capturing. The movies naturally have seized upon the tradition of the line in the dust, just as has the popular imagination. The Alamo movies usually end with some reference to victory at San

Death of Davy Crockett and the fall of the Alamo, a scene from the 1911 silent movie, *The Immortal Alamo*. Crockett lies on the ground as Jim Bowie fights from his sick bed. Courtesy Library of the Daughters of the Republic of Texas at the Alamo.

Jacinto. That victory, like the martyrdom at the Alamo, is typically presented as the success of righteous amateurs over the phalanxes of a corrupt military power. Again, history yields a fair analogue to the depiction on film. After the fall of the Alamo and the Mexican victories at Refugio and Goliad, all of Texas seemed ready to yield to Santa Anna's army. All he had to do was defeat the "so-called general Houston," and Santa Anna could return to Mexico a national hero, a role that was becoming familiar to him.[8] In retrospect, Santa Anna described his army's pursuit of Houston's rabble in striking terms: "Our campaign was a military parade."[9]

The image of such a parade might stand as the emblem of all the Mexican armies in all the Alamo movies. Against this proud display of uniformity, order, discipline, and hierarchal structure stand the isolated, defiant, idiosyncratic, ragtag sons of the frontier. These were the men whom Santa Anna characterized as "invaders . . . who, moved by the desire of conquest, with rights less apparent and plausible than those of Cortés and Pizarro, wished to take possession of that vast territory extending from Béxar to the Sabine belonging to Mexico."[10]

The Texas Revolution might be seen as a triumph over a military tradition as well as the natural expression of the Anglo-American character in warfare. T. R. Fehrenbach characterizes the Anglo-Celts who came to the Texas frontier as "aggressive, competitive, ambitious, and given to prejudice and hate. . . . They possessed the mental and moral equipment to wage a sustained campaign."[11] Certainly the unleashed furies at San Jacinto, with the Texans continuing the killing long after the battle was over, bespoke a deadliness that could match Santa Anna's own concept of the rules of war. This concept was demonstrated by his insistence, at the Alamo and at Goliad, to take no prisoners. Yet on the Anglo-American side, one must recall their treatment in 1835 of General Martín Perfecto de Cós and his men in the first battle of San Antonio, when the Texans captured Cós and simply bade him and his men return to Mexico. From the Anglo-American viewpoint, it was the Mexicans who first failed to play by the rules.

The Alamo movies do a good job of reflecting historical reality as it relates to this broad perspective of the enemy. They do so almost inevitably, so ingrained in American self-concept is this notion of the divine amateur confronting the Europeanized professional. Or in political terms, the equation becomes democracy versus whatever form of statist power happens to apply. In the Texas Revolution, as in the films about the Alamo, Mexican statism takes the form of a dictatorship. Texans liked to establish parallels between their cause and that of every previous struggle for freedom down through the annals of history, from Greece to the American Revolution.

The Alamo films are burdened with other problems, though, which they never seem to overcome. Chiefly, they tend to be tableaus instead of vivid drama: most of the Alamo films have all the emotional power of a Shriner parade. But there is one film that captures the emotions of what the Alamo might have been like and does so precisely in the context of Texan amateurism versus Mexican militarism. This is Sam Peckinpah's great Western, *The Wild Bunch* (1969). The outlaw heroes of Peckinpah's bloody film are hardly men to admire. They are neither patriots nor Texas Rangers; yet they are heroic, fatalistic, and doomed just as were the men in the Alamo. Pike Bishop (played by William Holden) and his gang finally make a stand against the hated Mapache, a stereotypical Mexican movie villain familiar to us from Wallace Beery to the bandit leader of *The Magnificent Seven* (1960). The four remaining members of the Wild Bunch walk into the heart of Mapache's stronghold to take back Angel, the only Mexican member of their gang, and the purest-hearted, the most idealistic. Mapache is drunk as usual and dressed in full military splendor. Beside him are the German military officers who act as advisers to Mapache. Bishop kills Mapache, then shoots the hated and arrogant German officer. The slaughter begins, and eventually, after an orgy of violence, the Wild Bunch are slain by overwhelming numbers of Mexican soldiers. But not before all the generals and officers have themselves been killed. This film, set in revolutionary Mexico in 1913, does more to create a sense of frontier individualism versus militaristic conformity than any other. It partakes of the Alamo spirit although it is not, of course, an Alamo film.

The Texas military experience has indirectly influenced a host of films dealing with Texas's most famous fighting organization: the Texas Rangers. All through the nineteenth century, the Rangers benefitted from an enormous amount of publicity generated by dime novels. By the time the movies came along, therefore, Ranger lore—like the Alamo story—was ripe for exploitation by this newest form of popular entertainment. The essence of the Ranger story was an idealization of the western fighter for law and order: a man with a six-shooter ready to defend schoolmarms and other icons of Anglo-Saxon civilization who were threatened by the forces of darkness. In fact, Rangers fought chiefly Indians and Mexicans, the latter along the border, during a half-century of skirmishing and killing that carried on old enmities dating from the Texas Revolution.

In most of these movies, the Ranger was extrapolated from history and pressed into service as a kind of dandified cowboy hero. He often worked undercover to help a lady take her herd of cattle to Abilene, prevent the rise of a dictatorship in West Texas, or generally help out when things were going badly for the forces of light. In many of these films the Ranger unit has a kind of quasi-military structure. There is usually a benign father figure who plays the Ranger captain, and the hero is cast in the role of a son. Often there is a sidekick who is a bit of a clown, and sometimes, as in Kind Vidor's *The Texas Rangers* (1936), there are three Rangers. In this film all the Rangers are former outlaws; the plot turns upon the conversion of two of them to the side of the law. They are won over by the majesty of the Ranger cause. Still, as a military structure, the Ranger command functioned as a pure free-lance operation.

The most famous of the Ranger stories illustrates this premise perfectly. There is a riot in a town, and the town sends for help from the Rangers. A delegation of citizens goes to the train station to greet the arriving Rangers, only to be surprised when just one Ranger steps off the train. Asked where the rest of the Rangers are, the hero laconically inquires how many riots there are. "One," say the townspeople. "Then all you need is one

Ranger," replies our hero. The story of the Lone Ranger, the most famous Texas Ranger of them all, illustrates the point as well. His detachment was ambushed in a canyon, and all were killed except him. Later, the Lone Ranger takes on a sidekick, Tonto, and thereafter the two of them perform endless feats of derring-do, saving the West from every possible brand of malfeasance. The Lone Ranger expands his field of opportunity outside Texas to include the entire mythic West, which is characteristic of Rangers in the movies. In Zane Grey's famous ground-breaking novel *Riders of the Purple Sage* (1912), set in Mormon country, his hero, Lassiter, is a Texas Ranger. Rangers, like the Central Intelligence Agency, see the world as their proper sphere of activity.

The myth of the Rangers in the movies, then, is primarily a myth of individualism. The typical Ranger is a cowboy who dresses well. He often wears a dandyish sort of uniform, not military in its trappings but not sodbuster plain, either. The Ranger movie, therefore, is little more than a formulaic exercise within the larger formula of the genre itself. Every cowboy star at the B level made a Ranger movie. Some of them, such as Wild Bill Elliot, an underrated 1940s B star, specialized in Ranger roles. Out of hundreds of Texas Ranger movies, not one is truly distinguished. The best are Elliot films such as *Gallant Legion* (1948), but these are simply B+ Westerns at best. One reason for this mediocrity is that the Ranger films made from the Anglo perspective—as they all were—never take a critical look at the legend. Indeed they cannot, because they are too busy recycling it.

The only such film that examines the Ranger legend in any critical way is John Ford's great movie *The Searchers* (1956). Even so, the Ranger presence is merely one of the subtexts in a complexly layered film. In the face of the Comanche threat, a band of Rangers organizes itself and sets out in pursuit of the marauders. Ethan Edwards, the hero played brilliantly by John Wayne, joins the Ranger contingent, only to be absent from his brother's homestead when the Comanches attack. The Indians kill the brother and his wife, whom Wayne loves, and carry off little Debbie and her sister, who is later killed. Ward Bond, a preacher who leads the Rangers, captures the old-time zeal of the militant Ranger very nicely as he embodies both a strong Christian fervor and a stern opposition to the Comanches. But Bond is a reasonable man compared to Ethan Edwards, who is singleminded to the point of fanaticism in his hatred of Comanches. Later in the film we see more of the Rangers and also the U.S. Army. Typically the latter is presented as a group of veterans mixed with greenhorn lieutenants (such as the character played by Patrick Wayne). In the final analysis,

The Searchers is a study in frontier individualism and not of the military tradition in a frontier society.

It was not until 1981 that the Ranger legend was subjected to a thoroughgoing critique in film. *The Ballad of Gregorio Cortéz* (1982), a small, independent production, looks at the Anglo legend from the Chicano perspective. The mirror held up to this revered police agency reveals striking criticism indeed. The result is a stimulating portrayal of the Rangers as a paramilitary unit instead of a romantic dramatization of the solitary Ranger hero. In this film the Rangers act in concert as a police organization with military trappings. They pursue with relentless zeal the Mexican Gregorio Cortéz, who murdered an Anglo sheriff and then fled toward the border attempting to escape. The Rangers in this film are desperate for a major success because the state legislature is threatening to disband them as an outmoded police agency whose time has passed. In this first movie critique of the Ranger attitude toward Mexicans, the aim is to make amends for the misrepresentation of Ranger-Mexican conflicts from the 1840s through at least the 1960s.

Indian warfare in Texas films has been mostly a matter of secondary action: attacks on wagon trains or trail herds bound to market. There are exceptions. John Ford's *The Searchers* (1956) and *Two Rode Together* (1961) are stunning meditations on captivity narratives, as is John Huston's *The Unforgiven* (1960). The latter bears a close relationship with *The Searchers*; both novels were written by Alan LeMay. Of even more interest is Ford's *Rio Grande* (1950). The third in his so-called cavalry trilogy, this film depicts the frustrating mission of a U.S. Army detachment stationed on the Rio Grande. Official American policy forbids Colonel Yorke (played by John Wayne) to pursue hostile Indians across the international boundary of the Rio Grande. This policy cripples the cavalry in its attempts to control the Indian threat. As John Lenihan has argued, the film, released in November, 1950, was a thinly veiled commentary on U.S. military policy in Korea, where U.S. troops were forbidden to pursue North Korean troops into Manchuria.[12] The film reaches a typically individualistic solution when Yorke's commanding officer gives him permission to lead a mission against the Apaches into Mexico. The general says, "I'm sick of diplomatic hide-and-seek." Here, once again, is underlined the free-lance military operation so characteristic of frontier Texas as portrayed in the movies (and in history).

Rio Grande, a Western that is really about its own era, the 1950s, marks a good place to shift the focus to films dealing with the military tradition in modern times. For many years there was no film about Texas that touched upon the First World War. Then Horton Foote's *1918* (1985) appeared, a wonderful film that memorably presents the impact of war propaganda on the men and women of a small Texas town. Scenes of battlefield carnage shown at the local theater stir the romantic longings of boys and men, but their dreams of military glory are presented ironically. This is best seen in the pathetic parades that celebrate the return of local boys once the Armistice is signed.

World War II, on the other hand, has stimulated both B- and A-budget films. The B Western in the forties sometimes commented on the war raging outside the localized territory of western props and Griffith Park sagebrush. *Texas to Bataan* (1942), for example, pitted three Texas cowboys against the Japanese. Set at the time of the Pearl Harbor attack, this fanciful little oater features Filipino spies in America's ranch country, Texas cowboys performing patriotic deeds in the Philippines, and other assorted absurdities. *Gallant Legion* (1948) was more serious and depicted the evil confronting Texas as a fascist-like desire to create a dictatorship in, of all places, West Texas.

But the film from this era that most completely defines and accepts a military tradition is that perennial favorite of the Texas A&M University campus, *We've Never Been Licked* (1942). In this film Japanese spies, posing as students, have infiltrated the Aggie Corps of Cadets. This is only one of the problems that the local patriots must solve. Another is the initiation of a smart-aleck rich kid into the true Aggie spirit, which, in this film, is identical to that found in any crack army regiment. The Japanese spies are caught red-handed, radioing information to the Orient, and the reluctant Aggie becomes a zealous convert. In this film the military tradition, Aggie-style, is the surest way to defeat the worldwide threat faced by the United States. Kyle Field (the football stadium) becomes a metaphor for the American spirit.

We've Never Been Licked is a rare exception to the thematic tradition traced above: that of frontier individualism as opposed to organized, hierarchal militarism. Certainly in later films, those of the 1950s and 1960s, the tradition of individualism is maintained. Two notable but representative examples can be cited. The first is Audie Murphy's *To Hell and Back* (1955), a classic film about combat in World War II. Starring America's most decorated soldier and based on Murphy's 1949 book about his war experiences, *To Hell and Back* sets out to celebrate the "dog-faced soldier." This is the infantryman, who fought the war at the grittiest, most desperate level—in the mud, rain, and agony of day-to-day ground fighting.

Although the film tries to honor the infantry company, always placing

Murphy within a group of friends in the company, what remains memorable are those isolated moments of remarkable individual courage and fighting skill exhibited by Murphy. Two moments stand out; one is highly symbolic. Murphy and his company have maneuvered under heavy fire to reach a farmhouse occupied by German machine gunners. Once inside the house, they check each room, looking for the enemy. Murphy steps into a room, rifle in position. Suddenly he sees the shape of a soldier and whirls to fire, only to realize that it is his own image in a mirror. One of the other soldiers remarks, "That's the first time I ever saw a Texan outdraw himself." Here the Texan as individual frontier gunfighter is invoked in a startling context—the middle of combat in Europe. The other unforgettable moment in the film, drawn meticulously from Murphy's Medal of Honor citation, is that of Murphy atop a blazing tank destroyer, stacking up Germans like cordwood.[13]

This incredible action is the kind of individual heroic feat that places Audie Murphy among the legends of warfare, equal to anything the heroes at the Alamo accomplished. In fact, the Alamo comparison is especially apt considering that Murphy's friends launched a campaign to get him a part in John Wayne's film *The Alamo* (1960). Even here, in the greatest mass war ever fought, the Texas hero is presented as an individual. But this emphasis on Texas may be too parochial, for it is clear that the real issue is the American suspicion of military traditions except as they are defined away from militarism and toward individualism. *Sergeant York* (1941), the Gary Cooper biographical film about an American hero in World War I, exhibits exactly the same characteristic tendency. It is hard to think of a combat film that does not.

The second notable example of individualism in later films may stand as a summation of the thematic opposition argued throughout this chapter. The film is *Dr. Strangelove* (1964). In this savagely funny satire on American militarism, the lone figure representing the old American tradition is Major King Kong. Commander of a B-52 carrying a nuclear payload, Major Kong (played unforgettably by Slim Pickens) is a distinct American—make that Texan—type. He has a heavy Texas drawl and wears a cowboy hat and boots, which lends a touch of frontier style and old-time individualism to his baggy flight suit. Ordered to drop a bomb on Russia, he carries out his orders with great efficiency. Damaged by flak, the bomb carriage jams, and Major Kong straddles the bomb as if it were a bucking bronco. Waving his hat and giving forth a cowboy whoop, he rides the bomb into Russia, thus setting off the Apocalypse.

In this film the real enemies are the generals and Pentagon planners.

It is one of these bureaucrats, played by George C. Scott, who has the classic line in the film regarding possible casualties from a nuclear exchange. Thirty million dead, he estimates. "We'd get our hair mussed." But Scott and the other members of the Joint Chiefs of Staff have made careful plans to secret themselves in underground shelters. They will survive to plan more wars, more wanton destruction.

From the first Alamo movie to *Dr. Strangelove,* the line runs straight and true: military traditions, which too often become militarism, are dangerous and suspect; what is valued most is frontier individualism. In this sense and this sense only can we speak of a military tradition in Texas films.[14]

THE TEXAS MILITARY EXPERIENCE IN LITERATURE

Tom Pilkington

A CRUCIAL FACET OF THE STEREOTYPICAL TEXAN—A figure recognized by nearly all citizens of the United States, indeed by most people of the world—is that he is a fighter. This element of the Texan character has ramifications both good and bad. At his best, the typical Texan is viewed as a man who takes seriously his duty to protect, by violence if necessary, his honor and the safety of his family and country. At his worst, he is seen as a trigger-happy thug who shoots first and asks questions later.

For soldiers—whether they are "good guys" or "bad guys"—most battles eventually escalate from the personal level to the collective level. It is at this point that they must submit themselves to the demands of concerted military action. Texans have never been slow to volunteer for such action. Throughout the history of the United States, its relations with other countries have been governed by a "traditional isolationism and neutrality,"[1] as one commentator put it. This position was compromised in the decades following World War II by the expansionist tendencies of Soviet communism and by America's own ambitions in the world. In the years preceding both world wars, it can be argued that American public opinion was mostly isolationist; in some regions, decidedly so. But not in Texas. It was no accident that Teddy Roosevelt came to San Antonio at the close of the nineteenth century to organize his Rough Riders for service in the Spanish-American War. Most of Roosevelt's volunteers, not surprisingly, were Texans and southwesterners. Of all the states of the Union, vocal support for intervention before each of the world wars was demonstrably strongest in Texas.[2] Moreover, a large percentage of American troops serving in the Vietnam War—many of them Mexican-American, incidentally—were Texans. More second lieutenants from Texas A&M University were casualties in Vietnam than were the graduates of any other university in the nation.

Texans, then, are fighters, and historically much of their fighting has been done within organized military campaigns. But through Texas military history, that fighting has been considerably more individualistic and quirky than most professional military officers would prefer. In this regard, if there is a Texas military tradition, it is only a mirror image of the *American* tradition, in a slightly distorted or exaggerated form. Because the United States emerged from a revolution that consciously violated due process of law, and—even more—because its national expansion was effected by wresting land from Indians and Mexicans and Frenchmen by means not always strictly legal, Americans have never had much respect for institutionalized forms of law and order such as the military. More than one American folk hero, historians tell us, was little more than a shady character whose actions "were legitimized because he fought in what appeared to be a good cause."[3] (If this is true of America's legendary heroes, consider the heroes of Texas. The defenders of the Alamo, for example, were adventurers who were transformed into valiant soldiers in the public mind.) As late as 1960 one of America's greatest generals and a two-term president, Dwight D. Eisenhower, warned his fellow citizens against the dangers of the "military-industrial complex." The recurrent American animosity toward militarism and a professional military establishment thereby comes more sharply into focus.[4]

If Texans, then, as freedom-loving individualists sometimes chafe under and even burst out of the constraints of the military code, they are only asserting their credentials as Americans—or, as John Bainbridge has put it, "super-Americans."[5] Certainly Texans have never adjusted well to the lockstep. It is interesting that a well-known Texas writer, George Sessions Perry, published in 1951 a history of what was then known as Texas A&M College that contains only two brief references to the Reserve Officers Training Corps. Perry talks at length about football and engineering and agriculture, and he spins many yarns about "Aggies I have known," but he scarcely mentions the corps.[6] Any Texas A&M graduate of 1951 or earlier would undoubtedly cite the corps as a major element of university life during those years. Perry saw action in World War II as a magazine and newspaper correspondent, which apparently initiated his downward spiral into alcoholism, mental illness, and ultimately, in 1956, suicide. Probably he witnessed too much of war and killing and, in *The Story of Texas A&M*, simply chose to ignore that institution's role as a military school. Perhaps also Perry was consciously cultivating the mildly rebellious attitude toward military discipline common to Texans.

The Texas military tradition, in whatever manner that phrase is defined, does not appear to be a significant theme in Texas literature. That does not mean, however, that examining a handful of literary works to see how they might illuminate the role of the military in Texas history is not a valid and important exercise. This chapter is intended as a preliminary—and by no means definitive—probe in this direction.

There are several fairly clear-cut events and periods in the history of Texas when the military and its actions have come to the fore: the Texas Revolution of 1836, the Civil War, the Indian wars of the late nineteenth century, and the four wars in this century (World War I, World War II, the Korean War, and the Vietnam War) in which the United States was involved. At least a few literary works have dealt provocatively and sometimes effectively with Texans' participation in these phenomena.

One of the earliest Texas novels, or at least one of the earliest novels set in Texas, was a book entitled *Mexico versus Texas*. Published in Philadelphia in 1838, it treats the Texas Revolution from an unusual perspective. In the first printing of the book, its author was identified only as "a Texian," although later editions suggested that his name was A. T. Myrthe, a Frenchman and a Catholic priest and missionary who had once been assigned to a post in Texas. The novel is dedicated to General Sam Houston. "To whom with more propriety than your Excellency can I inscribe a work whose principal theme consists of the glorious and successful struggles by which your fellow citizens attained their independence? It is, under God, to your valor, prudence and humanity they are indebted for their success, and now you stand before the world as one of those master-spirits by whom mighty changes are wrought in the economy of human affairs."[7]

As might be expected in a work by a priest, there is a good deal of religious conflict and turmoil, specifically between Catholics and Protestants. But the novel's most unusual aspect is that it is told from the vantage point of a young Mexican army officer who has an American mother and a Spanish father. The officer has some sympathy for the Texans' cause, and, perhaps as a result of his ambivalent feelings, he is treated kindly by the Texans when he is captured at San Jacinto. Despite an interesting premise, *Mexico versus Texas* is marred by the florid romanticism that characterizes most minor American novels of its period.

Two other nineteenth-century novels of some note with the Texas Revolution as their background are Augusta J. Evans's *Inez: A Tale of the Alamo* (1855) and Amelia E. Barr's *Remember the Alamo* (1888). Both works, for the most part, treat the turbulent historical events of the time from the perspective of female characters. And both suffer from the aesthetic flaws that weaken popular fiction in any era. Here, for example, is Evans's overwrought description of Fannin at Goliad: "Rumors of the fall of the Alamo, the overwhelming force of Santa Anna, and his own imminent danger, had reached Colonel Fanning [*sic*]. In vain he entreated reinforcements, in vain urged the risk hourly incurred. The Texan councils bade him save himself by flight. 'Retreat, fly from the post committed to my keeping!' The words sounded like a knell on the ear of the noble man to whom they were addressed. He groaned in the anguish of his spirit, 'I will not leave this fortress—Travis fell defending with his latest breath the Alamo! Oh, Crockett! Bowie! Can I do no better than follow thy example, and give my life in this true cause?'"[8] No more need be said about *Inez*.

In the twentieth century there have been surprisingly few attempts by Texas authors to come to grips with the Texas Revolution and its topsy-turvy outcome. In her novel *Star of the Wilderness* (1942), Karle Wilson Baker writes creditable historical fiction that, in its final chapters, provides an honest and generally believable account of the main events of the Revolution. Otherwise pickings are slim, except for a few works of popularized history such as *Thirteen Days to Glory* (1958), Lon Tinkle's narrative of the fall of the Alamo. James A. Michener's *Texas* (1985) contains a long, confused (and confusing) rehash of the three major battles of the Revolution: the Alamo, Goliad, and San Jacinto. Michener's account, however, adds nothing to the reader's understanding of those momentous occurrences.[9]

Overall, literature, like film, portrays the Texas Revolution—particularly the battle of the Alamo—in a melodramatic and superficial manner. In the Alamo literature no sense of an embryonic Texas military tradition emerges. The Texans are usually shown to be patriots, volunteers, and citizen-soldiers who have banded together to resist intolerable Mexican oppression. They must fight Santa Anna's dandified and Europeanized army, which they do more with extreme, even suicidal, acts of bravery than with military strategy and organization. Eventually, of course, motivated valor triumphs over superior force and merely mechanical military planning.

Another historical event that has received little attention in Texas literature is the state's participation in the Civil War. Texas was settled primarily by Southerners and, upon entry into the Union in 1845, was recognized as a slave state. Despite opposition by Sam Houston (himself a slave holder) and some scattered grumbling along the state's northern and western frontiers, Texans in 1861 voted overwhelmingly for secession and alliance with the Confederate States of America. Few battles took place on Texas soil during the Civil War, but thousands of Texans fought elsewhere for the Confederacy, most with honor and some with distinction.

The one certified (though minor) literary classic about Texans during the Civil War is *Lone Star Preacher* (1941) by John W. Thomason, Jr. It is subtitled "Being a Chronicle of the Acts of Praxiteles Swan, M.E. Church South, Sometime Captain, Fifth Texas Regiment, Confederate States Provisional Army." Thomason grew up in Huntsville and became a career military officer who reached the rank of lieutenant colonel in the United States Marine Corps. During his lifetime he was also a well-known writer and protégé of Maxwell Perkins, the famed editor of Scribner's who has been credited with discovering such renowned talents as F. Scott Fitzgerald, Ernest Hemingway, and Thomas Wolfe. Thomason's gifts as an artist and illustrator almost matched those he demonstrated as a writer; reviewers often commented that Thomason's illustrations were among the most interesting aspects of his works. He published several books in addition to fulfilling his military duties. One of these, *Fix Bayonets* (1926), is a collection of stories about the adventures of American military men around the world.[10]

Thomason's best work by far, however, is *Lone Star Preacher*. Its various chapters were originally self-contained stories published in the 1930s in the *Saturday Evening Post* and other popular periodicals. In the book the stories are brought together and strung along a rather loose plot line. Thomason describes his hero, Praxiteles Swan, as a "hot-headed and desirous young man, combatant officer in a most accomplished fighting army, and all his life a soldier of the Cross," who "did in every essential aspect exist, and move, and have his being in the southern regions of these United States, within the memory of living men."[11]

Praxiteles Swan, born in Virginia and an ordained Methodist minister, is sent by his church in the early 1850s to the village of Washington-on-the-Brazos in southeast Texas. Primarily an adherent to the God of the Old Testament, Swan is not averse to occasional instructive violence. In fact, he makes his first mark in Washington by whipping the town bully in a fistfight. "The engagement," the author says, "was like [the] San Jacinto fight in its brevity and violence and its astonishing and improbable outcome" (p. 36). In a few years Swan marries, starts a family, and establishes himself as a successful minister and prosperous farmer.

When the Civil War begins, Swan suffers a brief pang of conscience. He does not believe in secession, but his loyalties to the South are too strong to allow him to stay home while others march off to battle. On his way to war Swan encounters Sam Houston, who has just been removed from the office of governor of Texas because of his refusal to take an oath of allegiance to the Confederacy. Old Sam Houston's prophecy is as ominous as that of an oracle in Greek tragedy. "As the Gadarine swine," he tells Praxiteles Swan, "you rush on to destruction! And you who live will see your substance wasted, your women and children homeless, your very social order destroyed" (p. 55). Swan does not heed the warning.

He joins John Bell Hood's Texas Brigade, which throughout the war was attached to Robert E. Lee's Army of Northern Virginia. Swan is the brigade's chaplain, but before long he becomes involved in the fighting, eventually achieving the rank of captain. He is portrayed as a fierce warrior. At Gettysburg, "he rose to his knees and raised his immense voice—'Fifth Texas—Hood's Texans.'... An anger surged through him. He stood erect, and looked around. 'We air going,' he announced, 'to take that there hill. Come on.' He began to walk towards the hill.... A sort of moaning sigh ran from one man to another. A few of them got to their feet, and a few more, and then all of them" (p. 238). As they advance on the hill Swan urges the men on with a kind of song: "Come on, Fifth Texas,/ Come on, Fifth Texians—/ You boys from the Brazos/ And the Trinity" (p. 241). As the war drags on and bone-weariness and hopelessness begin to undermine the will of the Southern army, Praxiteles Swan never loses his optimism and exuberance. Even more remarkable, he somehow retains his sense of rough-and-ready humor.

Lone Star Preacher has an antique air about it. It springs from a simpler, more naive time, when war and fighting were deemed to be glorious occupations; when the stacking of the dead and maimed and even the certainty of defeat could not quench a man's thirst for battle. In this regard, the fictional Swan in the 1860s and the real-life John Thomason in the 1920s and 1930s seemed to share a common view. Both lived and fought before the mass, anonymous slaughter that characterized the final stages of World War II and before the ineffable horror of the threat of nuclear destruction. Praxiteles Swan, in any event, is a memorable character and a thoroughly representative Texian.

Lone Star Preacher helps a reader grasp the contours of the Texas military tradition. The Confederate army was, to Thomason, a Texan's kind of outfit. It was "as little bound by doctrine as any ever mustered for war, and the militia soldiers looked with cold suspicion upon anything emanating from West Point" (p. 70). The typical Confederate soldier, he continues, "was an individual, distrustful of anything that smacked of regimentation; jealous and ardent for his sectional ties; and peculiarly susceptible to leadership" (p. 281). Here, it appears, is the Texas attitude toward the military conveniently summarized: a Texan will follow a brave leader against the demons of hell if necessary, but he resists regimentation and maintains his individuality at all costs.

A period of Texas history in which the military played a major role and which has received a fair amount of coverage in the state's literature is the 1870s. At the beginning of that decade, Texas, like other Southern states, was occupied territory. Federal troops were present, at least in part, to enforce what many Anglo-Texans and other Southerners viewed as the harsh rule of Reconstruction. Unlike other Southern states at the time, however, Texas had a frontier, and the attitude of Texans toward the military was ambivalent. If most Texans saw the army troopers as hated reminders of their bitter defeat, some—especially those living on the West Texas frontier—welcomed the military as a guard against the depredations of hostile Indians. And indeed by the end of the 1870s the threat of Indian raids in Texas had been virtually eliminated, primarily because of the efforts of frontier cavalry units.

Unquestionably the most artistically accomplished work of Texas literature dealing with the military during this period is Elmer Kelton's novel *The Wolf and the Buffalo* (1980). Kelton, who has published more than two dozen novels set in nineteenth-century Texas, features vivid characterizations and plot lines as well as settings authentic in every detail. *The Wolf and the Buffalo* takes place in and around Fort Concho, near present-day San Angelo. At the beginning of the narrative, the feared Comanches are still making bloody forays onto the southern plains with impunity. They are generally contemptuous of the U.S. cavalry because the soldiers are "slow to get started. And unless they had the aid of good trackers. . . . were usually not hard to shake off the trail."[12]

The main character of the book is Gideon Ledbetter, a former slave from Louisiana who joins the army following the Civil War because there is nothing else for him to do. Gideon becomes a "buffalo soldier," one of those black troopers stationed in West Texas during the 1870s who acquired their name because their curly black hair resembled that of the buffalo, or bison. He discovers that, despite the useful service that he and his fellow black soldiers render on the frontier, he is not welcome in West Texas. "To ex-Confederates, a black man in a blue uniform represented misplaced authority, a swaggering symbol of a lost war. To Northerners moving in to seize upon rapidly opening business opportunities, Negroes were a social and economic burden. In a subtle way they also goaded the conscience, a reminder that much of the inspirational wartime talk about freedom and brotherhood and equality had come from the mouth and not from the heart" (p. 388).

But in the field Gideon prospers. He becomes increasingly confident of his ability to successfully pit himself against the land and the elements. Early on in the story he is tested and blooded as a leader of men. "He had tasted the land now. For all its strangeness, its continuous threat of disaster, it produced a stimulation he had never known before. Out there he seemed set free from the constraints of his blackness. The land made equal demands upon all men and neither gave credit nor demanded extra for their color" (p. 145). By the novel's end Gideon has been promoted to sergeant, about the highest rank a black man could aspire to, because all but a few officers were white.

Gideon's immediate superior, the white Lieutenant Hollander, is an honorable man who nevertheless realizes and accepts the violent and vengeful nature of his duty. "It is not army policy," Hollander tells his troop as they are about to attack an Indian village, "to brutalize these people, but it *is* army policy to see that every transgression is punished" (p. 250). The troopers, black and white, recognize that in a way they are just mercenaries, paid to perform an unpleasant task and then move on. "The soldier never gets to keep what he wins," a buffalo hunter tells Hollander. "We are tools of destiny, you and me and your darkies here. We'll do our bit and drift away with nothing to show for it" (p. 334). "We made the land safe for civilized people," Hollander later says to Gideon. "Now the danger is gone and we're in the way just as the Comanche was" (p. 386).

The inevitable resentment, even hostility, the army (mostly white officers from the North and black horse soldiers) and the civilians (mostly Southerners) feel for each other is never very far from the surface. "The army cannot watch over every outlying cabin of every ex-Confederate foolish enough to expose himself to the hazard of Indians," says a snippy Yankee major when the troopers come across a farm family slain by Comanches (pp. 184–85). Pat Maloney, a former Confederate who scouts for the army patrols, carries on a half-mocking, half-serious debate with the Northern cavalry officers. Once Maloney, along with Gideon and a few other buffalo soldiers, is trailing a band of Comanches, and Maloney comments on the glory they will share should they find the Indians. "They ain't goin' to let you and us have no glory," Gideon wisely tells Maloney. "We're too dark, and you're a Texican" (p. 241).

Interpolated into the story of Gideon Ledbetter are episodes from the life of a Comanche warrior named Gray Horse. The fate of Gray Horse is representative of that of all Plains Indians in the late nineteenth century. As the buffalo are slaughtered by white hunters, the cavalry slowly forces the nomadic tribes onto reservations in Oklahoma, and Anglo settlers make their way onto the plains, the old free life before white occupation quickly comes to an end. Frustrated and confused, Gray Horse makes a foolhardy assault on an army patrol, only to be killed by Gideon. The supreme irony of this iconographic scene is, as Kelton has written, that in "essence it was the black trooper's role to take the land away from the red man so that the white man could have it" (p. viii).

The Wolf and the Buffalo takes place in the early years of the 1870s. Another novel that explores the final eradication of the Indian menace on the West Texas plains in the mid-1870s is Max Crawford's *Lords of the Plain* (1985). Crawford's James John McSwain, commander of the 2nd Cavalry, is obviously a fictionalized version of Colonel Ranald S. Mackenzie. The author portrays McSwain as a Custer-like figure who entertains political ambitions. In real life Mackenzie seems to have been a decent, practical man and a superb commanding officer. In 1873 he was commended in a joint resolution of the Texas legislature for pursuing and punishing "a band of Kickapoo Indians who . . . have for years been waging a predatory warfare upon the frontiers of Texas." "Grateful thanks," the resolution continues, were due Mackenzie and his men "for their prompt action and gallant conduct in inflicting well-merited punishment upon these scourges of our frontier."[13] In 1874 Mackenzie became the hero of the battle of Palo Duro Canyon, in which his troops routed a large band of Comanches camped in the canyon, captured many of them, and slaughtered more than one thousand Indian ponies. Some saw the killing of the Indian horses as a draconian measure, but it had the salutary effect of severely diminishing the Comanches' mobility and, therefore, the threat they posed to Anglo settlers.

Lords of the Plain, in any event, is narrated by Captain Philip Chapman, a proper Bostonian who serves under Colonel McSwain.[14] Chapman, as an outsider, describes the Anglo-Texans he meets along the way with the scientific detachment of an entomologist examining some exotic new species of insect. Most of these Texans turn out to be very odd creatures indeed: violent, bigoted, and often half-crazed by loneliness and isolation. As in *The Wolf and the Buffalo,* relations between frontier Texans and the cavalrymen—most of whom, like Chapman, are from the North—are shown in *Lords of the Plain* to be, at best, wary.

Yet another noteworthy Texas novel that explores military campaigns against hostile Indians is Tom Lea's *The Wonderful Country* (1952). This tale is set near the end of the 1870s, and the only Indian problems remaining in Texas are in the far western part of the state. The buffalo soldiers have been moved westward from Fort Concho to places like Fort Jefflin

(Fort Bliss), near Puerto (El Paso). Indeed there is a character in *The Wonderful Country*, a black sergeant named Tobe Sutton, who is not as fully or believably developed as Elmer Kelton's Gideon Ledbetter but who resembles Gideon in many respects. In Lea's version of history the buffalo soldiers perform honorably in their campaigns against the Apaches, and their white commanding officer, Major Starke Colton, is somewhat foolhardy but nonetheless courageous. As he is dying, Colton asks to be remembered by the following epitaph: "When I found the enemy, I engaged him."[15]

In *The Wonderful Country*, Lea tosses a new element into the fictional history of the Indian wars of the 1870s: the Texas Rangers. The Rangers, who in this novel are portrayed as a semimilitary organization, have produced over the years a stormy and controversial history. Their demeanor has not always been in the best military tradition. By all accounts, for example, they were almost uncontrollable during their service in the Mexican War in the 1840s. They also participated in several grisly incidents that have not been forgotten in Mexico to this day.[16] Apparently, however, the Rangers were very effective—more so than the regular army—in combating the guerrilla warfare tactics of the Plains Indians. In *The Wolf and the Buffalo*, for instance, the Comanche warrior Gray Horse fears the "implacable . . . Texas Rangers—men always angry and always ready to travel" (p. 44).

The protagonist of *The Wonderful Country*, Martin Brady, eventually fulfills his ambition to become a Texas Ranger. He joins Captain John Rucker's Company E, Frontier Battalion, headquartered at Puerto at the tip of far West Texas. Rucker is a wise man and a good leader. His company takes part in a joint military operation on Mexican soil, including the Rangers, the U.S. Army's 10th Cavalry, and the private army of the governor of Chihuahua, Mexico. Their purpose is to flush out of their mountain stronghold the renegade Apache Fuego and his band of followers. The Mexican army does most of the fighting and appropriates most of the glory, a circumstance that does not sit well with the Rangers. "The wind kind of missing from my sails," one of them grouses. "Coming home from Mexico without a scrap" (p. 384). In general, though, the Rangers accept their disappointment with good grace. *The Wonderful Country*, then, perpetuates the notion (or myth) of the Texas Rangers as first-rate fighting men who work well together while retaining their frontier individualism.

Indeed, the Ranger myth has a long literary history, stretching back to the popular dime novels of the late nineteenth century. And it has made innumerable appearances in the literature of the twentieth century. One of the best fictional treatments of the mythical Ranger temperament is a scene in Larry McMurtry's trail-drive novel *Lonesome Dove* (1985). The prime mover behind the drive is Captain Woodrow Call, a former Texas Ranger. He is a man who is always on guard, always in control of his emotions, never allowing himself to be simply human. Until, that is, he goes berserk on the streets of Ogallala, Nebraska, when he sees some of his drovers being abused by an army scout.[17] Call's fury is awesome to behold. It is like a dam breaking, the emotional restraints of a lifetime bursting. In some ways, however, he is also a stereotype—the quintessential Texas Ranger.

After the 1870s most of the Texas forts were closed. The cavalry moved even farther west to New Mexico and Arizona, though a few army posts, such as those at San Antonio and El Paso, continued operations and became important American military installations. For the most part, Texans of the late nineteenth and early twentieth centuries turned their attention to economic matters and activities not concerned with military life: raising beef cattle and getting them to market, growing cotton, and, after 1901, extracting oil from the earth. Pro-war sentiment was strong during the brief Spanish-American War and, as mentioned earlier, before United States involvement in World War I. In all American wars of the twentieth century, numerous Texans have eagerly disrupted their normal civilian lives to volunteer for military service.

A literary work that covers the twentieth-century spectrum—from World War I to the Vietnam War—of Texans and their relation to the military is *A Time of Soldiers* (1976), a thought-provoking and thoroughly remarkable novel by Andrew Jolly. The tale follows the fortunes of three generations of a Texas military family, the Lears. In the first generation, as represented by Jack Lear, the flame of idealism burns with a hard intensity. Jack Lear is a New Englander who marries the daughter of a German saddle-maker from San Angelo. But he is really married to the army. Lear believes that the soldier's calling is akin to that of the priest. He writes a book, ostensibly a study of the interrelation of warfare and religion among the Apaches in the nineteenth century. It is titled *War and Faith*, and its first two sentences read: "War is an act of belief on the part of a people in their conception of the meaning of human life. The way in which people make war is influenced by this conception."[18]

Jack Lear once told a friend, the El Paso newspaperman Stefan Graf, that "he had become a soldier not to be only his own self alone, and in his romantic view the soldier was the incorruptible guardian of the City of Man and at the same time a part of that City" (p. 156). Lear's belief in the nobility of America's mission in the world seems unshakable. "If the profit motive is the bedrock of the nation's morality," he declares, "then I am only a hired killer, and I decline to accept that judgement" (p. 158). Graf sees in Jack Lear the embodiment of "some profound innocence and purity which could be murderous, bloody, and destructive. I thought of Lee and Stonewall Jackson and Lamar and Houston and Washington and of all those other saintly soldiers, and I felt that the enigma of our country sat before me" (p. 97).

Jack Lear becomes a kind of hero during the punitive expedition against Pancho Villa in northern Mexico. He antagonizes the "horse generals," however, by advocating a greater and more imaginative use of technology and is consequently assigned to a series of demeaning tasks. Eventually, in the 1930s, Lear is sent to the mountains of southern New Mexico to help train a group of quasi-religious counterrevolutionary Mexican nationals who call themselves the Cristeros. In due course, policy changes order Lear to abandon the mission. Instead of obeying orders, he chooses to stand with the Cristeros when they are attacked by the U.S. Army in the valley of La Luz in the Sacramento Mountains of New Mexico. He is one of the first to be killed.

Why this suicidal gesture? In Graf's view, Jack Lear had lost his idealism, his faith in his country, and the sanctity of his vocation. Training the Cristeros in the mountains, Graf says, Lear "must have halted upon some height within his mind and reasoned backward from technique and weapon and strategy to the faith from which he had himself asserted they sprang and to which they bore witness, and he must have seen that there was no faith at all, only a clutch of pure and mindless techniques in place of a common set of assumptions about the goodness and purpose of human existence, and that his beloved country was not a noble idea but a savage giant of a child, Browning's Caliban randomly smashing crabs on Setebos" (p. 180). Lear, Graf concludes, "had left to him only the gift of command. He must have thought that it was time for soldiers to protect whatever they could of the City by the naked example of command until some new civilizing faith should appear among men" (p. 181).

Jack Lear's son Ben is also an idealist and "a passionate man" who is betrayed at both the collective and personal levels. After serving honorably in World War II, Ben returns to a nation reveling in a "self-indulgent mood." He is repelled by the country's loose attitude, but "he did not know to what purpose he should discipline himself" (p. 261). His homecoming is made even more difficult by his wife, Kathleen, the only child of a famed history professor at the University of Texas at Austin. Ben wonders "whether it had always been this way for the soldier to come home and pick up the threads of that life for which he had fought only to find that it had changed through the very act of defending it" (p. 250).

His wife's promiscuity, which is somehow related in Ben's mind to his nation's promiscuity, is so dismaying that he kills her. He is not convicted of murder—Kathleen had been in bed with her Mexican lover at the time Ben shot her, and no jury in Texas in the 1940s would convict a man of killing his wife under those circumstances—but his promising military career is ended. At the close of the novel, however, in the late 1960s, Ben is still searching for "'the just war,' 'the good killing,' 'the pure act of service'" (p. 132). He is a mercenary fighting in Africa, or somewhere in the Third World. "It was not money and adventure that drove him but some kind of translation into a different quest of the love he had had for his wife who had . . . defiled it. Like a lover looking for a perfect beloved, he went about the world in search of the perfect cause for which to risk his life" (p. 133).

The third generation of Lears is embodied in Doniphan, Ben's son. In Doniphan the springs of idealism have dried up and been dusted over with the bitter ashes of cynicism. Graf tells Doniphan that his father and grandfather were "heroes and nobody gave a damn and never will in this forsaken country because any instance of the heroic is an unwanted reminder that there may be greater possibilities in life than stuffing your gut and making money and screwing your wife, or, better still, someone else's wife, and amassing things for which one has no taste or use, because, by God, the heroic is a call to order, to sacrifice, to honor—the dirty words of this sullen age" (p. 73).

Graf's outburst occurs in a Juárez restaurant the evening after Doniphan has been decorated at Fort Bliss for bravery in Vietnam. He has also been crippled overseas and must walk with a cane. Doniphan's disability is a none-too-subtle symbol of the disadvantages that afflict the aspiring idealist in modern America. Doniphan is confused and uncertain about his motivation for going to Vietnam. He recalls "shooting down women and children running over the bridges of the sluggish brown streams in a far land out of love of country, or freedom, or family, or honor, or some goddamned thing he could not remember anymore, which was just as well because it was not the truth since the mysterious passion that burned in his father and his father's father had never come to him at all so that he could not say he had done anything out of love of God, or country, or woman" (p. 133). "I mean no offense," Graf tells Doniphan, "when I say the serious business of your generation is to learn to live as a nation of cripples. You have less passion and therefore less meaning than your fathers and your sons will have less than you" (p. 194).

A Time of Soldiers is a remarkable book: not really a war or military novel but a novel of ideas, a philosophical novel. It takes seriously the concept of a "warrior class and its special code of behavior," and it assumes that faith and idealism must be the driving forces in the creation of such a class. It is set in Texas, mostly in El Paso and Austin, and traces the experiences of a trio of Texans who, in their different ways, fought their country's wars—only to have their country reveal itself corrupt and not worthy of their sacrifice.

While *A Time of Soldiers* projects the high motives that have often propelled Texans into battle, its bleak ending brings to the surface the dark side of the Texas military experience. This duality is apparently inescapable. A recurring and familiar figure in twentieth-century war novels and movies is the fighting Texan. He's brave, he's mean, and sometimes he's more than a touch crazy. A writer who has exploited this stereotype to the hilt is Norman Mailer. Mailer, a card-carrying member of the New York literary establishment, might plausibly be considered an honorary Texan, even though he usually does not have very nice things to say about Texas and Texans.

During World War II, Mailer served in the 112th Armored Cavalry Regiment, which entered the war as a Texas National Guard unit. Most of Mailer's comrades-in-arms were Texans. After the war, Mailer's sister said of him: "Norman would occasionally mention the men he was overseas with—which ones drank, which ones would fight, how they treated the . . . Jewish boys. He puts on his Texas accent now, but he didn't have it before he went in the army, and when he came back something was lost. A certain kindness, his softness. Because those Texas men were wild. . . . [The] army will never be out of his system. It scarred him."[19]

Mailer's portrait of the typical Texan gone to war is Sergeant Sam Croft in *The Naked and the Dead* (1948), a novel set in the South Pacific in the waning days of World War II. Croft is a fighting machine. Brown, one of Croft's fellow soldiers, describes him as follows:

> Listen, he's made of iron. He's the one man I'd *never* cross. He's probably the best platoon sergeant in the army and the meanest. He just doesn't have any nerves. . . . Out of all the old guys in recon, there ain't one of us whose nerves ain't shot. . . . But Croft—I tell you Croft loves combat, he *loves* it. There ain't a worse man you could be under or a better one, depending on how you look at it. We lost eleven guys out of seventeen in the platoon, counting the Lieu-

tenant we had then, some of the best guys in the world and the rest of us weren't good for anything for a week, but Croft asked for a patrol the next day.[20]

Croft is portrayed as a sadistic authoritarian who derives satisfaction and considerable personal magnetism from his capabilities as a killer. He is an expert at what he is supposed to do—disposing of the enemy—but clearly he takes too much pleasure in fulfilling the role. "But why *is* Croft that way? Oh, there are answers. He is that way because of the corruption-of-the-society. He is that way because the devil has claimed him for one of his own. It is because he is a Texan; it is because he has renounced God. . . . He was born that way" (p. 156).

Croft is prejudiced and creates division in the ranks by criticizing and irritating the Jewish soldiers in his outfit as well as a Mexican American, Martínez—who is also a Texan because he comes from the barrio of San Antonio. In one episode Croft indirectly causes the death of Roth (a Jew), who suffers a fatal fall as the men traverse a mountain trail. Roth's fear of Croft makes him attempt a jump across a gap in the trail, a jump Roth knows he cannot accomplish. Roth is aware that Croft will be furious if the men do not quickly leap across the ravine and continue toward their destination without delay. Roth's death upsets the other men in the platoon, but Croft is unconcerned about anything except completing the mission at hand.

Croft is thus shown to be merely an instrument of the officers, particularly the mean-spirited General Cummings. In Mailer's political morality, Croft is evil because he uses fascistic methods to implement the general's fascist program. A more generous view of Croft might see him, for better or worse, as a Texan. He is not really a military man at all but an extreme individualist, a gunslinger; not a military strategist, but a relentless frontiersman who leads by example.

In any event, *The Naked and the Dead* was hardly Norman Mailer's last word on the Texan at war. In 1967, at the height of United States' involvement in Southeast Asia, Mailer published a novel entitled *Why Are We in Vietnam?* He attempts to answer the title's question by telling the story of a group of male Texans who are in Alaska on a bear hunt. The three main characters are Rusty Jethroe, a wealthy corporation executive from Dallas; Rusty's sixteen-year-old son, D. J.; and D. J.'s friend Tex Hyde. Present time in the novel is actually two years after the bear hunt, and the setting is a dinner party in north Dallas in honor of D. J. and Tex, who are about to depart for military service in Vietnam. Most of the narrative is a kind of Joycean stream-of-consciousness recollection by D. J., interspersed between the various courses of the banquet, of the events of the bear hunt two summers back.

Rusty's reason for participating in the hunt is simply to confirm his manhood. He is a Texan (mythical mode) nonpareil. "His cells are filled with the biological inheritance and trait transmissions of his ancestors, all such rawhide, cactus hearts, eagle eggs, and coyote."[21] He is so competitive that once, in a game of one-on-one football with D. J., he became so "insane . . . with frustration" that he had lunged at his son and bitten him on the neck, bringing forth a spurt of blood (p. 40). In Alaska, Rusty declares, "I want to behold Bruin right in his pig red eye so I'll never have to be scared again, not until I got to face The Big Man" (p. 62).

For D. J. the hunt is of even more significance. In a way, Mailer's *Why Are We in Vietnam?* is a mean parody of William Faulkner's great short novel *The Bear*, which is also about a bear hunt. Traditionally the hunt, in American culture and thus in American literature, has been a ritual of initiation. In this ritual a boy meets a legendary animal in a mystically charged encounter, and as a result of his experience he becomes a man. Further, the hunt, because it excludes women, is ordinarily an exercise in what pop anthropologists call "male bonding."

Tex Hyde does not require initiation, for he was born with "that mean glint in the eye for which Texans are justly proud and famous" (p. 161). The party of Texans, especially D. J., is instructed in the rules of the hunt by a world-famous guide and hunter, Big Luke Fellinka, who is described simply as "a *man*!" (p. 47). Tex and D. J. each bag a "grizzer" fairly early in the hunt, but it is not until they leave behind their guns and supplies and trek into the mountains to face the grizzly unprotected that their mystical revelation occurs. In the wilderness there is a brief instant of sexual attraction that passes between the boys, an impulse they quickly reject. Instead they share an epiphany, a vision of God, who turns out to be "a beast, not a man, and God said, 'Go out and kill—fulfill my will, go and kill.'" From that moment they become "twins, never to be near as lovers again, but killer brothers, owned by something, prince of darkness, lord of light, they did not know" (p. 204).

Some of the surface parallels between the bear hunt and the then-current Vietnam War are obvious. The Texans in the hoodoo land of Alaska, like Americans in Vietnam, are invaders of an alien culture. The expedition, which besides the three main characters includes several of Rusty Jethroe's corporate underlings, carries an arsenal of sophisticated weaponry, which is described in lengthy and loving detail. The "grizzers" are hunted from a helicopter, a favored mode of transportation for American troops in Vietnam. After a couple of days of hunting, the body count is impressive: "twenty-five assorted grizzly, moose, ram, goat and caribou" (p. 100). There is no way the hunters can use all the meat, but the slaughter continues apace.

The point is, of course, that it is an *attitude*, a mind-set, that motivates Americans to invade places like Alaska and Vietnam. At the novel's end, Tex and D. J. are eager "to see the wizard in Vietnam." Says D. J., "Vietnam, hot damn" (p. 208). Mailer seems to be saying that America's frustrated sexuality—hetero and homo—crystallizes in a frenzied fascination with weapons and killing, which Americans force-feed the rest of the world as foreign policy. And, as usual, the Texan is seen as a super-American, possessing typically American traits in wildly exaggerated form. The Texans in Mailer's novel are examples of a type—"the ugly Texan," Don Graham has called him—[22] that was pervasive in American popular culture following the Kennedy assassination in Dallas and during Lyndon Johnson's increasingly controversial escalation of the war in Vietnam. For Mailer, the inevitable equation is that "the kink which resides in the heart of the Lone Star" (p. 167) is what got the United States into Vietnam. Regardless of whether there is any truth in such a simplistic explanation, it was—and maybe still is—a widely shared perception among Americans, particularly intellectuals, living outside Texas.

Texans may have taken a bum rap in having to shoulder most of the blame for the Vietnam fiasco. The state undeniably produced Lyndon Johnson, but not John Kennedy, who initiated the mess. It does seem fair to say that the Texas military experience is a double-edged sword. Texans' readiness to fight for their rights and beliefs can result in heroism, the subject of much Texas military lore. Or, in the cases of the Rangers in Mexico during the Mexican War and of Tex and D. J. in Vietnam, it can produce unbridled aggression and mindless violence. As with most things in life, the Texans' famed fighting abilities are a mixed blessing. At worst, they have put America, and perhaps the rest of the world, in some awkward and dangerous situations. At best, they are instruments by which tyranny and oppression are resisted in the name of honor and individual freedom. Literature, as a mirror of a people's culture, reflects these two sides of the Texas military experience with provocative fidelity.

EPILOGUE:

The Texas Military Experience

Roger Beaumont

THE DRAWING TOGETHER OF THESE CHAPTERS AROSE from the belief of several faculty at Texas A&M that a general overview of the Texas military experience was long overdue. Tracing patterns of meaning is an exercise that reacquainted the authors with the intricacies of a subject that, like so much else in history, has frequently been approached by vague allusion, anecdote, myth-making, or misapprehension. With Texas that has been especially true, given the Texan impulse to strike bold poses. Contrary to widespread impression, such posturing has not always taken the form of war or mayhem. Nevertheless, many throughout the world see Texans as more prone to violence than other Americans, in peace or war. This is perhaps because T. R. Fehrenbach is correct in viewing Texans as "closer in time and spirit and society to the frontier than in most of America . . . [in that they were] enormously self-sufficient,"[1] or, at least, believed they were.

The aggregate of history, anecdote, and experience of Texas can lead to many interpretations. Whatever their divergence in conclusions, most observers would probably agree that Texas's flavor, great scale, and diversity encompass more contradictions and extremes than other American states. As with any complex phenomenon, such perception is affected by the location and assumption of the observers. Thus, although these essays are arrayed chronologically, they can also be plotted across a gradient: from the inceptive microcosms of the Texas Revolution and the border and frontier wars to the projection of Texan style and attitude into broader arenas of conflict in the twentieth century. The following comments and allusions to the chapters do not follow either of those systems but reflect an attempt to consider issues raised both by the symposium as a whole and by some individual essays.

A central question throughout is, How much of the Texas military experience is substance, and how much is image? Furthermore, is there a Texas military tradition of such clarity and dimension that it stands forth as truly distinct from all others? The uncertainty of the answer to the latter question throws America's military history into a different light. Joseph Dawson, in citing the example of Virginia's rich military tapestry, suggests how much each state's individual military history may differ from those of the other states. It also raises the question of how far each history is from the general public view and from historians' beliefs. That is especially true when population and size are considered, as in the cases of South Carolina, New York, Massachusetts, Connecticut, Georgia, Ohio, and Wisconsin.

If nothing else, the sparsity of state military histories—beyond those popular or regionalist studies focused on events or people—reflects a centralist bias in academic American military history. This is true even in the case of the Civil War, where state military histories are also in short supply. This shortage may be traceable to a decline throughout the twentieth century in the longstanding practice of raising U.S. military units regionally in wartime. This phenomenon is noted by Martin Blumenson in his description of the composition of the 36th Infantry Division. Beyond the obscuring effects of that trend, it is not clear how much of Texas's military forces at any point was a synthesis of American, Southern, frontier, or other traditions. The blurring caused by such recurrent absorption and by the reshaping in popular culture and myth complicates the historian's task of searching amid that tangle for meaning. There is little comfort in the fact that such melanges of fiction, impression, and history can be found in all national military traditions. National models, however, may more aptly apply to the question because the hardihood and fame of Texas's military and paramilitary mythic images more closely resemble other nations than they do other states of the Union. It is axiomatic that popular enshrinement of virtues, prowess, and reputations far outweighs—and sometimes suppresses—careful appraisal of them. The iconic power of some subelements of the Texas military mystique, therefore, makes it especially difficult to move beyond fragments of myths and impressions and see a coherent whole: how the history and mythology of Texans-in-arms fit into the broader matrices of American or world history.

In reflecting on frontier societies worldwide, Walter Prescott Webb, dean of Texas historians, strove to look beyond the powerful tides of regionalism. He traced common patterns along the Great Frontier; that is, those regions of major European colonial incursions such as the United States, Siberia, Argentina, Canada, and South Africa. Across that far-flung archipelago, variants on a theme of paramilitarism included Texas Rangers,

Cossacks, *voorloopers*, *gauchos*, and Australian bush rangers. Beyond their not dissimilar equestrian swagger, each force confronted its enemies with a fierce pragmatism under variants of the *lex talionis*. In a corollary to Clausewitz, the citizen-soldiers projected culture as well as politics by violent means. Each of those cases also reflected the power of frontiers in reshaping traditional/conventional military formats and methods, as in the Anglo-French-Indian wars in North America.[2]

The sense of Texas as a savage frontier zone that stamped all dwellers with its harshness is conveyed by Thomas Cutrer's portrait of Ben McCulloch and the cruel, ruthless Texans in the Mexican War. It is not difficult to match that lusty bravado with Norman Mailer's recollections of his experiences with Texans in the Pacific a century later. It can also be aligned with the portrait of the shy Audie Murphy as an unlikely hero limned by Roger Spiller, or even to the Texas Rangers as described a generation later.[3] The paradoxical extremes of courage, shyness, reticence, and cold fury that Spiller found combined in Audie Murphy also comprise a leitmotif in Norman Mailer's novel *The Naked and the Dead* (1948). The characters in this book were drawn from his service with the 112th Armored Cavalry Regiment, a unit originally raised in the San Antonio area.[4] Both Don Graham's and Tom Pilkington's analyses of Texas's martial images in the cultural formats of cinema and literature found contradictions hard to reconcile with the haggard, yet gentle and youthful faces of the Texans of the 36th Infantry Division in John Huston's documentary film *The Battle of San Pietro* (1945). Further contradictions are found within the glossy production values of *To Hell and Back* (1955), the movie version of Audie Murphy's autobiography, and within the slimy politics of the Texas National Guard in *Attack* (1956), Robert Aldrich's film depicting American soldiers in the Battle of the Bulge.

How much can that sense of distinctiveness be attributed to a unique geographic or cultural setting? Texas was, after all, only one segment of the vast American frontier that bounded the great inland sea of grass. Yet no other state—not Colorado, with its infamous Sand Creek massacre, or Minnesota, with its Mankato massacre—matched the Texans' reputation for ferocity. Although the length and scale of Comanche depredations may be to blame, it is not easy to see why Texas more closely resembled such other fierce border realms as Argentina and Siberia in its style of guarding and advancing the frontier than it did the other territories and states of the Union, or Canada. Texas, after all, was not the only region of the United States that lay close to a populous foreign country with dissimilar mores and language, as well as a border marked by frequent open warfare and raiding.

Nor is there an easy way to measure the role of the Alamo as an icon. Most Americans know that Texas was once a separate country that won nationhood under arms, however confusedly, and had its own flag. Far less visible to Americans and many Texans is the complex interweaving of Anglo, Hispanic, African-American, and ethnic enclaves. An insight into this human tapestry is presented in Joseph Porter's description of the political and ethnic tangles on the border in the "American Congo."

Contrasting with such fusions is the relatively faint residue of Native American culture and imagery left within Texas military history, other than as adversaries. This is in sharp contrast to such other Great Plains states as New Mexico, Kansas, and the Dakotas. Was that because of the ferocious and prolonged Comanche threat in Texas? How much did that threat shape Texans' attitudes and behaviors toward war—and life? James Crisp's attempt to sort out the ethnic complexities of the Texas Revolution suggests how much more remains to be examined in this respect. Anomalies, beyond the African-American regular units described by William Leckie, include the role of black militia companies during Reconstruction and beyond, the role of Hispanic Texans in the Texas National Guard, and Texans in the armed services as a whole.

The Texas military experience is certainly a strong candidate for inclusion among examples of what William McNeill has deemed "mythistory."[5] Paul Andrew Hutton's "The Alamo As Icon" and Don Graham's and Tom Pilkington's respective analyses of Texas military imagery in film and literature bring that into sharp relief. A moderating perspective is Sandra Myres's evocation of the activities of women in and along the edges of Texas military life. Their sensitive, literate vignettes of the ordeals of life on the edge of their world can be found along other subsectors of Webb's Great Frontier, as well as in popular images of women struggling to survive and maintain courage and grace under grinding conditions. Such depictions range from O. E. Rolvaag's novel *Giants in the Earth* (1927) to film portrayals of pioneer women, such as those of Lillian Gish in *The Unforgiven* (1960), Anna Lee in *Fort Apache* (1948), and Olive Carey in *The Searchers* (1956).

Such insights into how life was lived, and how it tasted and felt, adds dimensionality to the stereotypical and often stilted martial images of the army's presence. They also serve as reminders that although studies of civil-military relations are usually couched in broad, statistical terms or concentrate on links between individual elites, interaction of institutions and cultures ultimately takes place between people. Such complex melding on military bases and their hinterlands, in peace and war, has been dealt with only fragmentarily—not only in Texas, but in the United States and its overseas bastions. The Brownsville affair of 1906 stands out because it prompted the U.S. Army to keep African-American regiments out of Texas for the next generation. These complex and variegated threads of the broader tapestry, however, deserve far more scrutiny from historians, sociologists, and cultural anthropologists.[6]

Although the frontier's powerful influence has faded with the passing of time, it shines through in half of these essays, even in those expressing skepticism about the uniqueness of a Texas military tradition. Focusing on race and ethnicity in the Texas Revolution and afterward, James Crisp offers a fresh sense of those times in which peaceful accommodation along the border contrasted sharply with religious conflicts in the eastern United States in the 1840s. These struggles were reflected in bloody riots as well as the tensions between Freemasons, various exclusionist groups, and Catholics that persisted for over a century.

Such anomalous features, brought to light in various essays, suggest how the symbols of the Texas military mystique have tended to obscure details and contrary subthemes. Paul Andrew Hutton notes how the distorted fictional and quasi-historical renderings of the Alamo siege not only thrust American-born Anglos forward as hero figures—to the near-exclusion of *tejano* revolutionaries—but also obscured the facts that no Anglo revolutionaries were Texans by birth except *tejanos* and that many Alamo defenders were foreign-born.[7] The dwelling on certain fixed mythic points has also served to blur the complex context of the Texas Revolution. Examples of other factors include the role of the British Empire as patron and would-be guardian, the revolutionary spirit of Latin America, and the strong support from other parts of America, such as the citizens of Cincinnati, Ohio.

Hutton's tracing of the Alamo-as-icon reflects the triumph of popular cultural imagery over formal historicism. By pointing out these distortions, he echoes the lament of numerous professional historians that many people, even those counted as educated, derive their sense of history from fragments and glimpses of the mass media. If nothing else, it helps to explain why certain details and personalities of the Alamo legend have remained fixed in the imagination of successive generations across the world, while a vast array of much grander sieges have faded from popular memory.[8]

Another major facet of the Texas martial image, prowess with weapons, is glimpsed in some of these essays, extending across the continuum of the military, the paramilitary, law enforcement, and the cowboy. This is particularly true of the Colt revolver, which appeared as the Texas Revolution began and subsequently flavored both historical and fictional portrayals of the Texas frontier.[9] After observing its usefulness in the Seminole wars in the early 1840s, Texas Rangers adopted the Paterson model Colt. This resulted in a spectacularly one-sided battle on the Pedernales, when fifteen Rangers killed or wounded half of a band of some eighty Comanches. The demand for revolvers swept Texas. Ranger captain Samuel Walker asked Samuel Colt to build a sturdier gun of heavier caliber that fired six, not five, shots. As a result, several hundred Walker Colts came into service in the Mexican War—but did not save Walker from death in the field. To what extent the Colt became a salient Texan symbol needs no belaboring,[10] nor does the persistent affinity of many Texans for using other weapons and for such legendary feats as the twelve-hundred-yard shot at the battle of Adobe Walls that brought down a Comanche warrior chief and stunned and demoralized his comrades. In the late twentieth century, foreign visitors to Texas are often shocked at seeing guns displayed on racks in pick-up trucks, while weapons of famous local peace officers are on display in police stations.

It is nevertheless difficult to account for Texans' reputation for ferocity in war as described by Thomas Cutrer and Ralph Wooster. At the battle of Gettysburg, Texans marched into the inferno of Pickett's charge after nearly taking Little Round Top. As Sir Garnet Wolseley (then a British observer with the Army of Northern Virginia and later a famous field marshal) watched Longstreet's shabby division march past, Robert E. Lee remarked to him, "Never mind the raggedness, Colonel. The enemy never sees the back of my Texas brigade." Wolseley recorded, much like observers of the Rangers in Mexico, that he had not seen a military unit that "looked more like work."[11] Texas units fought in over three hundred Civil War battles. Sul Ross's Texas brigade was reduced from almost five thousand in 1862 to about six hundred in 1865; Ross had five horses killed from under him and fought in 125 engagements. Ralph Wooster points out how much Texans bolstered the Confederacy's arms. This was reflected in the pride later felt that Galveston was the site of the last surrender of the Civil War.

These essays cannot encompass all dimensions of Texas military history. The Texas border before, during, and after the Mexican Revolution from 1900 to 1929; the specific activities of the 36th and 9th Infantry divisions and of other Texans in the First World War; the call-up of the

49th Armored Division in 1961–62; and Texans' service in the Korean and Vietnam wars await other treatments. Side channels to the main flow of Texas military history are the stories of Texans who served other nations or causes: the French Foreign Legion, the Mexican army, the Egyptian army. They also include those who, before U.S. entry into both world wars, volunteered for service with the British, Canadian, or French armed forces as well as Texans who fought as mercenaries in the Cold War era.

Another more muted, complex, but significant dimension of the American military tradition is the role that Texans as civilians played in American military history in the executive and legislative branches. These include Colonel Edward House, Bill Moyers, Lyndon Johnson, Jesse Jones, and John Connally; and in Congress, Tom Connally and Maury Maverick. Other prominent Texans who served in uniform include Colonel Oveta Culp Hobby, commander of the World War II Women's Auxiliary Army Corps (the WAACs); Tex Hill, of the Flying Tigers; intelligence expert Admiral Bobby Inman; and General Bernard Schriever, instrumental in the first phase of America's space program. Further yet from the domain of warfare—beyond the military, naval, and air installations in Texas noted by Joseph Dawson—lies Camp Mabry in Austin, where the entry arch proclaims "Headquarters—Texas Military Forces." There are also Texas's war-related industries and the contract airfields where British Empire pilots trained before and during World War II. Texas's martial spirit during the Cold War was not simply a product of federal funds. On the eve of the fall of the Berlin Wall, the state ranked third in absolute amounts of military money but only fortieth in per capita receipt of defense appropriations.[12]

Lesser known now but famous for a time were Ensign George Gay, sole survivor of the slaughter of Torpedo Squadron Eight at Midway in 1942, and Captain Tex McCrary, briefing officer for the ill-fated Ploesti raid in 1943. Those disastrous efforts, along with Martin Blumenson's grim saga of the 36th Infantry Division, touch on the darker side of the Texas military mystique. This is a litany encompassing Goliad, the Alamo, the Mier Expedition, the excesses of the Mexican War and border campaigns, Pickett's charge, Brownsville, the Aggie muster on Corregidor on the eve of the fall of the Philippines, the sinking of the USS *Houston*, the artillery battalion lost on Java in 1942, and Lyndon Johnson in Vietnam. Whether that panoply of frustrations and defeats is merely a random series of incidents, a time-series mirroring some Celtic-Jacobite or Southern tropism to lost causes, or reflects a susceptibility to taking risks are matters best weighed by those inclined to search for deeper meanings in the tangled flow of history.

Whatever the case, Texas history has encompassed signal military defeats and two harsh military occupations. That tension between triumph and disaster and between courage and inner uncertainty is evident in the evaluations of certain Texans in World War II. In keeping with F. Scott Fitzgerald's aphorism "Show me a hero and I will write you a tragedy," Spiller's portrait of Audie Murphy touches directly on that stress. The fate of another Texan in World War II throws the Murphy epic into sharper perspective. First Lieutenant William Deane Hawkins, a native of El Paso in the U.S. Marine Corps, played a key role in the first phase of the near-debacle at Tarawa. Pressing on in spite of his wounds, Hawkins, awarded a posthumous Medal of Honor, was deemed by *Time* magazine correspondent Robert Sherrod "the bravest man I ever knew."[13]

A similar tension is also reflected in Martin Blumenson's account of the anguish displayed by many Texans over the 36th Infantry Division's plight in Italy. This was true although two-thirds of the original Texans were gone from the unit by the time of the Rapido debacle.[14] The German view of the failed crossing as a minor attack that caused them "no particular anxiety" was galling, as was the Germans' initial claim that the division was in "headlong flight."[15] This furor—no doubt resulting from the 36th's reputation as "the Texas division"[16]—can be contrasted with the more muted reaction to the fate of the Wisconsin-Michigan 32nd and New York 27th Infantry divisions in the Pacific.[17]

Do all the incidents, personalities, and events constitute meaningful historical patterns? With respect to economics, politics, and social mores, Texas is far removed from its frontier days of the 1920s. Political candidates' military backgrounds have served less and less as a springboard to state or national office. As Texas's traditions and values change, what will be kept or thrown away, and how will the martial component fare in that sorting out? Does a magma of military esprit lie beneath all the changes, whose awakening from dormancy might yield unexpected force of the kind that erupted in Britain in the Falklands War?

The tainting of Texas's image by the assassination of John F. Kennedy in Dallas, the Whitman shootings in Austin, and Lyndon Johnson's role as architect of the least popular modern American war should be far enough in the past to allow clinical analysis. But those violent images were luridly recast in the films *JFK* (1991) and *Full Metal Jacket* (1987), echoing the demented martiality of Major Kong in *Dr. Strangelove* (1964). Those events had profound effects on the rest of the nation as well as on the Texas military experience/mystique. Most people in Texas and elsewhere realize that the state is no longer a raw frontier society and see Texans as less and less inclined to act out the role of violent Marcher Lords. But such incidents as the siege of the religious cultists' compound near Waco in 1993 by Texas law enforcement and federal agents throw that lurid perspective into fresh relief.

Historians do not and may not concur on how much the Texas military experience has resembled that of a sovereign state more than have the rest of the states, or if it is the most distinctly different of any state. As Lawrence Wright has observed, "Texas enjoys the singular blessing that every distinct culture must have, a sense of its own apartness."[18] As an aggregate, these essays suggest that the modern importance of the Texas military experience may be ebbing, but it remains a prominent element in the historical mosaic of the Lone Star State.

NOTES

Introduction

1. T. R. Fehrenbach, *The Seven Keys to Texas* (El Paso: Texas Western Press, 1983); Don Graham, James W. Lee, and William T. Pilkington, eds., *The Texas Literary Tradition* (Austin: College of Liberal Arts–University of Texas and the Texas State Historical Assoc., 1983); Robert F. O'Connor, ed., *Texas Myths* (College Station: Texas A&M University Press, 1986); Francis E. Abernethy, ed., *The Folklore of Texan Cultures* (Austin: Encino, 1974). See also Ross Phares, *Texas Tradition* (New York: Henry Holt, 1954); "Texas: A Special Issue," *The Atlantic* 235 (March, 1975); T. R. Fehrenbach, *Lone Star: A History of Texas and Texans* (New York: Macmillan, 1968); Ben Proctor and Archie P. McDonald, eds., *The Texas Heritage* (Arlington Heights, Ill.: Forum Press, 1980); Archie P. McDonald, comp., *The Texas Experience* (College Station: Texas A&M University Press, 1986); Ralph Wooster and Robert A. Calvert, eds., *Texas Vistas* (Austin: Texas State Historical Association, 1987); and Walter L. Buenger and Robert A. Calvert, eds., *Texas through Time: Evolving Interpretations* (College Station: Texas A&M University Press, 1991).

2. See, for example, Don Higginbotham, *George Washington and the American Military Tradition* (Athens: University of Georgia Press, 1985); Douglas E. Leach, *Arms for Empire: A Military History of the British Colonies in North America, 1607–1763* (New York: Macmillan, 1973); and Russell F. Weigley, *The American Way of War* (New York: Macmillan, 1973).

3. In addition to the historiographical citations for chapter 1 below, see also Edward T. Linenthal, "'A Reservoir of Spiritual Power': Patriotic Faith at the Alamo in the Twentieth Century," *Southwestern Historical Quarterly* 91 (April, 1988): 509–31.

4. James W. Pohl and Stephen L. Hardin, "The Military History of the Texas Revolution: An Overview," *Southwestern Historical Quarterly* 89 (January, 1986): 269–308 is an excellent study of military matters. Paul D. Lack, *The Texas Revolutionary Experience: A Political and Social History, 1835–36* (College Station: Texas A&M University Press, 1992) addresses military developments as well as social and political ones. See also Paul D. Lack, "Slavery and the Texas Revolution," *Southwestern Historical Quarterly* 89 (October, 1985): 181–202. Alwyn Barr, *Texans in Revolt: The Battle for San Antonio, 1835* (Austin: University of Texas Press, 1990) is a solid study of an important early revolutionary encounter. Also informative is Jakie L. Pruett and

Everett B. Cole, Sr., *Goliad Massacre: A Tragedy of the Texas Revolution* (Austin: Eakin, 1985). Archie P. McDonald provides an interesting analysis in "A Lusty Breed: The Military in Early Texas," *Military History of Texas and the Southwest* 9 (no. 3, 1971): 227-39.

5. All biographies of Houston discuss the battle of San Jacinto. For examples, see Marquis James, *The Raven: A Biography of Sam Houston* (Indianapolis: Bobbs, Merrill, 1929); and Llerena Friend, *Sam Houston: The Great Designer* (Austin: University of Texas Press, 1954). For a brief discussion, see James W. Pohl, *The Battle of San Jacinto* (Austin: Texas State Historical Assoc., 1989). An earlier study is Frank X. Tolbert, *The Day of San Jacinto* (New York: McGraw-Hill, 1959).

6. Tom H. Wells, *Commodore Moore and the Texas Navy* (Austin: University of Texas Press, 1960); Jim Dan Hill, *The Texas Navy* (Chicago: University of Chicago Press, 1937).

7. The most thorough studies of the state's military during the era of the Texas Republic are two works by Joseph Milton Nance: *After San Jacinto: The Texas-Mexican Frontier, 1836-41* (Austin: University of Texas Press, 1963); and *Attack and Counterattack: The Texas-Mexican Frontier, 1842* (Austin: University of Texas Press, 1964). See also Sam W. Haynes, *Soldiers of Misfortune: The Somervell and Mier Expeditions* (Austin: University of Texas Press, 1990); Gerald S. Pierce, "The Army of the Texas Republic, 1836-45" (Ph.D. dissertation, University of Mississippi, 1963); and the popular treatment by John E. Weems and Jane Weems, *Dream of Empire: A Human History of the Republic of Texas, 1836-46* (New York: Simon and Schuster, 1971).

8. A short introduction to the flamboyant Rangers is Ben Proctor, "The Texas Rangers: An Overview," in Proctor and McDonald, eds., *The Texas Heritage*, pp. 119-31. Covering the 1830s to the 1930s is Walter P. Webb, *The Texas Rangers: A Century of Frontier Defense* (Boston: Houghton Mifflin, 1935; 2nd ed., Austin: University of Texas Press, 1965). Rounding out Webb's work is Ben Proctor, *Just One Riot: Episodes of Texas Rangers and Rebels* (College Station: Texas A&M University Press, 1992). Sample studies of individual Rangers are James K. Greer, *Colonel Jack Hays* (New York: Dutton, 1952; rev. ed., College Station: Texas A&M University Press, 1987); Dora Neill Raymond, *Captain Lee Hall of Texas* (Norman: University of Oklahoma Press, 1940); and Harold J. Weiss, Jr., "'Yours to Command': Captain William J. 'Bill' McDonald and the Panhandle Rangers of Texas" (Ph.D. dissertation, Indiana University, 1980), pp. 44-47.

9. On Terry's unit see C. C. Jeffries, "The Character of Terry's Texas Rangers," *Southwestern Historical Quarterly* 64 (April, 1961): 454-62. For John Bell Hood's command, see Harold B. Simpson, *Hood's Texas Brigade, Lee's Grenadier Guard* (Waco: Texian Press, 1970). Other officers are covered in Jerry Thompson, *Henry Hopkins Sibley: Confederate General of the West* (Natchitoches, La.: Northwestern State University Press, 1987); Judith Ann Benner, *Sul Ross: Soldier, Statesman, Educator* (College Station: Texas A&M University Press, 1983); Norman D. Brown, ed., *One of Cleburne's Command: The Civil War Reminiscences and Diary of Captain Samuel T. Foster, Granbury's Texas Brigade, CSA* (Austin: University of Texas Press, 1980); Norman D. Brown, ed., *Journey to Pleasant Hill: The Civil War Letters of Captain Elijah P. Petty, Walker's Texas Division, CSA* (San Antonio: University of Texas/Institute of Texas Cultures, 1982); and Charles P. Roland, *Albert Sidney Johnston, Soldier of Three Republics* (Austin: University of Texas Press, 1964). For less conventional soldiering see Anne J.

Bailey, *Between the Enemy and Texas: Parsons's Texas Cavalry in the Civil War* (Fort Worth: Texas Christian University Press, 1989).

10. Randolph B. Campbell, *An Empire for Slavery: The Peculiar Institution in Texas* (Baton Rouge: Louisiana State University Press, 1989), pp. 1–2, 252–59; John Hope Franklin, *The Militant South, 1800–61* (Cambridge: Harvard University Press, 1961).

11. See, for example, Rollin G. Osterweis, *Romance and Nationalism in the Old South* (New Haven: Yale University Press, 1949); William R. Taylor, *Cavalier and Yankee: The Old South and American National Character* (New York: George Braziller, 1961); W. J. Cash, *The Mind of the South* (New York: Knopf, 1941); Bertram Wyatt-Brown, *Southern Honor* (New York: Oxford University Press, 1982); James C. Bonner, "The Historical Basis of Southern Military Tradition," *Georgia Review* 9 (Spring, 1955): 74–85, 90–91; and particularly Marcus Cunliffe, *Soldiers and Civilians: The Martial Spirit in America, 1785–1865* (New York: Free Press, 1968), pp. 337–42, 372–73, 380, 402. A tantalizing prospect for publication is the lectures of Russell F. Weigley, "The New Relevance of Southern Chivalry: The South and the Problem of the Control of War," one of the Walter Lynwood Fleming Lectures given at Louisiana State University in 1986. Refer to Burl Noggle, *The Fleming Lectures, 1937–90* (Baton Rouge: Louisiana State University Press, 1992), pp. 51, 82–83.

12. Robert E. May, "Dixie's Martial Image: A Continuing Historiographical Enigma," *Historian* 40 (February, 1978): 213–34, quotation on p. 213.

13. Broad overviews of the issue are found in Richard M. Brown, *Strain of Violence: Historical Studies of American Violence and Vigilantism* (New York: Oxford University Press, 1975); and Richard Slotkin, *Regeneration through Violence: The Mythology of the American Frontier, 1600–1860* (Middletown, Conn.: Wesleyan University Press, 1973). See also Robert R. Dykstra, *The Cattle Towns* (New York: Knopf, 1968), pp. 112–48; and W. Eugene Hollon, *Frontier Violence: Another Look* (New York: Oxford University Press, 1974). Focusing on Texas is Fehrenbach, *Seven Keys to Texas*, chap. 2, "The Frontier."

14. A summary is given in Bernard C. Nalty, *Strength for the Fight: A History of Black Americans in the Military* (New York: Free Press, 1986), pp. 50–62, 87–97; John D. Weaver, *The Brownsville Raid* (New York: Norton, 1970); and Robert V. Haynes, *A Night of Violence: The Houston Riot of 1917* (Baton Rouge: Louisiana State University Press, 1976).

15. An example of research into military families is Edward M. Coffman, *The Old Army: A Portrait of the American Army in Peacetime, 1784–1898* (New York: Oxford University Press, 1986), pp. 104–36, 287–327. For the "new military history," see Edward M. Coffman, "The New American Military History," *Military Affairs* 48 (January, 1984): 1–5; and Peter Karsten, "The New Military History: A Map of the Territory, Explored and Unexplored," *American Quarterly* 36 (Summer, 1984): 389–418.

16. An overview on the breadth of research is Michael L. Tate, "The Multi-Purpose Army on the Frontier: A Call for Further Research," in Ronald Lora, ed., *The American West: Essays in Honor of W. Eugene Hollon* (Toledo: University of Toledo, 1980), pp. 171–208.

17. Eric Morris, *Salerno* (New York: Stein and Day, 1983), p. 33.

18. *A Pictorial History of the Thirty-sixth "Texas" Infantry Division* (Austin: Thirty-sixth Division Association, n.d.), unpaged; Martin Blumenson, *Bloody River: The Real*

Tragedy of the Rapido (Boston: Houghton Mifflin, 1970).

19. Fred L. Walker, "The Thirty-sixth Was a Great Fighting Division," *Southwestern Historical Quarterly* 72 (July, 1968): 42, 43.

20. Martin Blumenson, *Mark Clark* (New York: Congdon and Weed, 1984), pp. 168–69, 255–56. See also Roger J. Spiller, "Crossing the Rapido," in Roger J. Spiller, ed., *Combined Arms in Battle since 1939* (Fort Leavenworth, Kan.: U.S. Army Command and General Staff College Press, 1992), pp. 221–29.

21. Robert Kemble, *The Image of the Army Officer in America* (Westport, Conn.: Greenwood Press, 1973), p. 192.

22. Richard Holmes, *Acts of War: Behavior of Men in Battle* (New York: Free Press, 1985), p. 68.

23. Ron Kovic, *Born on the Fourth of July* (New York: McGraw-Hill, 1976), p. 61.

24. Quoted in Holmes, *Acts of War*, p. 69.

25. Guenter Lewy, *America in Vietnam* (New York: Oxford University Press, 1978), p. 330.

26. E. B. Potter, *Nimitz* (Annapolis, Md.: Naval Institute Press, 1976); Ronald L. Lane, *Rudder's Rangers* (Manassas, Va.: Ranger Associates, 1979); Charles H. Taylor, *Omaha Beachhead* (Washington, D.C.: War Department Historical Division, 1946).

27. Thomas T. Smith, "Fort Inge and Texas Frontier Economy, 1849–69," *Military History of the Southwest* 21 (Fall, 1991): 135–56; Robert W. Frazer, *Forts of the West* (Norman: University of Oklahoma Press, 1965), pp. 139–64; Robert Wooster, *Soldiers, Sutlers, and Settlers: Garrison Life on the Texas Frontier* (College Station: Texas A&M University Press, 1987). In his bibliographic essay (pp. 217–31), Wooster discusses the many individual works on Texas forts.

28. An overview is Ann Markusen et al., *The Rise of the Gunbelt: The Military Remapping of Industrial America* (New York: Oxford University Press, 1992). See also Kenneth B. Ragsdale, *Wings over the Mexican Border: Pioneer Military Aviation in the Big Bend* (Austin: University of Texas Press, 1985); David R. Johnson, "The Failed Experiment: Military Aviation and Urban Development in San Antonio, 1910–40," in Roger W. Lotchin, ed., *The Martial Metropolis: U.S. Cities in War and Peace* (New York: Praeger, 1984), pp. 89–108; Barney M. Giles, "Early Military Aviation Activities in Texas," *Southwestern Historical Quarterly* 54 (October, 1950): 143–58; Gilbert S. Guinn, "A Different Frontier: Aviation, the Army Air Forces, and the Evolution of the Sunshine Belt," *Aerospace Historian* 29 (March, 1982): 34–35; Richard M. Bernard and Bradley R. Rice, eds., *Sunbelt Cities: Growth and Politics since World War II* (Austin: University of Texas Press, 1985); and especially Robert B. Fairbanks, "Dallas in the 1940s: The Challenges and Opportunities of Defense Mobilization," in Char Miller and Heywood Sanders, *Urban Texas: Politics and Development* (College Station: Texas A&M University Press, 1990), pp. 141–53.

29. For Texas contributions and losses in the world wars, see Seymour V. Connor, *Texas: A History* (Arlington Heights, Ill.: AHM Pub. Corp., 1971), pp. 311–14, 344–45; Rupert N. Richardson et al., *Texas: The Lone Star State* (3rd ed., Englewood Cliffs, N.J.: Prentice-Hall, 1970), pp. 315, 361–63; and Fehrenbach, *Lone Star*, pp. 643–44, 653–54. See also James W. Lee, ed., *1941: Texas Goes to War* (Denton: University of North Texas Press, 1991); and Char Miller, "Sunbelt Texas," in Buenger and Calvert, eds., *Texas through Time*, p. 295. For the federal government's toll of service deaths in World War II, consult Office of the Adjutant General, U.S. Army, *Army Battle Casualties*

and Nonbattle Deaths in World War II: Final Report (Washington, D.C.: U.S. War Department, 1946), p. 118.

30. Fred A. Daugherty and Pendleton Woods, "Oklahoma's Military Tradition," *Chronicles of Oklahoma* 57 (Winter, 1979–80): 427–45. Virginia has many active and former military installations, including the formidable Norfolk naval base, the U.S. Marine Corps facilities and schools at Quantico, and army posts such as Fort Monroe, Fort Belvoir, and Fort Eustis. Famous martial Virginians fill a gallery of their own: "Light Horse" Harry Lee, George Washington, Zachary Taylor, Winfield Scott, Robert E. Lee, Jeb Stuart, Jubal Early, Thomas J. Jackson, A. P. Hill, Joseph E. Johnston, Lewis "Chesty" Puller, and A. A. Vandegrift, among others. Battles in Virginia belong in their own category: Yorktown, First Bull Run, Second Bull Run, Richmond, Fredericksburg, Chancellorsville, the Wilderness, Cold Harbor, Petersburg, and Appomattox are among them. Virginia still maintains the Virginia Military Institute (established in 1839) as a military college. New York hosts the U.S. Military Academy at West Point and Fort Drum as well as the Brooklyn Navy Yard, Fort Hamilton, and the Brooklyn Army Terminal, among other bases. Prominent martial New Yorkers include Henry W. Halleck, Emory Upton, Evans Carlson, and James Gavin. Battles in New York include Saratoga, White Plains, Fort Ticonderoga, Stony Point, and Long Island in the American Revolution and the northern campaigns during the War of 1812.

31. For Texas A&M's contributions and activities in World War II see Henry C. Dethloff, *A Centennial History of Texas A&M University, 1876–1976* (College Station: Texas A&M University Press, 1975), pp. 450–75, especially 450. For LSU's claim, see *Oral History in Louisiana* 1 (Fall, 1992): 8; and Jack Fiser, "LSU Goes to War," *LSU Magazine* 68 (Spring, 1992): 23.

32. Donald E. Chipman, *Spanish Texas, 1519–1821* (Austin: University of Texas Press, 1992), pp. 242–59.

33. The Spanish encountered numerous difficulties as they established distant outposts in the New World. See Max L. Moorhead, *The Presidio: The Bastion of the Borderlands* (Norman: University of Oklahoma Press, 1975); and Odie B. Faulk, "The Presidio: Fortress or Farce?" in David J. Weber, ed., *New Spain's Far Northern Frontier: Essays on Spain in the American West, 1540–1821* (Albuquerque: University of New Mexico Press, 1979), pp. 67–76.

34. Chipman, *Spanish Texas*, p. 250; Arnoldo De León, *They Called Them Greasers: Anglo Attitudes toward Mexicans in Texas, 1821–1900* (Austin: University of Texas Press, 1983); David Montejano, *Anglos and Mexicans in the Making of Texas, 1836–1936* (Austin: University of Texas Press, 1987).

Chapter 1

1. This chapter is a revised version of Paul Andrew Hutton's introduction to Susan P. Schoelwer, *Alamo Images: Changing Perceptions of a Texas Experience* (Dallas: DeGolyer Library and Southern Methodist University Press, 1985). The author and the editor wish to thank the DeGolyer Library of Southern Methodist University for its permission to publish this revised essay.

Walter Lord, in *A Time to Stand* (New York: Harper, 1961), places the battle within a broader, national context, unlike many popularized accounts. Nevertheless, his documentation is hard to follow and the book has not satisfied scholars. One of the few academic works is Amelia W. Williams, "A Critical Study of the Siege of the Alamo and of the Personnel of Its Defenders" (Ph.D. dissertation, University of Texas, 1931). Although long considered the standard academic reference on the battle, it has numerous deficiencies. Parts of Williams's work were published in *Southwestern Historical Quarterly* 36 (April, 1933): 251–87; and *Southwestern Historical Quarterly* 37 (July, 1933): 1–44, (October, 1933): 79–115, (January, 1934): 157–84, (April, 1934): 237–312. For a brief modern summary of the battle see Paul Andrew Hutton, "The Alamo: An American Epic," *American History Illustrated* 20 (March, 1986): 12–37; and for the war see James W. Pohl and Stephen L. Hardin, "The Military History of the Texas Revolution: An Overview," *Southwestern Historical Quarterly* 89 (January, 1986): 269–308. See also John Myers, *The Alamo* (New York: Dutton, 1948), who focuses on personalities to present a heroic, traditional version of the story. Myers's book has been reprinted several times in paperback. See also Lon Tinkle, *Thirteen Days to Glory* (New York: McGraw-Hill, 1958), who emphasizes drama over analysis and scholarship; and the stridently revisionist history by Jeff Long, *Duel of Eagles: The Mexican and U.S. Fight for the Alamo* (New York: Morrow, 1990).

2. San Felipe *Telegraph and Texas Register,* March 24, 1836.

3. John Tower, ed., "A Nacogdoches Resolution on the Storming of the Alamo," *Southwestern Historical Quarterly* 78 (January, 1975): 303–306.

4. Sam W. Haynes, *Soldiers of Misfortune: The Somervell and Mier Expeditions* (Austin: University of Texas Press, 1990).

5. Martha Anne Turner, *William Barret Travis: His Sword and His Pen* (Waco: Texian Press, 1972), p. 230. See also Archie P. McDonald, *Travis* (Austin: Jenkins Pub. Co., 1976).

6. Jack Jackson, *Los Tejanos: The True Story of Juan Seguin and the Texas-Mexicans during the Rising of the Lone Star* (Stamford, Conn.: Fantagraphics Books, 1982). See also Jesús F. de la Teja, ed., *A Revolution Remembered: The Memoirs and Selected Correspondence of Juan N. Seguin* (Austin: State House Press, 1991).

7. Paul G. Levine, "Remember the Alamo?" *American Film* 7 (January, 1982): 47–48; *Dallas Morning News,* January 26, 1982.

8. Reuben M. Potter, *The Fall of the Alamo: A Reminiscence of the Revolution in Texas* (San Antonio: Herald Steam Press, 1860); R. M. Potter, "The Fall of the Alamo," *Magazine of American History* 2 (January, 1878).

9. Travis quoted in Lord, *A Time to Stand,* p. 142.

10. Quoted in *Lubbock Avalance-Journal,* September 8, 1979.

11. Ibid.

12. *Dallas Morning News,* September 7, 1979.

13. Bryan *Eagle,* September 8, 1979. See also *Phoenix Gazette,* September 10, 1979; *Arizona Republic,* September 8, 1979; *San Antonio News,* September 7, 1979; *Houston Chronicle,* September 18, 1979; *Houston Chronicle,* September 23, 1979; and *Houston Post,* September 7, 1979.

14. Tyler *Courier-Times Telegraph,* September 7, 1979; *Dallas Morning News,* September 7, 1979.

15. J. Frank Dobie, "The Line That Travis Drew," in J. Frank Dobie, Mody C. Boatright, and Harry H. Ransom, eds., *In the Shadow of History* (Dallas: Texas Folklore Society, 1939), p. 16.

16. William P. Zuber, "An Escape from the Alamo," *Texas Almanac for 1873*

(Galveston: Galveston News Printing Co., [1872]), pp. 80-85; Anna J. H. Pennybacker, *History of Texas for Schools* (Tyler, Tex.: Privately printed, 1888; rev. ed., Austin: by the author, 1924).

17. Clarence Wharton, *The Lone Star State: A School History* (Dallas: Southern Pub. Co., 1932); Dobie, "The Line That Travis Drew," p. 13.

18. R. B. Blake, "A Vindication of Rose and His Story," in Dobie, Boatright, and Ransom, eds., *In the Shadow of History*, p. 39.

19. Lord, *A Time to Stand*, pp. 201-204.

20. Dobie, "The Line That Travis Drew," p. 20.

21. John H. Jenkins, ed., "Did Davy Crockett Survive the Alamo?" *Texana* 1 (Summer, 1963): 287; Theodore Roosevelt, *Hero Tales from American History* (1895; New York: Century Co., 1908), pp. 171-81.

22. Edward S. Ellis, *The Life of Colonel David Crockett* (Philadelphia: Porter and Coates, 1884), p. 260.

23. Lord, *A Time to Stand*, pp. 206-207.

24. José Enrique de la Peña, *With Santa Anna in Texas: A Personal Narrative of the Revolution*, trans. Carmen Perry (College Station: Texas A&M University Press, 1975), p. 53.

25. *Denver Post*, October 24, 1975; *Jackson* [Tennessee] *Sun*, September 23, 1975.

26. *People*, October 13, 1975, p. 41; *Jackson* [Tennessee] *Sun*, September 23, 1975; *San Antonio Express*, April 4, 1976; *El Paso Times*, September 10, 1975.

27. Dan Kilgore, *How Did Davy Die?* (College Station: Texas A&M University Press, 1978). See also Dan Kilgore, "Why Davy Didn't Die," in Michael A. Lofaro and Joe Cummings, eds., *Crockett at Two Hundred: New Perspectives on the Man and the Myth* (Knoxville: University of Tennessee Press, 1989), pp. 7-19.

28. *Corpus Christi Times* information quoted in "Kent Biffle's Texana," *Dallas Morning News*, January 13, 1985. See also Kevin R. Young, "Facts and Footnotes," *Goliad Texan-Express*, February 4, 1987.

29. *Dallas Morning News*, January 13, 1985. See also *Dallas Times Herald*, November 24, 1985.

30. Eric von Schmidt, "How is the Alamo Remembered?" *Smithsonian* 16 (March, 1986): 54-67; Susan Prendergast Schoelwer with Tom W. Glaser, *Alamo Images: Changing Perceptions of a Texas Experience* (Dallas: DeGolyer Library and Southern Methodist University Press, 1985); James C. Kelly and Frederick S. Voss, *Davy Crockett: Gentleman from the Cane. An Exhibition Commemorating Crockett's Life and Legend on the 200th Anniversary of His Birth* (Washington and Nashville: Smithsonian Institution and Tennessee State Museum, 1986).

31. Frank Thompson, *Alamo Movies* (East Berlin, Penn.: Old Mill Books, 1991), pp. 45, 91-109, 120. For more on Alamo films, see Paul Andrew Hutton, "The Celluloid Alamo," *Arizona and the West* 28 (Spring, 1986): 5-22; Don Graham, "Remembering the Alamo: The Story of the Texas Revolution in Popular Culture," *Southwestern Historical Quarterly* 79 (July, 1985): 35-66; and Brian Huberman and Ed Hugetz, "Fabled Facade," *Southwest Media Review* 3 (Spring, 1985): 30-41.

32. *A Narrative of the Life of David Crockett of the State of Tennessee* (Lincoln: University of Nebraska Press, 1987); James A. Shackford and Stanley J. Folmsbee, eds., *A Narrative of the Life of David Crockett of the State of Tennessee by David Crockett* (Knoxville: University of Tennessee Press, 1987); Virgil E. Baugh, *Rendezvous at the*

Alamo: Highlights in the Lives of Bowie, Crockett, and Travis (Lincoln: University of Nebraska Press, 1986); Richard Boyd Hauck, *David Crockett: A Handbook* (Lincoln: University of Nebraska Press, 1986); James Atkins Shackford, *David Crockett: The Man and the Legend* (Chapel Hill: University of North Carolina Press, 1986); James Wakefield Burke, *David Crockett: The Man behind the Myth* (Austin: Eakin, 1984); Gary L. Foreman, *Crockett: The Gentleman from the Cane* (Dallas: Taylor Pub. Co., 1986); Walter Blair, *Davy Crockett: Legendary Frontier Hero* (Springfield, Ill.: Lincoln-Herndon Press, 1986).

33. Michael A. Lofaro, ed., *Davy Crockett: The Man, the Legend, the Legacy, 1786–1986* (Knoxville: University of Tennessee Press, 1985); *Knoxville Journal,* April 17, 19, 1986.

34. Bob Boyd, *The Texas Revolution: A Day-by-Day Account* (San Angelo: San Angelo Standard, 1986), p. 54; *Wall Street Journal,* July 10, 1986.

35. Paul Andrew Hutton, "The Alamo: An American Epic," *American History Illustrated* 20 (March, 1986): 12–37; Paul Andrew Hutton, "Davy Crockett: Still King of the Wild Frontier," *Texas Monthly* 14 (November, 1986): 122–30, 244–48.

36. "The Roar of the Crowd," *Texas Monthly* 15 (January, 1987): 10.

37. Unpublished letters to *Texas Monthly* and to the author in author's possession. See also *USA Today,* November 14, 1986; *Arkansas Gazette,* November 9, 1986; *Albuquerque Journal,* December 21, 1986; and *El Paso Times,* December 22, 1986. For two scholarly views of the Alamo myth see David J. Weber, *Myth and the History of the Hispanic Southwest* (Albuquerque: University of New Mexico Press, 1988), pp. 133–51; and Edward Tabor Linenthal, *Sacred Ground: Americans and Their Battlefields* (Urbana: University of Illinois Press, 1991), pp. 53–86. See also David Montejano, *Anglos and Mexicans in the Making of Texas, 1836–1986* (Austin: University of Texas Press, 1987), pp. 223–25, 231, 305–306.

38. *Dallas Morning News,* November 9, 1986.

Chapter 2

1. There have been several notable contributions to the literature of the Texas Revolution since this paper was delivered in 1986, though none of these has fully met the challenge laid down by the late John H. Jenkins. Two of the most important—though strikingly different in form and content—are Paul D. Lack, *The Texas Revolutionary Experience: A Political and Social History, 1835–36* (College Station: Texas A&M University Press, 1992); and Jeff Long, *Duel of Eagles: The Mexican and U.S. Fight for the Alamo* (New York: Morrow, 1990). Both of these books, however, overemphasize the role of Anglo-American racism in causing, or in guiding the development of, the Texas Revolution.

Their conclusions are brought into question, moreover, by three other important recent studies of the rebellion: Andreas V. Reichstein, *Rise of the Lone Star: The Making of Texas,* trans. Jeanne R. Willson (College Station: Texas A&M University Press, 1989), which explicitly rejects ethnic animosity as a major factor in fomenting the uprising; Alwyn Barr, *Texans in Revolt: The Battle for San Antonio, 1835* (Austin: University of Texas Press, 1990), which shows Anglo and native Mexican military cooperation to be far more important in the early phases of the rebellion than Long suggests; and *A Revolution Remembered: The Memoirs and Selected Correspondence of Juan N.*

Seguín, ed. Jesús F. de la Teja (Austin: State House Press, 1991), which lends very little support to Lack's assertion that the Texas Revolution "had become a race war" by 1836.

For Jenkins's challenge, see John H. Jenkins, "The Texas Revolution: The Need for Solid Research and a New Interpretation," an address delivered at the Annual Meeting of the Texas State Historical Association, Daughters of the Republic of Texas Library, San Antonio, March 10, 1979, p. 2.

The author wishes to thank Mr. Jenkins for supplying a typescript of his speech and for his words of encouragement during the preparation of this essay. Thanks are also due to David J. Weber and Felix D. Almaráz, Jr., for their comments on earlier versions of the work and to Joseph P. Hobbs and John David Smith, my colleagues at North Carolina State University, for their critical reading of the manuscript.

2. Jenkins, "The Texas Revolution," p. 6. For the most extensive collection of documents, see John H. Jenkins, ed., *Papers of the Texas Revolution,* 10 vols. (Austin: Presidial Press, 1973).

3. Jenkins, "The Texas Revolution," pp. 6-7. See also John H. Jenkins, *Basic Texas Books: An Annotated Bibliography of Selected Works for a Research Library* (Austin: Jenkins Pub. Co., 1983), pp. 273-74.

4. Jenkins, "The Texas Revolution"; David J. Weber, "Mexico's Far Northern Frontier, 1821-54: Historiography Askew," *Western Historical Quarterly* 7 (July, 1976): 279-93.

5. David J. Weber, *The Mexican Frontier, 1821-46: The American Southwest under Mexico* (Albuquerque: University of New Mexico Press, 1982).

6. Archie P. McDonald, *Travis* (Austin: Jenkins Pub. Co., 1976); Dan Kilgore, *How Did Davy Die?* (College Station: Texas A&M University Press, 1978).

7. Margaret Swett Henson, *Juan Davis Bradburn: A Reappraisal of the Mexican Commander of Anahuac* (College Station: Texas A&M University Press, 1982).

8. David Hackett Fischer, *Historians' Fallacies: Toward a Logic of Historical Thought* (New York: Harper, 1970), pp. 172-75.

9. Malcolm D. McLean, *Papers Concerning Robertson's Colony in Texas,* 13 vols. to date (Fort Worth: Texas Christian University Press [vols. 1-3], 1974-76; and Arlington: University of Texas at Arlington Press [intro. vol. and vols. 4-12], 1977-86), vol. 10, pp. 65-66.

10. Ibid., vol. 11, p. 60. For further comments by McLean on the causes of the Revolution, see ibid., vol. 10, p. 80; and ibid., vol. 11, pp. 51, 59-60.

11. Arnoldo De León, *They Called Them Greasers: Anglo Attitudes toward Mexicans in Texas, 1821-1900* (Austin: University of Texas Press, 1983), p. 12.

12. Ibid. (De León's emphasis.)

13. Ibid., p. 13.

14. Walter Nugent, "Western History: Stocktakings and New Crops," review of Michael P. Malone, ed., *Historians and the American West* (Lincoln: University of Nebraska Press, 1983), in *Reviews in American History* 13 (September, 1985): 325.

15. Weber's and De León's analyses of the role of negative attitudes in bringing about conflict have never been identical. De León's approach is psychohistorical: he claims that westward-moving Anglos "felt a compelling need to control all that was beastly—sexuality, vice, nature, and colored peoples." His emphasis is on interpersonal relations, on "the deep-seated resentment whites felt toward darker-skinned people

whenever they came into contact with them" and on "the motivating force of white supremacy" that he believes traditional histories of the Texas Revolution have overlooked (De León, *They Called Them Greasers*, pp. 1, 12). Weber, on the other hand, does not disregard racism as a factor but has been less inclined than De León to see interpersonal conflict as an automatic consequence of interracial contact. He has been more attentive to what might be called "public opinion" in the respective Anglo-American and Mexican societies. Weber argued in the early 1970s that although the "infiltration" of Americans into Mexico convinced many frontier Mexicans "that it was possible to live and work with Yankees," the circumstances of the meeting of the two peoples on the north Mexican frontier nevertheless "contributed to shaping stereotypes in Mexico and the United States which made war between the two nations nearly unavoidable by 1846" (David J. Weber, ed., *Foreigners in Their Native Land: Historical Roots of the Mexican Americans* [Albuquerque: University of New Mexico Press, 1973], pp. 51–53, 59–61).

16. Arnoldo De León, "White Racial Attitudes toward Mexicanos in Texas, 1821–1900" (Ph.D. dissertation, Texas Christian University, 1974), p. 32, n. 9. De León may be splitting hairs in this criticism, for Weber certainly acknowledged the relevance of American racism and conceded that Anglo-Americans added a distaste for racial mixture to their antipathy toward Spain's heirs in the New World. "Especially evident to Mexicans," he noted, "was the Americans' [negative] attitude toward people of color—Indians and Negroes" (Weber, *Foreigners in Their Native Land*, pp. 58–61). See also David J. Weber, "'Scarce More Than Apes': Historical Roots of Anglo-American Stereotypes of Mexicans in the Border Region," in *New Spain's Northern Frontier: Essays on Spain in the American West, 1540–1821*, ed. David J. Weber (Albuquerque: University of New Mexico Press, 1979), pp. 298–304.

Some scholars, who share Weber's appreciation of the strength of the Black Legend as well as his assumption that the negative preconceptions carried by Anglo-Americans into Mexico helped bring about conflict, have argued that the *Leyenda Negra* itself had racial overtones. See Raymund A. Paredes, "The Origins of Anti-Mexican Sentiment in the United States," *New Scholar* 6 (1977): 139–65; and Philip Anthony Hernandez, "The Other North Americans: The American Image of Mexico and Mexicans, 1550–1850" (Ph.D. dissertation, University of California at Berkeley, 1974), pp. 1–3, 35–36, 134.

Interestingly, although Weber gives even less attention to the role of racism in *The Mexican Frontier* (1982) than in his writings of the 1970s, De León's recent work retains intact the basic conclusions of his dissertation. He maintains that the anti-Mexican prejudice that guided white actions was heavily racial, that it was present at initial contact and remained a constant source of friction, and that it was the chief underlying cause of the Texas revolt against Mexico. See Arnoldo De León, *The Tejano Community, 1836–1900* (Albuquerque: University of New Mexico Press, 1982); and De León, *They Called Them Greasers*, especially pp. 1–23.

17. Paredes, "Origins of Anti-Mexican Sentiment," p. 145.

18. David Thomas Leary, "The Attitudes of Certain United States Citizens toward Mexico, 1821–46" (Ph.D. dissertation, University of Southern California, 1970), pp. 42–43.

19. Edward Thornton Tayloe, *Mexico, 1825–28: The Journal and Correspondence of Edward Thornton Tayloe*, ed. C. Harvey Gardiner (Chapel Hill: University of North

Carolina Press, 1959), p. 69.

20. Weber, *Foreigners in Their Native Land,* p. 59.

21. Ibid., pp. 58–60. See also David J. Weber, "Stereotyping of Mexico's Far Northern Frontier," in *An Awakened Minority: The Mexican-Americans,* ed. Manuel P. Servín (2nd ed.; Beverly Hills, Calif.: Glencoe Press, 1974), pp. 22–23.

22. In addition to the works already cited by Weber, De León, Paredes, Hernandez, and Leary, see the following: Cecil Robinson, *Mexico and the Hispanic Southwest in American Literature,* a revised edition of *With the Ears of Strangers: The Mexican in American Literature,* 1963 (Tucson: University of Arizona Press, 1977); and Norman David Smith, "Stereotypical Enemies: American Frontiersmen and Mexican Caricatures in the Literature of an Expanding White Nation" (Ph.D. dissertation, Oklahoma State University, 1975). See also James E. Crisp, "Anglo-Texan Attitudes toward the Mexican, 1821–1845" (Ph.D. dissertation, Yale University, 1976).

23. Glenda Riley, *Women and Indians on the Frontier: 1825–1915* (Albuquerque: University of New Mexico Press, 1984); Sandra L. Myres, *Westering Women and the Frontier Experience, 1800–1915* (Albuquerque: University of New Mexico Press, 1982); Sandra L. Myres, "Mexican Americans and Westering Anglos: A Feminine Perspective," *New Mexico Historical Review* 57 (October, 1982): 317–33.

24. Riley, *Women and Indians,* p. 92.

25. Ibid., especially chap. 6, "The Selective Nature of Frontierswomen's Sympathies." Riley's evidence shows that both Mormons and Panamanian Indians continued to be the targets of white women's fear and loathing, largely because "there was seldom little more than superficial contact" between them and these groups and therefore few actual experiences to offset rumor and stereotype (see pp. 229, 244). Inexplicably, Riley generalizes from the cases of the Mormons and Panamanian Indians that blacks, Orientals, and Mexicans also failed to receive the kind of sympathy and understanding shown by white women to Indians. Her book, however, contains no supporting evidence for (or even discussion of) these claims (see p. 205 and chapter 6, passim).

26. McLean, *Robertson's Colony,* vol. 5, p. 33. The process by which initial alienation from people of an unfamiliar culture may be supplanted by a more understanding and sympathetic point of view is outlined in *The Face of the Fox* (Chicago: Aldine Pub. Co., 1970), a study of white-Indian cross-cultural contact by anthropologist Frederick O. Gearing. What most often occurs at first is a distorted interpretation of an alien people's unintelligible social structure—a distortion expressed as alleged character flaws. Gearing's analysis of this phenomenon, which he labels "nondescription by the notion of character," has been applied to American views of Mexicans by Philip Hernandez ("Other North Americans," pp. 135ff.). In the cases of both the Fox Indians and the Mexicans, outsiders who have no actual knowledge or understanding of a people's thought and behavior are forced by their ignorance to report not what these people *are,* but what they are *not.* This "nondescription," in tandem with the characterization of behavior as vice or virtue in lieu of any explanation of its structure or function, produces a descriptive mode that is "certain to be empirically unassailable and powerfully comforting," even if its truth-value is zero. "Nondescription by notion of character" leads to the finding of the virtues which are *not* present; it is an explanatory device that is very likely to result in a negative image. Notes Gearing, it "seems certain to estrange" (see pp. 30–77). What is present but unnoted by Hernandez, in

both Gearing's theoretical model and among the Americans in Mexico, is evidence that a negative first impression is not necessarily the end of the story. Familiarity need not breed even deeper contempt.

"The opposite of being estranged," writes Gearing, "is to find the life of a people believable" (p. 109). Besides Stephen F. Austin and Edward Tayloe, a surprisingly large number of Americans, even in Texas, had the opportunity to learn something of the lives and values of their Hispanic hosts and countrymen and to find them less strange. This does not mean that profound cultural differences between Mexicans and Americans did not exist but that they did not inevitably produce discord. According to Gearing, the inability to see and understand genuine cultural differences may cause the observer to see great differences in character. But a careful observer's increasing familiarity with an alien people can lead to a sympathetic understanding of cultural variations and the discovery of a common humanity with these people (pp. 127–28).

David J. Weber, in *Foreigners in Their Native Land*, p. 60, has noticed that it was "often those Americans who had least contact with Mexicans [who] denounced them most virulently." Likewise, the greater the separation (measured not only in physical distance but also in language and social contacts) between the observer and the observed, the more likely it is that the descriptions will be guided by the special interests, cultural baggage, psychic needs, or ulterior motives of the observer. They will be less likely to reflect any familiarity with or concrete understanding of the people or things described.

27. Weber, "Stereotyping of Mexico's Far Northern Frontier," pp. 20–21, p. 25, n. 17. This charge against Poinsett and Tayloe is repeated in Weber, "'Scarce More Than Apes,'" pp. 297–98.

Weber acknowledges that Mexican females were an exception to the rule of the automatically negative image. He argues that in forming a positive image of the Mexican woman, "American males allowed their hormones to overcome their ethnocentrism" (see Weber, "'Scarce More Than Apes,'" p. 296). Space does not permit the discussion of this complex subject here.

28. Weber, "'Scarce More Than Apes,'" p. 298.

29. Tayloe, *Mexico*, pp. 53–55. It is important to keep in mind in interpreting the responses of both Tayloe and Poinsett that both men's works were written primarily from diary entries and, therefore, often reveal the growth and change of attitudes. Poinsett's change of attitudes toward Mexicans was similar to, though less drastic than, Tayloe's. See Joel Poinsett, *Notes on Mexico, Made in the Autumn of 1822* (Philadelphia: H. C. Carey and I. Lea, 1824; reprint ed., New York: Praeger, 1969), pp. 119–21, 178, 200–201.

Hernandez, "Other North Americans," pp. 191–98, notes that the perceptive observers Brantz Mayer and Madame Francis Calderón de la Barca also moderated considerably their negative first impressions of Mexicans after lengthy stays in Mexico. For evidence of a similar progression of views, see Bill Karras, ed., "First Impressions of Mexico, 1828, by Reuben Potter," *Southwestern Historical Quarterly* 79 (July, 1975): 55–68.

30. Tayloe, *Mexico*, pp. 69–71.
31. Ibid., pp. 97–100, 108.
32. Ibid., pp. 30, 48, 128, 154, 159–64.
33. See Richard Henry Dana, *Two Years before the Mast* (New York: Harper, 1840;

reprint ed., New York: Airmont Pub. Co., 1965), p. 53; James Ohio Pattie, *The Personal Narrative of James O. Pattie, of Kentucky*, ed. Timothy Flint (Cincinnati: John H. Wood, 1831; reprint ed., New York: Arno Press, 1973), pp. 41-42; and Weber's comment on Pattie in *Foreigners in Their Native Land*, p. 60.

34. Tayloe, *Mexico*, pp. 18, 25.

35. Ibid., p. 159.

36. See Rae Sherwood, *The Psychodynamics of Race: Vicious and Benign Spirals* (Atlantic Heights, N.J.: Humanities Press, 1980), pp. 9, 493, 498, 520-28, 556-57, 565; T. H. Breen and Stephen Innes, *"Myne Owne Ground": Race and Freedom on Virginia's Eastern Shore* (New York: Oxford University Press, 1980), pp. 23, 32-33; Fredrik Barth, ed., *Ethnic Groups and Boundaries: The Social Organization of Culture Difference* (London: Allen & Unwin, 1969), p. 15; and Pierre van den Berghe, *Race and Racism: A Comparative Perspective*, 2nd ed. (New York: John Wiley & Sons, 1978), p. xiii.

37. George M. Fredrickson, "Toward a Social Interpretation of the Development of American Racism," in *Key Issues in the Afro-American Experience*, ed. Nathan I. Huggins, Martin Kilson, and Daniel M. Fox, 2 vols. (New York: Harcourt Brace Jovanovich, 1971), vol. 1, pp. 240-49, 254. (Emphasis added.) For another version of this essay, see George M. Fredrickson, *The Arrogance of Race: Historical Perspectives on Slavery, Racism, and Social Inequality* (Middletown, Conn.: Wesleyan University Press, 1988). Some of the more important sociological treatises that lend support to Fredrickson's approach are Tamotsu Shibutani and Kian M. Kwan, *Ethnic Stratification: A Comparative Approach* (New York: Macmillan, 1965); Hubert M. Blalock, Jr., *Toward a Theory of Minority-Group Relations* (New York: John Wiley & Sons, 1967); John Rex, *Race Relations in Sociological Theory* (New York: Schocken Books, 1970); Robert Blauner, *Racial Oppression in America* (New York: Harper, 1972); William J. Wilson, *Power, Racism, and Privilege: Race Relations in Theoretical and Sociohistorical Perspectives* (New York: Macmillan, 1973); and Graham C. Kinlock, *The Dynamics of Race Relations: A Sociological Analysis* (New York: McGraw-Hill, 1974).

It should be noted that Arnoldo De León explicitly dissents from Fredrickson's "social" interpretation of the development of racism. To establish the decisive role of racial prejudice in Texas, he cites the works of a diverse group of scholars who attribute significantly more influence than does Fredrickson to deeply rooted cultural and psychological factors (see De León, *They Called Them Greasers*, pp. xi, 1-2, 107-108). These works include Richard Drinnon, *Facing West: The Metaphysics of Indian-Hating and Empire-Building* (Minneapolis: University of Minnesota Press, 1980); Ronald Sanders, *Lost Tribes and Promised Lands: The Origins of American Racism* (Boston: Little, Brown and Co., 1978); Thomas F. Gossett, *Race: The History of an Idea in America* (Dallas: Southern Methodist University Press, 1963); Ronald T. Takaki, *Iron Cages: Race and Culture in Nineteenth-Century America* (New York: Knopf, 1979); Gary B. Nash, *Red, White, and Black: The Peoples of Early America*, 2nd ed. (Englewood Cliffs, N.J.: Prentice-Hall, 1982); David Brion Davis, *The Problem of Slavery in Western Culture* (Ithaca: Cornell University Press, 1966); and Robert F. Berkhofer, Jr., *The White Man's Indian: Images of the American Indian from Columbus to the Present* (New York: Knopf, 1978).

What I find most questionable about De León's use of this literature is his attempt to offer such very general works as these in direct refutation of other scholars' conclusions (including my own) concerning racial attitudes and interethnic relations in pre-annexation Texas (see De León, *They Called Them Greasers*, pp. 1, 107).

I believe that there is more complexity to the role of racism in the westward movement of Anglo-Americans than De León's psychohistorical approach appears to acknowledge. For a contrasting view of manifest destiny ideology in particular and theories of racial inferiority in general, see Mario Barrera, *Race and Class in the Southwest: A Theory of Racial Inequality* (Notre Dame, Ind.: University of Notre Dame Press, 1979), pp. 12–18, 197–202. See also two superb articles by Reginald Horsman: "American Indian Policy and the Origins of Manifest Destiny," *University of Birmingham Historical Journal* 11 (December, 1968): 128–40; and "Scientific Racism and the American Indian in the Mid-Nineteenth Century," *American Quarterly* 27 (May, 1975): 152–68. On the inadequacy of the "culture-conflict" model to explain subordination of Hispanics, see also Albert Camarillo, *Chicanos in a Changing Society: From Mexican Pueblos to American Barrios in Santa Barbara and Southern California, 1848–1930* (Cambridge: Harvard University Press, 1979), p. 4.

38. See Thomas E. Sheridan, *Los Tucsonenses: The Mexican Community in Tucson, 1854–1941* (Tucson: University of Arizona Press, 1986); Rebecca McDowell Craver, *The Impact of Intimacy: Mexican-Anglo Intermarriage in New Mexico, 1821–46*, Southwestern Studies Monograph no. 66 (El Paso: Texas Western Press, 1982); Gilbert Miguel Hinojosa, *A Borderlands Town in Transition: Laredo, 1755–1870* (College Station: Texas A&M University Press, 1983); Arthur J. Rubel, *Across the Tracks: Mexican-Americans in a Texas City* (Austin: University of Texas Press, 1966); Leonard Pitt, *The Decline of the Californios: A Social History of the Spanish-Speaking Californians, 1846–1890* (Berkeley: University of California Press, 1970); and David J. Weber, *Foreigners in Their Native Land*.

Both Weber (pp. 58, 211–12) and Pitt (pp. 14, 123–29) describe Anglo-Mexican relations (in Texas and California, respectively) as a cultural conflict, in which Anglo racism and anti-Catholicism also played major roles. Yet both show that where Anglos were in the minority, they quickly sought a modus vivendi that included frequent intermarriage, at least nominal conversions to Catholicism, and the development of a "business elite" that transcended racial and ethnic barriers.

Such an elite apparently held sway for several decades in Laredo, where Hinojosa (pp. 68–70) found that "the complex relationship that developed between Anglo-Americans and Mexican Americans was often mutually beneficial and never outwardly hostile. In Laredo the coalitions that evolved were not principally ethnic; instead, they pitted the privileged, whether Anglo, European, or Mexican, against the poor." At least before the coming of the railroads in 1881, "interaction between Mexican Americans and Anglo-Americans was to a great extent characterized by cooperation, blending, and mixing." Significantly, Hinojosa contrasts Laredo's experience with that of Brownsville, where ethnic clashes resulted in armed conflict during the same period, and he notes the very different economic and demographic circumstances in the two cities. Sheridan (p. 33) offers a very similar explanation of the contrast between mercantile Tucson's atmosphere of "cordiality and respect" and the more exploitative and explosive mining districts of southern Arizona. Sheridan also implies that what he says explicitly with regard to findings of Mexican cultural "backwardness" holds for Anglo "racism" as well: researchers should recognize "that attitudes changed in response to social and economic opportunities, not vice versa" (pp. 232–33).

39. See Paul D. Lack, "Slavery and the Texas Revolution," *Southwestern Historical Quarterly* 89 (October, 1985): 181–202. Lack (p. 188) argues that "the approach of war was attended by more complaints about Mexican abolitionism and by heightened racial invective." He makes an excellent case for his thesis that Santa Anna's impending destruction of the federal system made many Anglo-Texans defensive of their peculiar institution of black slavery. But all of the quotations that he marshals to support his racial invective argument are from the desperate days of late February and early March, 1836. What seemed to be approaching at that time was not war but imminent defeat by Santa Anna's armies.

40. Margaret Swett Henson, "Tory Sentiment in Anglo-Texan Public Opinion, 1832–36," *Southwestern Historical Quarterly* 90 (July, 1986): 1–34.

41. Even aside from theoretical considerations regarding the primacy of attitudes and preconceptions versus specific circumstances in determining the character of ethnic relations, great care must be exercised to avoid such mundane methodological pitfalls as errors of logic, chronology, or unwarranted assumption. Even among careful and judicious historians such mistakes can occur, especially in the context of the nearly universal assumption of early and prevailing Anglo-Mexican hostility in Texas.

For example, Sandra L. Myres, in two studies of white female attitudes toward Mexicans (*Westering Women*, p. 75; and "Mexican Americans and Westering Anglos: A Feminine Perspective," *New Mexico Historical Review* 57 [October, 1982]: 319), quotes anti-Mexican remarks by Mary Austin Holley to illustrate negative preconceptions among Anglo-Texan women. But these comments, which she attributes to the first edition (Baltimore: Armstrong & Plaskitt, 1833) of Holley's *Texas*, are actually found only in the later version (Lexington, Ky.: J. Clarke & Co., 1836), which is a product of the immediate circumstances of the Texas Revolution. The earlier edition conveys a far more favorable impression of Mexicans. Moreover, in providing corroborating remarks hostile to Mexicans, Myres cites the reminiscences of three Texan women (all of whom lived far from the Mexican settlements), all written well after the notion of Mexican perversity had become an Anglo-Texan article of faith. The two more favorable estimates of Mexicans in contrast are, significantly, by female Anglos (Mary Maverick and Jane Cazneau) who lived close to and had numerous contacts with Mexicans.

The expectation of Mexican alienation upon contact with immigrating Americans, as well as vice versa, may have contributed to the apparent misreading of a document from the Texas Revolution by David J. Weber. In *The Mexican Frontier* (p. 254), Weber refers to the *tejanos*' evaluation of recently arrived Anglo aliens as "a worse than Savage set." However, a close reading of the substantiating letter (which is far from being clearly written or interpreted) suggests that the reference to the newcomers who are "polluting the country" is not to Anglos but to the centralist Mexican soldiers who have occupied San Antonio de Béxar! (See John J. Linn to James Kerr, July 30, 1835, in Jenkins, *Papers of the Texas Revolution*, vol. 1, pp. 288–89.) After reviewing an earlier version of this essay, Professor Weber graciously acknowledged his probable error in interpreting this letter.

The possibility of an alternative reading of this minor document echoes a similar variance of opinion concerning the meaning of a much more important (perhaps *the* most important) statement of prerevolutionary *tejano* sentiment: the *Representación dirijida por el ilustre ayuntamiento de la Ciudad de Béxar al honorable Congreso del Estado* of December, 1832. Weber's view is that the failure of the San Antonio *ayun-*

tamiento to explicitly endorse the demand for separate Texan statehood indicates a degree of separation and alienation of these *tejanos* from the Anglo-Texans who would dominate a separate state by their numbers (see Weber, *Mexican Frontier*, pp. 253–54; and David J. Weber, ed., *Troubles in Texas, 1832: A Tejano Viewpoint from San Antonio with a Translation and Facsimile*, trans. Conchita Hassell Winn and David J. Weber, DeGolyer Library Publication Series, vol. 1 [Dallas: DeGolyer Library and Southern Methodist University Press, 1983]). Another recent study of the *bejareños*, however, interprets this document as a "consonance of Tejano concerns with those of the Anglos" and an implication of the "goal of eventual independent statehood." See Jesús F. de la Teja and John Wheat, "Béxar: Profile of a Tejano Community, 1820–32," *Southwestern Historical Quarterly* 89 (July, 1985): 33–34.

42. De León, *They Called Them Greasers*, p. 13. George R. Woolfolk, who shares De León's disdain for the racist regimes that followed the Revolution in nineteenth-century Texas, has attempted to explain the apparent lack of racial cleavage in the early years of Anglo settlement. He suggests that the first arrivals from the United States in Hispanic Texas were refugees from a stifling, restrictive, racist Protestantism but that later immigrants came "freighted with the full weight of Protestant oriented cotton-slavery culture," seeking to reconstruct this oppressive system in their new home. See Woolfolk, *The Free Negro in Texas, 1800–60: A Study in Cultural Compromise* (Ann Arbor, Mich.: published for *The Journal of Mexican-American History* by University Microfilms International, 1976). Although there is undoubtedly some truth in both of these formulations, I believe that both De León's and Woolfolk's views are overly simplistic: both beg critical questions deserving of more sophisticated sociological analysis. Both, in a manner similar to the process of nondescription outlined by Frederick O. Gearing (above, see n. 27), label by *individual character traits* what are essentially different social and demographic situations.

43. De León, *They Called Them Greasers*, p. 13. See above, n. 14.

44. Lack, "Slavery and the Texas Revolution," pp. 188–96.

45. "Address of W. H. Jack," August 9, 1835, *The Papers of Mirabeau Buonaparte Lamar*, ed. Charles A. Gulick et al., 6 vols. (Austin: A. C. Baldwin & Sons, 1920–27), vol. 1, pp. 223–28; "Address of B. T. Archer," November 3, 1835, *Texas Republican* (Brazoria), November 14, 1835.

46. "Report of Committee on State and Judiciary," December 23, 1835, in H. P. N. Gammel, *The Laws of Texas, 1821–97*, 10 vols. (Austin: Gammel Book Co., 1898), vol. 1, pp. 643–44.

47. "Report of the Committee on Military Affairs," December 8, 1835, in *Official Correspondence of the Texas Revolution, 1835–36*, comp. William C. Binkley, 2 vols. (New York: Appleton-Century Co., 1936), vol. 1, pp. 166–68.

48. Stephen F. Austin to Senator L. F. Linn, May 4, 1836, *Papers of the Texas Revolution* 6: 160–164. Arnoldo De León incorrectly attributes this statement to a private letter written by Austin to his cousin Mary Austin Holley on August 21, 1835. (See De León, *They Called Them Greasers*, pp. 12, 110.) No such statement occurs in the 1835 letter. (See Jenkins, *Papers of the Texas Revolution* 1: 359–62) See also above, note 42.

49. De León, *They Called Them Greasers*, pp. 12–13.

50. Stephen F. Austin to W. S. Archer, August 15, 1836, *The Austin Papers*, ed. Eugene C. Barker, 3 vols. (vol. 1, in two parts, published as vol. 2 of the *Annual*

Report of the American Historical Association for the Year 1919 [Washington, D.C.: Government Printing Office, 1924], vol. 2 published as vol. 2 of the *Annual Report of the American Historical Association for the Year 1922* [Washington, D.C.: Government Printing Office, 1928], vol. 3 [Austin: University of Texas Press, 1927], vol. 3, p. 416).

51. Crisp, "Anglo-Texan Attitudes toward the Mexican," pp. 352–63.
52. *Telegraph and Texas Register* (Houston), March 13 and April 10, 1839.
53. Frederick C. Chabot, ed., *The Perote Prisoners, Being the Diary of James L. Truehart* (San Antonio: Naylor, 1934), pp. 39–40.
54. Crisp, "Anglo-Texan Attitudes toward the Mexican," pp. 326–31, 438, and chaps. 8 and 9, passim.
55. See Stephen Stagner, "Epics, Science, and the Lost Frontier: Texas Historical Writing, 1836–1936," *Western Historical Quarterly* 12 (April, 1981): 165–81; and Don Graham, "Remembering the Alamo: The Story of the Texas Revolution in Popular Culture," *Southwestern Historical Quarterly* 89 (July, 1985): 35–66.
56. Graham, "Remembering the Alamo," pp. 46–48.
57. Seymour V. Connor, *Texas: A History* (New York: Thomas Y. Crowell Co., 1971), pp. 120–22, 351.
58. Eugene C. Barker, *Mexico and Texas, 1821–35* (Dallas: P. L. Turner Co., 1928), p. 146. See the almost identical conclusion of William C. Binkley, in *The Texas Revolution* (Baton Rouge: Louisiana State University Press, 1952), p. 129.
59. Barker, *Mexico and Texas*, pp. 143–46, 148–49; Binkley, *The Texas Revolution*, pp. 69, 129–30. Barker's strongest statement concerning Anglo-Texan racism as a basis of the Revolution was written by 1911. "At the close of the summer in 1835 the Texans saw themselves in danger of becoming the alien subjects of a people to whom they deliberately believed themselves morally, intellectually, and politically superior" (Barker, *Mexico and Texas*, p. 148). This quotation is from chapter 5, which was originally published as "Public Opinion in Texas Preceding the Revolution," in the *Annual Report of the American Historical Association for the Year 1911*, 2 vols. (Washington, D.C.: n.p., 1913), vol. 1, pp. 217–28. Note the similarity to De León's statement of the issue seventy-two years later in *They Called Them Greasers*, pp. 12–13.
60. Samuel H. Lowrie, *Culture Conflict in Texas, 1821–35* (New York: Columbia University Press, 1932); Cecil Robinson, "Flag of Illusion: The Texas Revolution Viewed As a Conflict of Cultures," in Stephen B. Oates, ed., *The Republic of Texas* (Palo Alto: American West Pub. Co., 1968), pp. 10–17. Lowrie cogently criticizes Barker's imprecise use of the term *racial* (*Culture Conflict*, pp. 59–60).
61. Robinson, "Flag of Illusion," p. 17.
62. Weber, *Mexican Frontier*, pp. xxii, 254–55, and chap. 12, passim.
63. See Arnoldo De León, "Tejanos and the Texas War for Independence: Historiography's Judgment," *New Mexico Historical Review* 61 (April, 1986): 137–46; and Robert A. Calvert and Arnoldo De León, *The History of Texas* (Arlington Heights, Ill.: Harlan-Davidson, 1990), pp. 47–71.
64. Andrew Anthony Tijerina, "Tejanos and Texans: The Native Mexicans of Texas, 1820–50" (Ph.D. dissertation, University of Texas at Austin, 1977), especially chap. 7.
65. Ibid., p. 318.
66. Weber, *Mexican Frontier*, pp. 245–46.

67. The best studies linking economic and demographic change to changes in ethnic relations in early Texas are of the geographic and demographic extremes of Nacogdoches in the northeast and Laredo in the southwest. They are generally supportive of the thesis of this essay. See James Michael McReynolds, "Family Life in a Borderland Community: Nacogdoches, Texas, 1779–1861" (Ph.D. dissertation, Texas Tech University, 1978); and Hinojosa, *A Borderlands Town in Transition*. The critical story of San Antonio and Central Texas has yet to be adequately told, although a beginning was made by Ray F. Broussard, *San Antonio during the Texas Republic: A City in Transition*, Southwestern Studies Monograph no. 18 (El Paso: Texas Western Press, 1967).

68. See, for instance, Barrera, *Race and Class in the Southwest*, pp. 30, 218; and Felix D. Almaráz, Jr., "The Historical Heritage of the Mexican American in Nineteenth-Century Texas: An Interpretation," in *The Role of the Mexican American in the History of the Southwest*, (Edinburg, Tex.: Inter-American Institute, Pan American College, 1969), pp. 12–23.

69. See William Ransom Hogan, *The Texas Republic: A Social and Economic History*, (Austin: University of Texas Press [Texas History Paperback], 1969); Stanley Siegel, *A Political History of the Texas Republic, 1836–45*, (Austin: University of Texas Press, 1956). For a similar omission in more recent histories, see Joe B. Frantz, *Texas: A History* (New York: Norton, 1984), pp. 71–89; and Archie P. McDonald, "Lone Star on the Rise," in *Texas: A Sesquicentennial Celebration*, ed. Donald W. Whisenhunt (Austin: Eakin, 1984), pp. 59–91.

70. *Telegraph and Texas Register* (Columbia), March 28, 1837.

71. Notwithstanding its comic-book format, the best and most complete account of Seguín's life and his significance for the Republic of Texas is Jack Jackson, *Los Tejanos: The True Story of Juan N. Seguín and the Texas-Mexicans during the Rising of the Lone Star* (Stamford, Conn.: Fantagraphics Books, 1982). The author is grateful to Jackson for his comments regarding an earlier version of this essay.

Chapter 3

1. Justin H. Smith, *The War with Mexico*, 2 vols. (New York: Macmillan, 1919), vol. 1, p. 161.

2. Ibid., p. 464n.

3. *Telegraph and Texas Register*, May 6, 1846, p. 2, col. 5.

4. T. R. Fehrenbach, *Lone Star* (New York: Macmillan, 1968), pp. 85–92.

5. *Telegraph and Texas Register*, May 6, 1846, p. 2, col. 5.

6. Walter Prescott Webb, *The Texas Rangers* (Boston: Houghton Mifflin, 1935; reprint, Austin: University of Texas Press, 1965).

7. Russell Buchanan, ed., "George Washington Trahern: Texan Cowboy from Mier to Buena Vista," *Southwestern Historical Quarterly* 58 (July, 1954): 72–73.

8. Samuel E. Chamberlain, *My Confession* (New York: Harper, 1956), p. 39.

9. Buchanan, ed., "Trahern: Texan Cowboy," p. 72.

10. Albert G. Brackett, *History of the United States Cavalry* (New York: Harper, 1865; reprint, New York: Greenwood Press, 1968), p. 60. See also R. S. Ripley, *The War with Mexico* (1849; reprint, New York: Burt Franklin, 1970), vol. 1, p. 98.

11. Ethan Allen Hitchcock, *Fifty Years in Camp and Field* (New York: Putnam, 1909), p. 310.
12. Walter Prescott Webb, *The Texas Rangers in the Mexican War* (Austin: Jenkins Garrett Press, 1975), p. 9.
13. Memucan Hunt, quoted in *Telegraph and Texas Register,* January 18, 1843, 1:4.
14. Houston to J. Pinckney Henderson, February 20, 1844, in Amelia W. Williams and Eugene C. Barker, *The Writings of Sam Houston, 1813–63* (Austin: University of Texas Press, 1943), vol. 4, p. 269.
15. *Telegraph and Texas Register,* January 18, 1843, 1:4.
16. Samuel C. Reid, *The Scouting Expeditions of McCulloch's Texas Rangers* (Philadelphia: John E. Potter, n.d.), p. 23.
17. Ibid., p. 26.
18. Jonathan D. Brown, "Reminiscences of Jno. Duff Brown," *Quarterly of the Texas State Historical Association* 12 (April, 1909): 305.
19. Undated newspaper clipping, McCulloch Papers, Barker Texas History Center, University of Texas at Austin (hereafter BTHC).
20. George Wilkins Kendall, quoted in Fayette Copeland, *Kendall of the Picayune* (Norman: University of Oklahoma Press, 1943), p. 169.
21. Victor M. Rose, *The Life and Services of Gen. Ben McCulloch* (Philadelphia: Pictorial Bureau of the Press, 1888), p. 69.
22. Brown, "Reminiscences," pp. 304–305.
23. Reid, *Scouting Expeditions,* p. 43.
24. Ibid., p. 44.
25. Ibid., pp. 47–52.
26. Ibid., pp. 60–61.
27. Smith, *War with Mexico,* vol. 1, p. 204.
28. *Journal of the Executive Proceedings of the Senate* 7 (Washington: Government Printing Office, 1887), pp. 114, 120.
29. Taylor to Wood, July 7, 1846, "Governors' Letters," Texas State Archives, Austin.
30. Kendall, quoted in Copeland, *Kendall of the Picayune,* p. 163.
31. Brown, "Reminiscences," p. 305.
32. John N. Seguín, *Personal Memoirs of John N. Seguín from the Year 1834 to the Retreat of General Woll from the City of San Antonio, 1842* (San Antonio: Ledger Book and Job Office, 1858), pp. 28–29; reprinted in David J. Weber, ed., *Northern Mexico on the Eve of the United States' Invasion* (New York: Arno Press, 1976), n.p.
33. McCulloch to Taylor, July 20, 1846, McCulloch Papers, BTHC.
34. Ibid., McCulloch to Bliss, July 23, 1846.
35. Reid, *Scouting Expeditions,* p. 53.
36. William S. Henry, *Campaign Sketches of the War with Mexico* (New York: Harper, 1847), p. 123.
37. Williams and Barker, *Writings of Houston,* vol. 5, pp. 172–73.
38. McCulloch to Bliss, June 23, 1846, McCulloch Papers, BTHC.
39. Thomas J. Green, *Journal of the Texian Expedition against Mier* (New York: Harper, 1845; reprint, New York: Arno Press, 1973), p. 33.
40. McCulloch to Bliss, McCulloch Papers, BTHC.

41. Kendall, quoted in Copeland, *Kendall of the Picayune*, p. 163.

42. Mexican War Papers, Special Collections Division, Manuscripts Section, Howard-Tilton Memorial Library, Tulane University, New Orleans, La.

43. Kendall, in New Orleans *Picayune*, October 6, 1846.

44. Ibid.

45. James K. Greer, ed., *A Texas Ranger and Frontiersman: The Days of Buck Barry in Texas, 1845–1906* (Dallas: Southwest Press, 1932), p. 40.

46. [Luther Giddings], *Sketches of the Campaign in Northern Mexico* (New York: Putnam, 1853), p. 143.

47. Reid, *Scouting Expeditions*, pp. 151–54.

48. Greer, ed., *Buck Barry*, p. 38.

49. William J. Worth, quoted in Dunbar Roland, ed., *Jefferson Davis, Constitutionalist* (Jackson: Mississippi Department of Archives and History, 1923), vol. 1, p. 454.

50. Greer, ed., *Buck Barry*, p. 34.

51. Worth, quoted in Roland, ed., *Davis*, vol. 1, p. 454.

52. Greer, ed., *Buck Barry*, p. 34.

53. Reid, *Scouting Expeditions*, p. 157.

54. Kendall, in Copeland, *Kendall of the Picayune*, pp. 171–73.

55. Reid, *Scouting Expeditions*, pp. 157–58.

56. Copeland, *Kendall of the Picayune*, p. 173.

57. Clarksville *Northern Standard*, November 7, 1846, 2:3.

58. Greer, ed., *Buck Barry*, p. 35.

59. Reid, *Scouting Expeditions*, p. 162.

60. George Gordon Meade, *The Life and Letters of George Gordon Meade, Major General United States Army* (New York: Scribner's Sons, 1913), vol. 1, p. 134.

61. Reid, *Scouting Expeditions*, p. 165.

62. Ibid.

63. *General Taylor and His Staff* (Philadelphia: Grigg, Elliot & Co., 1848), p. 203.

64. Meade, *Life and Letters*, vol. 1, pp. 136–37.

65. Greer, ed., *Buck Barry*, p. 38.

66. Ibid.

67. Reid, *Scouting Expeditions*, pp. 200–204.

68. Chamberlain, *My Confession*, p. 56.

69. Otis A. Singletary, *The Mexican War* (Chicago: University of Chicago Press, 1960), p. 42.

70. General Order No. Thirty-nine, September 28, 1847, quoted in Reid, *Scouting Expeditions*, p. 224.

71. Greer, ed., *Buck Barry*, p. 40; Reid, *Scouting Expeditions*, p. 255.

72. Muster Roll, 1st Texas Mounted Riflemen, October 2, 1846, McCulloch Papers, BTHC; Reid, *Scouting Expeditions*, p. 233.

73. House Executive Document 60, 30th Cong., 1st sess., pp. 430, 508.

74. Ben McCulloch to Francis LeNoir McCulloch, November 30, 1846, McCulloch Papers, BTHC.

75. Clarksville *Northern Standard*, March 6, 1847, 2:1.

76. Ben McCulloch to Richardson Scurry, April 30, 1849, in Pat B. Clark, *The History of Clarksville and Old Red River County* (Dallas: Mathis, Van Nort & Co., 1937), p. 247.

77. Ibid. Quotations attributed to McCulloch, unless otherwise noted, are drawn from this remarkable letter appendixed to this most improbable source.
78. Ann Fears Crawford, ed., *The Eagle: The Autobiography of Santa Anna* (Austin: Pemberton Press, 1967), p. 90.
79. McCulloch to Scurry, in Clark, *History of Clarksville*, p. 247.
80. Singletary, *The Mexican War*, p. 50.
81. McCulloch to Scurry, in Clark, *History of Clarksville*, pp. 256–59.
82. Ibid.
83. Quoted in Benjamin Franklin Scribner, *Camp Life of a Volunteer* (Philadelphia: Grigg, Elliot & Co., 1847; reprint, Austin: Jenkins Pub. Co., 1975), p. 59.
84. House Executive Document 60, 30th Cong., 1st sess., p. 1176.
85. Zachary Taylor, June 10, 1847, quoted in Williams and Barker, *Writings of Houston*, vol. 5, p. 169.
86. H. P. N. Gammel, *Laws of Texas, 1822–97* (Austin: Gammel Book Co., 1898), vol. 2, pp. 137–39.
87. Ben McCulloch to Francis LeNoir McCulloch, November 9, 1849, McCulloch Papers, BTHC.
88. Walter P. Lane, *The Adventures and Recollections of General Walter P. Lane* (Marshall, Tex.: News Messenger Publishing Co., 1887; reprint, Austin: Pemberton Press, 1970), p. 94.
89. Williams and Barker, *Writings of Houston*, vol. 5, p. 172.
90. Ibid., p. 173.
91. McCulloch to Scurry, in Clark, *History of Clarksville*, p. 259.

Chapter 4

1. Walter L. Buenger, *Secession and the Union in Texas* (Austin: University of Texas Press, 1984), pp. 6–7. For other accounts, see Edward R. Maher, Jr., "Secession in Texas" (Ph.D. dissertation, Fordham University, 1960); Anna Irene Sandbo, "Beginnings of the Secession Movement in Texas," *Southwestern Historical Quarterly* 18 (July, 1914): 41–73; and Anna Irene Sandbo, "The First Session of the Secession Convention of Texas," *Southwestern Historical Quarterly* 18 (October, 1914): 162–94.
2. Ernest W. Winkler, ed., *Journal of the Secession Convention of Texas, 1861* (Austin: Austin Printing Co., 1912), pp. 13–14; *Dallas Herald*, January 30, 1861; Edward R. Maher, Jr., "Sam Houston and Secession," *Southwestern Historical Quarterly* 60 (April, 1952): 453–54.
3. Buenger, *Secession and the Union in Texas*, pp. 174–76; Joe T. Timmons, "The Referendum in Texas on the Ordinance of Secession, February 23, 1861: The Vote," *East Texas Historical Journal* 11 (Fall, 1973): 15–16; *Journal of the Secession Convention*, pp. 90–102; Maher, "Sam Houston and Secession," pp. 454–58.
4. D. E. Twiggs to C. L. Thomas, February 19, 1861, *The War of the Rebellion: A Compilation of the Official Records of the Union and Confederate Armies* (70 vols. in 128 parts; Washington: Government Printing Office, 1880–1901), ser. 1, vol. 1, p. 504. Hereafter cited as *Official Records*. See also reports of Colonel C. A. Waite, 1st Infantry, HQ, Dept. of Texas, February 26, 1861, *Official Records*, ser. 1, vol. 1, pp. 521–22; *Journal of the Secession Convention*, pp. 262–64, 317–24, 366–68; Stephen B. Oates, "Texas under the Secessionists," *Southwestern Historical Quarterly* 67

(October, 1963): 173–74; Allan Coleman Ashcraft, "Texas: 1860–66: The Lone Star State in the Civil War" (Ph.D. dissertation, Columbia University, 1960), pp. 60–64; and Thomas W. Cutrer, *Ben McCulloch and the Frontier Military Tradition* (Chapel Hill: University of North Carolina Press, 1993), pp. 177–86.

5. Stephen B. Oates, *Confederate Cavalry West of the River* (Austin: University of Texas Press, 1961), p. 5; Henry M. Henderson, *Texas in the Confederacy* (San Antonio: Naylor, 1955), p. 141.

6. For Ford's experiences in the war, see John S. "Rip" Ford, *Rip Ford's Texas*, ed. Stephen B. Oates (Austin: University of Texas Press, 1963); Stephen B. Oates, "John S. 'Rip' Ford: Prudent Cavalryman, CSA," *Southwestern Historical Quarterly* 64 (January, 1961): 289–314; and W. J. Hughes, *Rebellious Ranger: Rip Ford and the Old Southwest* (Norman: University of Oklahoma Press, 1964), pp. 187–245.

7. Edward Clark to the people of Texas, April 17, 1861, and April 24, 1861, in Executive Record Book, Texas State Archives, Austin; appointment of Nichols, May 13, 14, 1861, in Executive Record Book, Texas State Archives, Austin; Fredericka Ann Meiners, "The Texas Governorship, 1861–65: Biography of an Office" (Ph.D. dissertation, Rice University, 1974), pp. 48–50.

8. Proclamation of Governor Clark, June 8, 1861, in Executive Record Book; W. Buck Yearns, ed., *The Confederate Governors* (Athens: University of Georgia Press, 1985), p. 197.

9. Arthur James L. Fremantle, *The Fremantle Diary: Being the Journal of Lieutenant Colonel James Arthur Fremantle, Coldstream Guards, on His Three Months in the Southern States*, ed. Walter Lord (1863; reprint, Boston: Little, Brown & Co., 1954), p. 58.

10. Message of Edward Clark to the Senate and House of Representatives, November 1, 1861, *Official Records*, ser. 4, vol. 1, p. 717.

11. Oates, *Confederate Cavalry*, pp. 8–29; Stephen B. Oates, "Recruiting Confederate Cavalry in Texas," *Southwestern Historical Quarterly* 64 (April, 1961): 463–77; Henderson, *Texas in the Confederacy*, pp. 69–74. For the story of Sibley's brigade, see Martin Hardwick Hall, "The Formation of Sibley's Brigade and the March to New Mexico," *Southwestern Historical Quarterly* 64 (January, 1958): 383–405; and Martin Hardwick Hall, *Sibley's New Mexico Campaign* (Austin: University of Texas Press, 1960). For Terry's Texas Rangers, see Leonidas B. Giles, *Terry's Texas Rangers* (Austin: Von Boeckmann-Jones Co., 1911); C. C. Jeffries, *Terry's Rangers* (New York: Vantage Press, 1961); C. C. Jeffries, "The Character of Terry's Texas Rangers," *Southwestern Historical Quarterly* 64 (April, 1961): 454–62; and J. K. P. Blackburn, "Reminiscences of the Terry Rangers," *Southwestern Historical Quarterly* 22 (July, 1918): 38–78.

12. Mrs. A. V. Winkler, *The Confederate Capital and Hood's Texas Brigade* (Austin: Von Boeckmann, 1894), p. 209. The modern works on Hood's Texas Brigade are by Harold B. Simpson: *Hood's Texas Brigade, Lee's Grenadier Guard* (Waco: Texian Press, 1970); *Hood's Texas Brigade in Poetry and Song* (Waco: Texian Press, 1968); *Hood's Texas Brigade in Reunion and Memory* (Waco: Texian Press, 1974); and *Hood's Texas Brigade: A Compendium* (Waco: Texian Press, 1977). See also an important earlier work: J. B. Polley, *Hood's Texas Brigade: Its Marches, Its Battles, Its Achievements* (New York: Neale Pub. Co., 1910).

13. Joseph E. Chance, *The Second Texas Infantry: From Shiloh to Vicksburg* (Aus-

tin: Eakin, 1984); Elizabeth Silverthorne, *Ashbel Smith of Texas: Pioneer, Patriot, Statesman, 1805-86* (College Station: Texas A&M University Press, 1982), pp. 147-59.

14. Meiners, "The Texas Governorship, 1861-65," pp. 32-38, 45-47, 59-65, 124-38, 197-98, 226-30, 289-301. See also Yearns, ed., *Confederate Governors*, pp. 203-13.

15. Francis R. Lubbock, *Six Decades in Texas: The Memoirs of Francis R. Lubbock, Confederate Governor of Texas*, ed. C. W. Raines (Austin: Pemberton Press, 1968), p. 471; Lubbock to the legislature, November 4, 1863, James M. Day, comp. and ed., *Senate Journal of the Tenth Legislature, Regular Session of the State of Texas, November 3, 1863-December 16, 1863* (Austin: Texas State Library, 1965), pp. 7-33. Stephen B. Oates, in "Texas under the Secessionists," p. 187, estimates that fifty-eight thousand Texans served in the cavalry and thirty thousand served in the infantry and artillery. Robert P. Felgar, in "Texas in the War for Southern Independence, 1861-65" (Ph.D. dissertation, University of Texas, 1935), p. 106, states that only fifty to sixty thousand Texans served in the Confederate army.

16. Oates, *Confederate Cavalry*, pp. 10-11, 44, 177-78; Henderson, *Texas in the Confederacy*, pp. 142-43; Marcus J. Wright, *Texas in the War, 1861-65*, ed. Harold B. Simpson (Hillsboro: Hill Junior College Press, 1965), p. 123; Ernest Wallace, *Texas in Turmoil* (Austin: Steck Vaughn, 1965), pp. 86-87, 237-39.

17. Major James Cooper McKee, *Narrative of the Surrender of a Command of U.S. Forces at Fort Fillmore, New Mexico, in July, A.D. 1861, with Related Reports by John R. Baylor, C.S.A. & Others* (Houston: Stagecoach Press, 1960); Hall, *Sibley's New Mexico Campaign*, pp. 26-28; Martin Hardwick Hall, "Planter vs. Frontiersman: Conflict in Confederate Indian Policy," in William F. Homes and Harold M. Hollingsworth, eds., *Essays on the American Civil War* (Austin: University of Texas Press for University of Texas at Arlington, 1968), pp. 46-50; Jerry Don Thompson, *Colonel John Robert Baylor: Texas Indian Fighter and Confederate Soldier* (Hillsboro, Tex.: Hill Junior College Press, 1971), pp. 24-36. For Confederate expansionism see W. H. Watford, "Confederate Western Ambitions," *Southwestern Historical Quarterly* 44 (October, 1940): 161-87; and Jason H. Silverman, "Confederate Ambitions for the Southwest: A New Perspective," *Red River Valley Historical Review* 4 (Winter, 1979): 62-71.

18. Hall, *Sibley's New Mexico Campaign*, pp. 18-43; Wright, *Texas in the War, 1861-65*, pp. 78-79, 93, 112. For more on Tom Green, see Odie Faulk, *General Tom Green, Fightin' Texan* (Waco: Texian Press, 1963).

19. Oates, "Texas under the Secessionists," p. 178. See also Theodore Noel, *A Campaign from Santa Fe to the Mississippi: Being a History of the Old Sibley Brigade* (Shreveport: Shreveport News Printing, 1865), pp. 8-17. Two companies of Green's regiment were armed with lances, which one soldier described as spears. See Oscar Haas, trans., "The Diary of Julius Giesecke, 1861-62," *Texas Military History* 3 (Winter, 1963): 233.

20. Hall, *Sibley's New Mexico Campaign*, p. 54. Drinking was not confined to Sibley. William Henry Smith, a private in the 5th Cavalry, complained that the officers of the brigade were "drunk all the time, unfit for duty—incompetent to attend to the duty" (Walter A. Faulkner, ed., "With Sibley in New Mexico: The Journal of William Henry Smith," *West Texas Historical Association Year Book* 27 [October, 1951]: 137).

21. *Official Records*, ser. 1, vol. 9, pp. 490-521; Hall, *Sibley's New Mexico Cam-*

paign, pp. 83–103; M. L. Crimmins, "The Battle of Val Verde," *New Mexico Historical Review* 7 (October, 1932): 348–52.

22. David B. Gracy II, ed., "New Mexico Campaign Letters of Frank Starr, 1861–62," *Military History of Texas and the Southwest* 4 (Fall, 1964): 182.

23. Hall, *Sibley's New Mexico Campaign,* pp. 105–21.

24. Ibid., pp. 141–60; J. F. Santee, "The Battle of La Glorieta Pass," *New Mexico Historical Review* 6 (January, 1931): 66–75.

25. Noel, *A Campaign from Santa Fe to the Mississippi,* pp. 26–39; Hall, *Sibley's New Mexico Campaign,* pp. 161–226; Sibley to Samuel Cooper, May 4, 1862, *Official Records,* ser. 1, vol. 9, pp. 509–12. For more on Sibley and his career, see Jerry Thompson, *Henry Hopkins Sibley: Confederate General of the West* (Natchitoches, La.: Northwestern State University Press, 1987).

26. Rupert N. Richardson, Ernest Wallace, Adrian Anderson, *Texas, the Lone Star State* (4th ed., Englewood Cliffs, N.J.: Prentice-Hall, 1981), p. 229. The best overall account of Texas coastal defense is Alwyn Barr, "The Texas Coastal Defense, 1861–65," *Southwestern Historical Quarterly* 45 (July, 1961): 1–31.

27. Barr, "Texas Coastal Defense," pp. 5–6; Henderson, *Texas in the Confederacy,* pp. 117, 122–23, 145; Robert G. Hartje, *Van Dorn: The Life and Times of a Confederate General* (Nashville: Vanderbilt University Press, 1967), pp. 79–91.

28. Thomas North, *Five Years in Texas; or, What You Did Not Hear during the War from January, 1861, to January, 1866* (Cincinnati: Elm Street Printing Co., 1871), pp. 105–106.

29. General Hébert to Secretary of War Judah P. Benjamin, October 24, 1861, *Official Records,* ser. 1, vol. 4, p. 127.

30. *Official Records of the Union and Confederate Navies in the War of the Rebellion* (31 vols.; Washington: Government Printing Office, 1894–1927), ser. 1, vol. 17, pp. 79–80, vol. 18, pp. 690–91, hereafter cited as *Official Records, Navies; Official Records,* ser. 1, vol. 4, pp. 153–57.

31. Barr, "Texas Coastal Defense," pp. 11–13; Major A. M. Hobby's reports, August 16, 18, 1862, *Official Records,* ser. 1, vol. 9, pp. 621–23; Lieutenant Colonel A. W. Spaight's reports, September 26, October 2, 1862, *Official Records,* ser. 1, vol. 15, pp. 144–47; W. T. Block, "A History of Jefferson County from Wilderness to Reconstruction" (M.A. thesis, Lamar University, 1974), pp. 273–77.

32. Barr, "Texas Coastal Defense," p. 13; Galveston *Weekly News,* October 15, 1862; Earl Wesley Fornell, *The Galveston Era: The Texas Crescent on the Eve of Secession* (Austin: University of Texas Press, 1961), pp. 297–98.

33. Commander W. B. Renshaw to Admiral David G. Farragut, October 8, 1862, *Official Records, Navies,* ser. 1, vol. 19. pp. 254–60; Colonel J. J. Cook's report, October 9, 1862, *Official Records,* ser. 1, vol. 15, pp. 151–53; Charles C. Cumberland, "The Confederate Loss and Recapture of Galveston," *Southwestern Historical Quarterly* 51 (October, 1947): 109–30.

34. Ford, *Rip Ford's Texas,* p. 343. For Magruder's early career, see Timothy Spell, "John Bankhead Magruder: Defender of the Texas Coast" (M.A. thesis, Lamar University, 1981), pp. 1–28. Magruder's position in Texas was enhanced by his kinship with several prominent Texas families, including that of agricultural reformer and planter Thomas Affleck. See Ralph A. Wooster, "With the Confederate Cavalry in the War: The Civil War Experiences of Isaac Dunbar Affleck," *Southwestern Historical*

Quarterly 83 (July, 1979): 11–12.

35. General Magruder to General Samuel Cooper, February 21, 1863, *Official Records, Navies*, ser. 1, vol. 19, p. 474; Oates, "Texas under the Secessionists," pp. 203–204; Barr, "Texas Coastal Defense," pp. 15–18.

36. General Banks's report, January 3, 1863, *Official Records*, ser. 1, vol. 15, pp. 199–206; General Magruder's report, February 26, 1863, *Official Records*, ser. 1, vol. 15, pp. 211–20; Commander Henry Wilson to Admiral Farragut, January 8, 1863, *Official Records, Navies*, ser. 1, vol. 19, p. 439.

37. Ashcraft, "Texas: 1860–66," pp. 124–25; Fremantle, *The Fremantle Diary*, pp. 54–56; Barr, "Texas Coastal Defense," pp. 18–23; Maury Darst, "Artillery Defenses of Galveston, 1863," *Military History of Texas and the Southwest* 12 (no. 1, 1975): 63–67.

38. Commodore H. H. Bell to Secretary of the Navy Gideon Welles, September 9, 1863, *Official Records, Navies*, ser. 1, vol. 20, pp. 515–16; General N. P. Banks's report, September 5, 1863, *Official Records*, ser. 1, vol. 26, pt. 1, pp. 286–92.

39. Barr, "Texas Coastal Defense," pp. 24–25. Lieutenant Commander W. H. Dana to Commodore H. H. Bell, September 9, 1863, *Official Records, Navies*, ser. 1, vol. 20, p. 522; Captain F. H. Odlum's report, September 8, 9, 1863, *Official Records*, ser. 1, vol. 26, pt. 1, pp. 309–10; Block, "History of Jefferson County," pp. 298–99.

40. Lieutenant R. W. Dowling's report, September 9, 1863, *Official Records*, ser. 1, vol. 26, pt. 1, pp. 311–12; Major General Franklin's report, September 11, 1863, *Official Records*, ser. 1, vol. 26, pt. 1, pp. 294–97. For descriptions of the battle, see Alwyn Barr, "Sabine Pass, September, 1863," *Texas Military History* 2 (February, 1962): 17–22; Andrew Forest Muir, "Dick Dowling and the Battle of Sabine Pass," *Civil War History* 4 (December, 1958): 399–428; Lieutenant H. L. Sandefur and Archie P. McDonald, "Sabine Pass: David and Goliath," *Texana* 7 (Fall, 1969): 177–188; Harold B. Simpson, "The Battle of Sabine Pass," in *Battles of Texas* (Waco: Texian Press, 1967), pp. 137–69; Frank X. Tolbert, *Dick Dowling at Sabine Pass* (New York: McGraw-Hill, 1962); and Jo Young, "The Battle of Sabine Pass," *Southwestern Historical Quarterly* 52 (April, 1949): 398–409.

41. Oates, "Texas under the Secessionists," pp. 206–209; Barr, "Texas Coastal Defense," pp. 27–29; Lester N. Fitzhugh, "Saluria, Fort Esperanza, and Military Operations on the Texas Coast, 1861–64," *Southwestern Historical Quarterly* 61 (July, 1957): 66–100; Ford, *Rip Ford's Texas*, pp. 342–66. It should be noted that even though he commanded Confederate troops, Ford was never commissioned by the Confederate War Department. Throughout the war, however, he claimed the rank of colonel, CSA Cavalry, and various district commanders of Texas recognized him as such. See Oates, "John S. 'Rip' Ford," p. 297.

42. Louise Horton, *Samuel Bell Maxey, A Biography* (Austin: University of Texas Press, 1974), pp. 36–38. See also Louise Horton, "General Sam Bell Maxey: His Defense of North Texas and the Indian Territory," *Southwestern Historical Quarterly* 74 (April, 1971): 507–24; Ira Don Richards, "The Battle of Poison Spring," *Arkansas Historical Quarterly* 18 (Winter, 1959): 339–42; and Anne J. Bailey, "Was There a Massacre at Poison Spring?" *Military History of the Southwest* 20 (Fall, 1990): 157–68.

43. Richard Taylor, *Destruction and Reconstruction* (New York: Longman's, 1955), pp. 186–212; Alwyn Barr, *Polignac's Texas Brigade*, Texas Gulf Historical Assoc. Pub. Ser. 8 (November, 1964): 39–41; Wright, *Texas in the War, 1861–65*, pp. 100–101,

164–65; John W. Spencer, *Terrell's Texas Cavalry* (Burnet, Tex.: Eakin, 1982), pp. 1–41; Alwyn Barr, ed., "William T. Mechling's Journal of the Red River Campaign, April 7–May 10, 1864," *Texana* 1 (Fall, 1963): 365–68; J. P. Blessington, *The Campaigns of Walker's Texas Division* (1875; reprint, Austin: State House Press, 1994), pp. 182–206.

44. Taylor was critical of his superior, General Edmund Kirby Smith, for not giving him sufficient manpower to crush Banks's retreating army. Taylor, *Destruction and Reconstruction*, pp. 212–33; Barr, *Polignac's Texas Brigade*, pp. 42–47; Alwyn Barr, "Texan Losses in the Red River Campaign, 1864," *Texas Military History* 3 (Summer, 1963): 103–10; Fredericka Meiners, "Hamilton P. Bee in the Red River Campaign," *Southwestern Historical Quarterly* 78 (July, 1974): 21–44; Carl P. Tyson, "Highway of War," *Red River Valley Historical Review* 3 (Summer, 1978): 28–51; Anne J. Bailey, *Between the Enemy and Texas: Parsons's Texas Cavalry in the Civil War* (Fort Worth: Texas Christian University Press, 1989), pp. 165–94. The most complete account of the whole campaign is Ludwell H. Johnson, *Red River Campaign: Politics and Cotton in the Civil War* (Baltimore: Johns Hopkins University Press, 1958).

45. Charles P. Roland, *Albert Sidney Johnston: Soldier of Three Republics* (Austin: University of Texas Press, 1964), pp. 339–51; T. Harry Williams, *P. G. T. Beauregard: Napoleon in Gray* (Baton Rouge: Louisiana State University Press, 1954), pp. 116, 141–42; James Lee McDonough, *Shiloh: In Hell before Night* (Knoxville: University of Tennessee Press, 1977), pp. 152–54, 221–22; Wiley Sword, *Shiloh: Bloody April* (New York: Morrow, 1974), pp. 365–66, 439–40, 443.

46. Simpson, *Hood's Texas Brigade*, pp. 176, 276, 325–26; Judith Ann Benner, *Sul Ross: Soldier, Statesman, Educator* (College Station: Texas A&M University Press, 1983), pp. 101–104; Henderson, *Texas in the Confederacy*, pp. 94–100; Wright, *Texas in the War, 1861–65*, pp. 78, 91–92.

47. Frank H. Smyrl, "Texans in the Union Army, 1861–65," *Southwestern Historical Quarterly* 65 (October, 1961): 234–50; Claude Elliott, "Union Sentiment in Texas, 1861–65," *Southwestern Historical Quarterly* 50 (July, 1946): 449–77; Floyd F. Ewing, Jr., "Unionist Sentiment on the Northwest Texas Frontier," *West Texas Historical Association Yearbook* 33 (October, 1957): 58–70. For more on Davis and Hamilton, see Ronald Norman Gray, "Edmund J. Davis: Radical Republican and Reconstruction Governor of Texas" (Ph.D. dissertation, Texas Tech University, 1976); and John L. Waller, *Colossal Hamilton of Texas: A Biography of Andrew Jackson Hamilton* (El Paso: Texas Western Press, 1964). See also James A. Marten, *Texas Divided: Loyalty and Dissent in the Lone Star State* (Lexington: University of Kentucky Press, 1990).

48. Robert W. Shook, "The Battle of the Nueces, August 10, 1862," *Southwestern Historical Quarterly* 66 (July, 1962): 31–42; Sam Acheson and Julie Ann Hudson, eds., "George Washington Diamond's Account of the Great Hanging at Gainesville, 1862," *Southwestern Historical Quarterly* 66 (January, 1963): 331–414; Thomas Barrett, *The Great Hanging at Gainesville, Cooke County, Texas, October, A.D., 1862* (Gainesville, 1885; reprint, Austin: Texas State Historical Assoc., 1961); James Smallwood, "Disaffection in Confederate Texas: The Great Hanging at Gainesville," *Civil War History* 22 (December, 1976): 349–60; L. D. Clark, ed., *Civil War Recollections of James Lemuel Clark, Including Previously Unpublished Material on the Great Hanging at Gainesville, Texas, in October, 1862* (College Station: Texas A&M University Press, 1984), pp. 94–112; Richard B. McCaslin, *Tainted Breeze: The Great Hanging*

at Gainesville, Texas, 1862 (Baton Rouge: Louisiana State University Press, 1994).

49. Lucia Rutherford Douglas, comp. and ed., *Douglas's Texas Battery, CSA* (Tyler: Smith County Historical Society, 1966), p. 153.

50. Norman Brown, ed., *One of Cleburne's Command: The Civil War Reminiscences and Diary of Capt. Samuel T. Foster, Granbury's Texas Brigade, CSA* (Austin: University of Texas Press, 1980), p. 163; Robertson to Julia, May 8, 1865, Robertson Papers, Texas State Archives, Austin; and W. W. Heartsill, *Fourteen Hundred and Ninety-one Days in the Confederate Army; or, Camp Life, Day by Day, of the W. P. Lane Rangers from April 19, 1861, to May 20, 1865,* ed. Bell I. Wiley (1876; reprint, Jackson, Tenn.: McCowat-Mercer Press, 1954), p. 239.

51. Ford, *Rip Ford's Texas,* pp. 386–92; *Official Records,* ser. 1, vol. 48, pt. 2, pp. 600–601; Oates, "John S. 'Rip' Ford," pp. 310–14.

Chapter 5

KEY

AG: Adjutant General
AGO: Adjutant General's Office
AAG: Assistant Adjutant General
LR: Letters Received
NA: National Archives
RG: Record Group
SDLR: Selected Documents, Letters Received
SLR: Selected Letters Received

1. L. D. Reddick, "The Negro Policy of the United States Army," *The Journal of Negro History* 34 (January, 1949): 14–18; Benjamin Quarles, *The Negro in the Civil War* (Boston: Little, Brown & Co., 1953), p. 188; Dudley T. Cornish, *The Sable Arm* (New York: Longman's, 1956), p. 288.

2. Arlen L. Fowler, *Black Infantry in the West, 1869–81* (Westport, Conn.: Greenwood Press, 1971), pp. 116–17; William H. Leckie, *The Buffalo Soldiers: A Narrative of the Negro Cavalry in the West* (Norman: University of Oklahoma Press, 1967), pp. 8–9.

3. Leckie, *Buffalo Soldiers,* pp. 6–7; *Annual Report of the Secretary of War for 1869,* vol. 1, pp. 96–99.

4. Fowler, *Black Infantry in the West,* pp. 17–19.

5. General U. S. Grant to General W. T. Sherman and General P. H. Sheridan, August 4, 1866, SLR, relating to the 9th and 10th Cavalry, Adjutant General's Office, Record Group 94, National Archives (hereafter cited as AGO, RG 94, NA); William H. and Shirley A. Leckie, *Unlikely Warriors: General Benjamin Grierson and His Family* (Norman: University of Oklahoma Press, 1984), p. 101.

6. Leckie, *Buffalo Soldiers,* pp. 10–11.

7. Ibid., p. 11; Organizational returns, 9th Cavalry, February–April, 1867, AGO, RG 94, NA; Theodore R. Davis, "A Summer on the Plains," *Harper's Monthly Magazine* 36 (February, 1868): 306.

8. Organizational returns, 10th Cavalry, February–May, 1867, AGO, RG 94, NA; Leckie, *Buffalo Soldiers,* pp. 12–17.

9. Leckie and Leckie, *Unlikely Warriors*, p. 150; Organizational returns, 10th Cavalry, August, 1867, AGO, RG 94, NA.

10. Arrel M. Gibson, *The Kickapoos: Lords of the Middle Border* (Norman: University of Oklahoma Press, 1963), p. 210; Henry B. Parkes, *A History of Mexico* (Boston: Houghton Mifflin, 1928), pp. 242–50; Leckie, *Buffalo Soldiers*, pp. 82–83.

11. *Annual Report of the Secretary of War for 1872*, pp. 59–60; Organizational returns, 9th Cavalry, January–December, 1871, AGO, RG 94, NA.

12. Leckie, *Buffalo Soldiers*, pp. 107–109.

13. Mackenzie to the AAG, Department of Texas, SDLR, 1872–76, AGO, NA; Governor Richard Coke of Texas to President U. S. Grant, May 29, 1875, AGO, LR, Consolidated File no. 1653, Affairs on the Rio Grande and Texas Frontier, 1875–81, AGO, RG 94, NA.

14. Organizational returns, 9th Cavalry, July–September, 1875, AGO, RG 94, NA.

15. Leckie, *Buffalo Soldiers*, pp. 47–49.

16. Loring B. Priest, *Uncle Sam's Stepchildren: The Reformation of United States Indian Policy, 1865–87* (New Brunswick, N.J.: Rutgers University Press, 1942), pp. 44–47; William H. Leckie, *The Military Conquest of the Southern Plains* (Norman: University of Oklahoma Press, 1963), p. 138.

17. Leckie, *Military Conquest*, pp. 198–99; *Annual Report of the Secretary of War for 1874*, p. 40; Leckie, *Buffalo Soldiers*, pp 123–24.

18. Leckie, *Buffalo Soldiers*, pp. 135–40. For a detailed account of the Red River War, see James L. Haley, *The Buffalo War: The History of the Red River Indian Uprising* (Garden City, N.Y.: Doubleday, 1976).

19. Quoted in Leckie and Leckie, *Unlikely Warriors*, p. 257.

20. For a complete account of the Victorio War, see Dan L. Thrapp, *Victorio and the Mimbres Apaches* (Norman: University of Oklahoma Press, 1974).

21. Fowler, *Black Infantry in the West*, p. 38.

22. Organizational returns, 10th Cavalry, September, 1886, AGO, RG 94, NA.

23. Leckie and Leckie, *Unlikely Warriors*, p. 231. See also Paul H. Carlson, *"Pecos Bill": A Military Biography of William R. Shafter* (College Station: Texas A&M University Press, 1989).

24. General Sheridan to Adjutant General Edward Townsend, October 21, 1877, File no. 1653, AGO, RG 94, NA; Colonel Hatch to General John Pope, December 27, 1877, File no. 1653, AGO, RG 94, NA; Walter P. Webb, *The Texas Rangers: A Century of Frontier Defense* (Boston: Houghton Mifflin, 1935), pp. 353–55.

25. Leckie, *Buffalo Soldiers*, pp. 136–40.

26. General Sherman to General W. S. Hancock, January 24, 1867, Grierson Papers, Newberry Library, Chicago.

27. Alex E. Sweet and J. Armoy Know, *On a Mustang through Texas, from the Gulf to the Rio Grande* (Saint Louis: T. N. James and Co., 1884), p. 525; Douglas C. McChristian, "Grierson's Fight at Tinaja de las Palmas: An Episode in the Victorio Campaign," *Red River Valley Historical Review* 7 (Winter, 1982): 45–63.

28. Leckie and Leckie, *Unlikely Warriors*, pp. 274–75.

29. Captain Nolan to Mr. R. N. Price, September 24, 1879, Benjamin H. Grierson Papers, 1827–1941, Southwest Collection, Texas Technological University, Lubbock, Texas.

30. Henry O. Flipper, *Negro Frontiersman* (El Paso: Texas Western College Press, 1963), pp. 15–20.

31. For details of the Flipper case, see Army Board for Correction of Military Records, NNM 372-2, AGO, RG 94, NA. See also Bruce J. Dinges, "Court-Martial of Henry O. Flipper: An Example of Black-White Relationships in the Army," *American West* 9 (January 1972): 12–17, 59–61.

32. *Annual Report of the Secretary of War for 1889*, pp. 799–800.

33. Organizational returns of the 9th and 10th Cavalry and the 24th and 25th Infantry for the years 1869–80, AGO, RG 94, NA.

34. Buell to the AAG, Department of Texas, February 24, 1875, SLR, Department of Texas, AGO, NA. For an account of Buell's campaign, see William H. Leckie, "Buell's Campaign," *Red River Valley Historical Review* 3 (Spring, 1978): 186–93.

35. Galveston *Daily News*, March 1, 1878.

36. Susan Miles, "The Soldiers' Riot," *Fort Concho Report* 13 (Spring, 1981): 1–19.

37. Leckie and Leckie, *Unlikely Warriors*, p. 274. For an additional analysis on the role of black soldiers in the West, see Robert M. Utley, *Frontier Regulars: The United States Army and the Indian, 1866–91* (New York: Macmillan, 1973), pp. 20, 25–28, 146–48, 209–11, 220–22, 350, 361–65.

Chapter 6

1. Patricia Y. Stallard, *Glittering Misery: Dependents of the Indian Fighting Army* (San Rafael, Calif., and Fort Collins, Colo.: Presidio Press/Old Army Press, 1978), p. vii.

2. For a discussion of the frontier army's nonmilitary roles, see Richard N. Ellis, "The Political Role of the Military," and Jack D. Foner, "The Socializing Role of the Military," both in James P. Tate, ed., *The American Military on the Frontier: Proceedings of the Seventh Military History Symposium, United States Air Force Academy, 30 September–October 1976* (Washington, D.C.: Office of Air Force History and United States Air Force Academy, 1978), pp. 71–84, 85–100; and Sandra L. Myres, "Fort Graham, Listening Post on the Texas Frontier," *West Texas Historical Association Yearbook* 59 (1983): 33–51.

3. Stallard, *Glittering Misery*, p. vii.

4. In compiling a bibliography of accounts by army wives in the trans-Mississippi West in the nineteenth century, I was able to find only two written by enlisted men's wives. See Sandra L. Myres, "Army Wives in the Trans-Mississippi West: A Bibliography," in Teresa Viele, *Following the Drum: A Glimpse of Frontier Life* (Lincoln: University of Nebraska Press, 1984), pp. 257–73.

5. Sandra L. Myres, "Romance and Reality on the American Frontier: Views of Army Wives," *Western Historical Quarterly* 13 (October, 1982): 410; Darlis A. Miller, "Introduction," in Mrs. Orsemus B. Boyd, *Cavalry Life in Tent and Field* (Lincoln: University of Nebraska Press, 1982), p. v.

6. Myres, "Romance and Reality," pp. 409–10. See also Edward M. Coffman, *The Old Army: A Portrait of the American Army in Peacetime, 1784–1898* (New York: Oxford University Press, 1986), pp. 287–327.

7. Elizabeth B. Custer, *"Boots and Saddles"; or, Life in Dakota with General Custer*

(Norman: University of Oklahoma Press, 1961), p. xxix.

8. Viele, *Following the Drum,* pp. 13–15.

9. Custer, *"Boots and Saddles,"* p. xv.

10. Quoted in Robert M. Utley, *Frontiersmen in Blue: The United States Army and the Indian, 1848–65* (New York: Macmillan, 1967), p. 31.

11. Lydia Spencer Lane, *I Married a Soldier; or, Old Days in the Army* (Albuquerque: Horn and Wallace, 1964), pp. 30–31; Lou Conway Roberts, *A Woman's Reminiscences of Six Years in Camp with the Texas Rangers* (Austin: Von Boeckmann-Jones Company, 1928), p. 202; Viele, *Following the Drum,* pp. 137, 140.

12. Boyd, *Cavalry Life,* p. 250.

13. Alice Kirk Grierson, *An Army Wife's Cookbook with Household Hints and Home Remedies,* ed. Mary L. Williams (Tucson: Southwest Parks and Monuments Assoc., 1972), pp. 24, 27, 43; Ellen Biddle, *Reminiscences of a Soldier's Wife* (Philadelphia: J. B. Lippincott, 1907), p. 173.

14. Myres, "Romance and Reality," p. 422.

15. Biddle, *Reminiscences,* p. 252. An excellent discussion of the problems posed by raising children and growing up on a frontier army post can be found in Stallard, *Glittering Misery,* pp. 75–101; and Forrest R. Blackburn, "Army Families in Frontier Forts," *Military Review* 44 (October, 1969): 17–28.

16. Sandra L. Myres, ed., "A Woman's View of the Texas Frontier, 1874: The Diary of Emily K. Andrews," *Southwestern Historical Quarterly* 84 (July, 1982): 76.

17. Boyd, *Cavalry Life,* p. 247; Viele, *Following the Drum,* pp. 142–54, 176–90; Boyd, *Cavalry Life,* p. 288; "The Diary of Eliza (Mrs. Albert Sidney) Johnston," Charles P. Roland and Richard C. Robbins, eds., *Southwestern Historical Quarterly* 60 (April, 1957): 497.

18. Myres, "Romance and Reality," p. 422.

19. Boyd, *Cavalry Life,* p. 250; Roland and Robbins, eds., "Diary of Eliza Johnston," p. 487; Myres, "A Woman's View," p. 66.

20. Lane, *I Married a Soldier,* pp. 25, 28; Viele, *Following the Drum,* p. 95.

21. Roland and Robbins, eds., "Diary of Eliza Johnston," p. 487; Myres, "A Woman's View," pp. 65, 70–71; anonymous, "Diary of My Trip," MSS, Garrett Library, University of Texas at Arlington.

22. Robert M. Utley, *Frontier Regulars: The United States Army and the Indian, 1866–91* (New York: Macmillan, 1973), p. 45.

23. Martha Summerhayes, *Vanishing Arizona: Recollections of the Army Life of a New England Woman* (Glorieta, N.Mex.: Rio Grande Press, 1970), p. 124.

24. Lane, *I Married a Soldier,* pp. 38, 45; Myres, "A Woman's View," pp. 77–78.

25. For more detailed information, see Myres, "Romance and Reality," pp. 413–14, n. 11.

26. Viele, *Following the Drum,* pp. 216–17.

27. Boyd, *Cavalry Life,* p. 64; Lane, *I Married a Soldier,* p. 66.

28. Viele, *Following the Drum,* pp. 121, 124. There is an extensive literature on army women and their impressions and experiences with Indians. See especially Myres, "Romance and Reality," pp. 412–15; Sandra L. Myres, "The Ladies of the Army: Views of Western Life," in Tate, ed., *American Military on the Frontier,* pp. 140–42; Glenda Riley, *Women and Indians on the Frontier* (Albuquerque: University of New Mexico Press, 1984); and Sherry L. Smith, "Officer's Wives, Indians and the Indian

Wars," *Journal of the Order of the Indian Wars* 1 (Winter, 1980): 35-46.

29. Boyd, *Cavalry Life*, pp. 172-73; Viele, *Following the Drum*, pp. 155-56.

30. Boyd, *Cavalry Life*, pp. 223-24. For other women's views, see Myres, "Romance and Reality," p. 415.

31. Viele, *Following the Drum*, pp. 113, 156, 183.

32. For views of women in other parts of the West, see Myres, "The Ladies of the Army," pp. 143-45; and Myres, "Romance and Reality," pp. 416-17.

33. Viele, *Following the Drum*, pp. 80-81, 84, 105, 151-52.

34. Elizabeth B. Custer, *Tenting on the Plains; or, General Custer in Kansas and Texas*, 3 vols. (Norman: University of Oklahoma Press, 1971), vol. 1, pp. 120-21.

35. Myres, "A Woman's View," pp. 53-54, 65.

36. Custer, *Tenting on the Plains*, vol. 1, pp. 216, 211-15; vol. 2, pp. 206, 267. Custer, of course, was in Texas immediately after the Civil War. The tone of her book, however, implied that the conditions she described were typical behavior instead of the result of the dislocations of war and Reconstruction.

37. Lane, *I Married a Soldier*, pp. 146-47. Interestingly, the women made very few comments about blacks, either in or out of the army. Only Elizabeth Custer recorded any extensive description when she described a ball in Austin attended by friends of her black servant, Eliza (Custer, *Tenting on the Plains*, vol. 1, pp. 232-36). Although Emily Andrews traveled with black troops, her only comment was a brief description of "our gallant '*brunette*' escort waiting for a chance to cross, so fresh and far from fatigue that it was hard to believe they had come so many miles day after day" (Myres, "A Woman's View," p. 61-62). For other western women's views of blacks, see Sandra L. Myres, *Westering Women and the Frontier Experience, 1800-1915* (Albuquerque: University of New Mexico Press, 1982): 85-86. Custer also repeated the commonly held belief that "the negroes of Texas and Louisiana were the worst in all the South" (Custer, *Tenting on the Plains*, vol. 1, p. 224).

38. Robert M. Utley, ed., "Campaigning with Custer: Letters and Diaries Sketch Life in Camp and Field during the Indian Wars," *American West* 14 (July-August, 1977): 4; Myres, "Romance and Reality," pp. 417-18.

39. Myres, *Westering Women*, pp. 6-7. A great deal has been written about the Cult of True Womanhood and the Cult of Domesticity. See especially the seminal article by Barbara Welter, "The Cult of True Womanhood: 1820-60," *American Quarterly* 18 (Summer, 1966): 151.

40. Myres, *Westering Women*, p. 185. See also Julie Roy Jeffrey, *Frontier Women: The Trans-Mississippi West, 1840-80* (New York: Hill and Wang, 1979), pp. 11-14.

41. Custer, *"Boots and Saddles,"* p. 181. See also Myres, "Romance and Reality," p. 423 and especially note 41; and Roland and Robbins, eds., "Diary of Eliza Johnston," pp. 493-94.

42. Duane N. Greene, *Ladies and Officers of the United States Army; or, American Aristocracy, A Sketch of the Social Life and Character of the Army* (Chicago: Central Pub. Co., 1880), pp. 13, 17-18.

43. *Army and Navy Journal* 15 (June 15, 1878): 721, as quoted in Utley, *Frontier Regulars*, p. 89. In his earlier study of the frontier army, Utley characterized the officer corps as exhibiting "contrasts of competence and incompetence, youth and age, energy and lethargy" ranging from "vigorous and ambitious young line officers glorying in the traditions of professionalism . . . older officers who laid the ground-

work for the new professionalism . . . [and] on the other hand . . . the deadbeats, timeservers and narrow martinets" (Utley, *Frontiersmen in Blue,* pp. 29–30).

44. Roland and Robbins, eds., "Diary of Eliza Johnston," p. 493.

45. Ibid., p. 467; Viele, *Following the Drum,* p. 222.

46. See Myres, "Foreword," in Viele, *Following the Drum,* pp. 1–2; and Myres, "Romance and Reality," pp. 426–27.

47. Myres, "Romance and Reality," pp. 425-26; and Myres, "The Ladies of the Army," pp. 149–50.

48. Ellis, "The Political Role of the Military"; Foner, "The Socializing Role of the Military"; and Roger L. Nichols, "Commentary," in Tate, *The American Military.* The quote is from Nichols, "Commentary," p. 110.

49. General Sherman is quoted in Foner, "The Socializing Role of the Military," p. 86. However, without the army the frontier would not have been safe either for settlers or for the railroad. Many western towns grew up around military posts that offered not only protection but an economic base. On the impact of the frontier on the army women, see Myres, "Romance and Reality," pp. 425–26, and the sources listed in note 49 of that article.

50. Boyd, *Cavalry Life,* p. 222; Utley, *Frontier Regulars,* p. 89.

51. Information on the Vieles can be found in Myres, "Foreword," in Viele, *Following the Drum,* and the sources cited therein. See especially the family history by her granddaughter, Elise Strother Tuckerman, *The Pendulum Swings* (New York: Vantage Press, 1971).

52. See Sandra L. Myres, *Cavalry Wife: The Diary of Eveline M. Alexander, 1866–67* (College Station: Texas A&M University Press, 1977).

53. On friendships and family networks and rivalries, see Paul A. Hutton, *Phil Sheridan and His Army* (Lincoln: University of Nebraska Press, 1985), especially chap. 6; and Edward M. Coffman, *The Old Army, A Portrait of the American Army in Peacetime, 1784–1898* (New York: Oxford University Press, 1986), pp. 215–86.

54. Foner, "The Socializing Role of the Military," p. 87.

55. Mattes, quoted in Jo Beth Jacobs, "The Westering Male through Victorian Eyes," paper presented at the Thirteenth Annual Conference of the Western Historical Assoc., Fort Worth, Texas, October, 1973; Robert M. Utley, "Arizona Vanquished: Impressions and Reflections Concerning the Quality of Life on a Military Frontier," *American West* 6 (November, 1969): 16.

Chapter 7

1. John G. Bourke, *An Apache Campaign in the Sierra Madre: An Account of the Expedition in Pursuit of the Hostile Chiricahua Apaches in the Spring of 1883* (New York: Scribner's Sons, 1886; reprint ed., 1958); John G. Bourke, *Mackenzie's Last Fight with the Cheyennes: A Winter Campaign in Wyoming and Montana* (Governor's Island, N.Y.: Military Service Institution; reprint, Bellevue, Neb.: Old Army Press, 1970); John G. Bourke, *On the Border with Crook* (New York: Scribner's Sons, 1891; reprint, Glorieta, N.Mex.: Rio Grande Press, 1971). For a complete list of Bourke's many publications devoted to anthropology, folklore, and history, see the bibliography in Joseph C. Porter, *Paper Medicine Man: John Gregory Bourke and His American West* (Norman: University of Oklahoma Press, 1986). For a summary of Bourke's

career, see Joseph C. Porter's chapter on John G. Bourke in *Soldiers West: Biographies of the Frontier Military*, ed. Paul Andrew Hutton (Lincoln: University of Nebraska Press, 1986), pp. 137–56. I would like to acknowledge the permission of the University of Oklahoma Press to reprint this material, which first appeared in Porter, *Paper Medicine Man*.

2. Bourke Diary 88 (October 19–November 30, 1888): 45–49. Bourke faithfully kept a diary from his arrival in the Southwest in 1869 until his death in 1896. Probably lost or stolen, the diaries encompassing the years 1869–72 have vanished. Except for the diary covering the dates December 1–16, 1888, all of the surviving volumes of the diaries are in the Library of the United States Military Academy (USMA) at West Point, New York. My research is based on the Bell and Howell microfilm edition of the West Point volumes. Citations will follow the USMA classification giving volume number.

3. Ibid., p. 52.

4. Brigadier General William E. Carraway, U.S. Army (retired), to Joseph C. Porter, April 9, 1976; Bourke Diary 90 (February 3–March 27, 1889): 13–14. The late General Carraway studied the history of the 15th Pennsylvania Volunteer Cavalry. Bourke Diary 31: 234; Edwin V. Sutherland, "The Diaries of John Gregory Bourke: Their Anthropological and Folklore Content" (Ph.D. dissertation, University of Pennsylvania, 1965), p. 7.

5. Bourke Diary, December 1–16, 1888, ed. Lansing Bloom, "Bourke on the Southwest," *New Mexico Historical Review* 8 (January, 1933): 26.

6. George Crook (1828–90) was born in Ohio. He graduated from West Point in 1852. After serving in the Pacific Northwest, Crook returned east with the outbreak of the Civil War. During that struggle, he rose to the rank of major general of volunteers. Crook was certainly one of the army's most successful Indian-fighting generals. The best sources on Crook are Porter, *Paper Medicine Man*; Bourke, *On the Border with Crook*; and Martin F. Schmitt, ed., *General George Crook: His Autobiography* (Norman: University of Oklahoma Press, 1946, 1960, 1986). See also Joseph C. Porter, "Foreword," in the 1986 edition of Schmitt, ed., *General George Crook: His Autobiography*. The army ordered Crook, a lieutenant colonel in 1871, to assume command of the Military Department of Arizona (normally a position for a brigadier general) because of his brevet rank of major general. Crook achieved the actual rank of brigadier general in the regular army in 1873 and of major general in 1888.

7. The Southern Athapascans included seven tribes: the Navajo and six distinct Apache tribes. Bourke was most involved with the western Apache and the Chiricahua Apache. The western Apaches were further divided into five major groups: the White Mountain, the Cibecue, the San Carlos, the Southern Tonto, and the Northern Tonto. The term *Chiricahua* has been applied to four related groups: the Bedonkohe, the Chokonen, the Chihenne, and the Nednai. For a good introduction to the history and culture of these two Apache tribes and their conflict with outsiders, see Grenville Goodwin, *The Social Organization of the Western Apache* (Chicago: University of Chicago Press, 1942); Morris E. Opler, *An Apache Life Way: The Economic, Social, and Religious Institutions of the Chiricahua Indians* (Chicago: University of Chicago Press, 1941); and Dan L. Thrapp, *The Conquest of Apachería* (Norman: University of Oklahoma Press, 1967). Bourke Diary 1: 175.

8. Concerning the Sioux War of 1876 and its various battles, consult Robert M.

Utley, *Frontier Regulars: The United States Army and the Indian, 1866–91* (New York: Macmillan, 1973), pp. 236–91; John S. Gray, *Centennial Campaign: The Sioux War of 1876* (Fort Collins, Colo.: Old Army Press, 1976); J. W. Vaughn, *With Crook at the Rosebud* (Harrisburg, Pa.: Stackpole Co., 1956); Bourke, *On the Border with Crook;* Porter, *Paper Medicine Man;* Jerome A. Greene, *Slim Buttes, 1876: An Episode of the Great Sioux War* (Norman: University of Oklahoma Press, 1982); Paul Andrew Hutton, *Phil Sheridan and His Army* (Lincoln: University of Nebraska Press, 1985), pp. 302–30; Paul L. Hedren, *With Crook in the Black Hills: Stanley J. Morrow's 1876 Photographic Legacy* (Boulder, Colo.: Pruett Pub. Co., 1985); and John G. Bourke, *Mackenzie's Last Fight with the Cheyennes* (1890; reprint, Bellevue, Neb.: Old Army Press, 1970). It is difficult to ponder the Sioux War without thinking about George A. Custer and the Battle of the Little Bighorn. An excellent study of this is Evan S. Connell, *Son of the Morning Star: Custer and the Little Bighorn* (San Francisco: North Point Press, 1984).

9. For a comprehensive analysis of Bourke's development as an anthropologist, see Porter, *Paper Medicine Man.*

10. Bourke, *On the Border with Crook,* p. 1; Bourke Diary 30: 145–46.

11. Bourke, *On the Border with Crook,* p. 87.

12. See Porter, *Paper Medicine Man,* for details about Bourke's activities in Washington, D.C., between 1886 and 1891.

13. Bourke Diary 102: 111. See Porter, *Paper Medicine Man,* especially chaps. 13 and 14, which deal with Bourke's years in Texas.

14. Arnoldo De León, *The Tejano Community, 1836–1900* (Albuquerque: University of New Mexico Press, 1982), p. 200; Bourke Diary 106: 32, 65.

15. Bourke Diary 106: 72.

16. Ibid., p. 84.

17. Ibid., p. 81.

18. Ibid., pp. 77–82.

19. Ibid., pp. 98, 153.

20. Ibid., pp. 98–100, 175–91; 107: 1–5, 30.

21. Ibid., 107: 138–41.

22. Ibid., 141–43; William Warren Stirling, *Trails and Trials of a Texas Ranger* (Norman: University of Oklahoma Press, 1959), p. 374.

23. Bourke Diary 107: 145–47.

24. Ibid., pp. 151–57.

25. Ibid., p. 157; 108: 6–8.

26. Ibid., 108: 13–15.

27. Ibid., pp. 33–38.

28. Ibid., pp. 58–59.

29. Ibid., 109: 9–10. Bourke sent his note to Haynes on July 3, 1892. The offensive remarks appeared in the *Chicago Tribune* on March 19, 1892.

30. Ibid., p. 15.

31. Ibid., p. 30, has text of Bourke telegram to A. J. Evans, U.S. District Attorney, San Antonio, Texas, dated July 31, 1892.

32. Ibid., p. 156.

33. Ibid., 111: 31.

34. *War against Peace; or, A New Attila* (Rio Grande City, Tex.: El Bien Público, 1895).
35. Bourke Diary 111: 32, 56–57.
36. John G. Bourke, "Folk-Foods of the Rio Grande Valley," *Journal of American Folk-Lore* 8 (no. 28): 55; John G. Bourke, "Popular Medicine, Customs, and Superstitions of the Rio Grande," *Journal of American Folk-Lore* 7 (no. 25): 131.
37. John G. Bourke, "Folk-Lore of the Plants and Animals Near Fort Ringgold on the Lower Rio Grande, Texas," unpub., Christlieb Collection, University of Nebraska Library, Lincoln; O. T. Mason to Bourke, July 11, 1891, Folder 14; and F. W. Ture, curator-in-charge, U.S. National Museum, to Bourke, January 16, 1892, Folder 17, Bourke Collection, Nebraska State Historical Society; Bourke Diary 107: 17–28.
38. Bourke Diary 107: 12–18; John G. Bourke, "Popular Medicine, Customs, and Superstitions of the Rio Grande," p. 119. In his diary, Bourke calls his informant Antonia Maria Cabazo de García, but in the *Journal of American Folk-Lore* he spells her name as Maria Antonia Cavazo de Garza.
39. Bourke Diary 107: 48–49.
40. Ibid., pp. 63–119; W. W. Newell to Bourke, February 2, 1894, Folder 21, Bourke Collection, Nebraska State Historical Society; John G. Bourke, "The Miracle Play of the Rio Grande," *Journal of American Folk-Lore* 6 (no. 21): 89–95; *Los Pastores: A Mexican Play of the Nativity*, translated and annotated by M. R. Cole (Boston: American Folk-Lore Society, 1907).
41. John G. Bourke, "Popular Medicine, Customs, and Superstitions of the Rio Grande," p. 131.
42. John G. Bourke, "The American Congo," *Scribner's Magazine* 15 (May, 1894): 596–610. "The American Congo" was reprinted in *War against Peace; or, A New Attila* (Rio Grande City, Tex.: *El Bien Público*, 1895). Bourke's quotes are from the reprint, pp. 9, 5.
43. *War against Peace*, p. 37.
44. General Orders, no. 33, Headquarters of the Army, Adjutant General's Office, Washington, D.C., May 16, 1892, Personal File, Bourke, Box 863, Record Group 94, National Archives, Washington, D.C.

Chapter 8

1. Information furnished by Janice McKenney, U.S. Army Center of Military History, Washington, D.C., January 3, 1986. See also Lonnie J. White, *Panthers to Arrowheads: The Thirty-sixth (Texas-Oklahoma) Division in World War I* (Austin: Presidial Press, 1984); and Paul Braim, *The Test of Battle* (Newark: University of Delaware Press, 1987).
2. See Ann Larson, *Volunteer Citizen Soldiers of Southwest Iowa, 1930–45*, a 1981 National Endowment for the Humanities project.
3. Ibid.
4. See Martin Blumenson, *Mark Clark* (New York: Congdon and Weed, 1984), p. 50. See also John K. Mahon, *History of the Militia and National Guard* (New York: Macmillan, 1983), p. 180; and *Historical and Pictorial Review: National Guard of the State of Texas, 1940* (Baton Rouge, La.: Army & Navy Co., 1940).

5. Janice McKenney to Martin Blumenson, January 3, 1986; Shelby L. Stanton, *Order of Battle, U.S. Army, World War II* (Novato, Cal.: Presidio Press, 1984), p. 119.

6. GHQ became the Army Ground Forces under General McNair in February, 1942.

7. Blumenson, *Mark Clark*, p. 125.

8. Interview with author, General Fred L. Walker, 1957; interview with author, General Mark W. Clark, 1974.

9. See Fred L. Walker, *From Texas to Rome* (Dallas: Taylor Pub. Co., 1969).

10. Stanton, *Order of Battle*, p. 119.

11. Ibid.

12. Henry G. Phillips, *Heavy Weapons: An Account of the World War II Travels and Travails of M Company, Forty-seventh Infantry* (Penn Valley, Calif.: privately printed, 1985), p. 2.

13. Lieutenant Colonel Albert N. Garland and Howard McGaw Smyth, *Sicily and the Surrender of Italy*, U.S. Army in World War II (Washington: Government Printing Office, 1965), p. 57.

14. The following account is based on Martin Blumenson, *Salerno to Cassino*, U.S. Army in World War II (Washington: Government Printing Office, 1969), pp. 73–152.

15. Ibid., pp. 237–38, 240.

16. Ibid., p. 285.

17. Ibid., p. 286.

18. Ibid., p. 346.

19. For additional details and analysis, see Martin Blumenson, *Bloody River: The Real Tragedy of the Rapido* (Boston: Houghton Mifflin, 1970), p. 92.

20. Interview with author, General J. Lawton Collins, 1981.

21. Ernest F. Fisher, Jr., *Cassino to the Alps*, U.S. Army in World War II (Washington: Government Printing Office, 1977), pp. 184ff.

22. Blumenson, *Bloody River*, p. 128.

23. Charles B. MacDonald, *The Mighty Endeavor* (New York: Oxford University Press, 1969), pp. 320–22; Jeffrey Clarke and Robert Ross Smith, *Riviera to the Rhine*, U.S. Army in World War II (Washington: Government Printing Office, 1993); Alan F. Wilt, *The French Riviera Campaign of August, 1944* (Carbondale: Southern Illinois University Press, 1981).

24. Stanton, *Order of Battle*, pp. 119–20.

25. See also *A Pictorial History of the Thirty-sixth "Texas" Infantry Division* (Austin: Thirty-sixth Division Assoc., n.d.); and Robert L. Wagner, *The Texas Army: A History of the Thirty-sixth Division in the Italian Campaign* (Austin: R. L. Wagner, 1972).

Chapter 9

1. Donald G. Taggart, ed., *History of the Third Infantry Division* (Washington, D.C.: Infantry Journal Press, 1947), pp. 307–10. The crossing of the L'Ill was part of a general Allied attempt to reduce the Colmar Pocket, an important salient of German resistance still west of the Rhine. After worrying about the pocket during most of November and December, 1944, General Dwight D. Eisenhower directed General

Jacob Devers, the commander of the VI Army Group, to eliminate the pocket once and for all. See also Dwight D. Eisenhower, *Crusade in Europe* (Garden City, N.Y.: Doubleday, 1948), p. 31; and D. D. Eisenhower to G. C. Marshall, December 1, 1945, in Alfred Chandler et al., eds., *The Papers of Dwight D. Eisenhower: The War Years* (Baltimore: Johns Hopkins University Press), vol. 4, pp. 2426, 2431.

    2. Harold Simpson, *Audie Murphy: American Hero* (Dallas: Alcor Pub. Co., 1982), pp. 153–54. This work is an indispensable study. See also Don Graham, *No Name on the Bullet: A Biography of Audie Murphy* (New York: Viking, 1989).

    3. Lucian K. Truscott, Jr., *Command Missions: A Personal Story* (New York: Dutton, 1954), pp. 544–45.

    4. Replacements were most vulnerable to being killed, wounded, captured, or suffering a neuropsychiatric collapse. As reckoned by Swank and Marchand, the soldier's period of adjustment was five to seven days. If he survived, he supposedly became battle-wise. His effectiveness improved until about the twenty-first day in combat, when a slight decline set in and increased in severity until the forty-fifth day, when true combat exhaustion took over. Once again, the period following that of "peak effectiveness" was one of great danger for the infantryman. The state of infantry training was frequently criticized by front-line officers as being utterly inadequate. Quite often, soldiers complained of replacements who arrived in their units ignorant of such rudimentary combat skills as knowing how to clean, load, and fire their rifles. (Roy L. Swank and Walter E. Marchand, "Combat Neuroses: Development of Combat Exhaustion," *Archives of Neurology and Psychology* 55 [1946]: 238–41.) See also United States Forces, European Theater, Report of the General Board, United States Forces, Europe: Medical Section, "Combat Fatigue," Study no. 91 (1945 ?); U.S. Army, Headquarters, Army Ground Forces: Plans Section, "Study of Army Ground Force Casualties," September 23, 1946, p. 3; James Jones, *WW II* (New York: Ballantine Books, 1975), p. 68; and John Ellis, *The Sharp End* (New York: Scribner's Sons, 1980), pp. 335–39.

    5. Audie Murphy, *To Hell and Back* (New York: Holt, Rinehart and Winston, 1949), p. 7; Simpson, *Murphy*, p. 153. *To Hell and Back* is Murphy's autobiography, ghostwritten by David McClure, a Hollywood writer. McClure took a year off to write the book. Murphy talked with McClure about his war experiences and McClure wrote them for Murphy's inspection, but Murphy did very little of the actual writing, despite McClure's urging. For all that, *To Hell and Back* is a classic of its kind. McClure and Murphy remained friends for the rest of Murphy's career. See Simpson, *Murphy*, pp. 258, 363–65.

    6. The foregoing narrative is based upon Murphy's Medal of Honor citation as it appears in U.S. Congress, Senate Committee on Veterans' Affairs, *Medal of Honor Recipients, 1863–1973*, 96th Cong., 1st sess., February 14, 1979, pp. 638–39. See also Simpson, *Murphy*, pp. 152–60.

    7. Murphy's decorations for valor were the Medal of Honor; the Distinguished Service Cross; the Silver Star with one oak leaf cluster; the Bronze Star with "V" device and one oak leaf cluster; the Legion of Merit; the French Croix de Guerre with palm; the French Legion d'honneur, grade of Chevalier; and the Belgian Croix de Guerre with palm. For the wounds he suffered in combat, Murphy wore the Purple Heart with two oak leaf clusters. See Simpson, *Murphy*, p. 442, for a complete list of Murphy's awards and badges.

8. U.S. Army Infantry School, "Decorations, Commendations, and Other Awards," *The Infantry School Mailing List* 26 (February, 1944): 230.

9. There is a very large body of literature on the transformation of war in the nineteenth century. See, for example, William McElwee, *The Art of War from Waterloo to Mons* (Bloomington: Indiana University Press, 1978); Grady McWhiney and Perry Jamieson, *Attack and Die: Civil War Military Tactics and the Southern Heritage* (Tuscaloosa: University of Alabama Press, 1982); Theodore Ropp, *War in the Modern World* (New York: Collier Books, 1962); Walter Millis, *Arms and Men* (New York: Mentor Books, 1956); and Jay Luvaas, *The Military Legacy of the Civil War* (Chicago: University of Chicago Press, 1959).

10. I have been asking this question of my students at the U.S. Army Command and General Staff College, as well as other serving officers, since 1978 and have never had a different answer.

11. Hook is quoted in Anthony Kellett, *Combat Motivation: The Behavior of Soldiers in Battle* (Boston: Kluwer Nijhoff Co., 1982), p. 205. As American soldiers fought their way into Buna, New Guinea, during World War II, Lieutenant General Robert L. Eichelberger offered the Distinguished Service Cross to three infantrymen if they would go down a trail they knew was covered by a Japanese machine gun. Much to Eichelberger's disappointment, the soldiers refused his offer. Eventually, the position was taken by stratagem instead of assault. Major Herbert M. Smith, the men's battalion commander, recalled, "Decorations look damn artificial to a soldier who is filthy, fever-ridden, practically starved, living in a tidal swamp and frustrated from seeing his buddies killed." See Lida Mayo, *Bloody Buna* (Garden City, N.Y.: Doubleday, 1974), pp. 118–19.

12. S. L. A. Marshall and Bill Davidson, "Do the Real Heroes Get the Medal of Honor?" *Collier's*, February 21, 1953, pp. 13–15.

13. U.S. Army Infantry School, "Decorations, Commendations, and Other Awards," 230.

14. Michael Novosel, a combat aviator who won the Medal of Honor in Vietnam, offers two reasons for the hero's reluctance to parade too much. He recalls another aviator saying to him, "I know damn well I did as much as you did, and they didn't give me anything." Too, Novosel admits frankly that he harbors "a fear, the possibility that . . . [I] did not deserve the medal." Novosel is quoted in Robert Manning, ed., *Above and Beyond: A History of the Medal of Honor from the Civil War to Vietnam* (Boston: Boston Pub. Co., 1985), p. 310.

15. Author's notes, conversation with an unnamed retired senior U.S. Army officer, December 19, 1984.

16. Bill Mauldin, *Up Front* (New York: Henry Holt, 1945; reprint, New York: Bantam, 1984), pp. 56–57.

17. Simpson, *Murphy*, p. 163.

18. Audie Murphy to Mr. and Mrs. J. H. Cawthon, April 1, 1945, in Simpson, *Murphy*, p. 213.

19. Ibid., p. 176. See also pp. 216–37 for a chronicle of Murphy's homecoming ordeal. Cagney is quoted on p. 257.

20. *Life* 19 (July 16, 1945): 94ff.

21. John Winton, "The High Price of Valour," *The Illustrated London News* 267, no. 6974 (September, 1979): 51–53.

22. Senate, *Medal of Honor Citations*, pp. 483–720, 1079.
23. Charles B. MacDonald, *The Last Offensive*, U.S. Army in World War II (Washington, D.C.: Government Printing Office, 1973), p. 425, n. 27.
24. There were seven Medal of Honor winners in the 30th Infantry Regiment and five in the 7th Infantry Regiment. See Senate, *Medal of Honor Citations*, pp. 483–720.
25. See Truscott, *Command Missions*, p. 544; and Simpson, *Murphy*, pp. 66, 176. Kesselring is quoted on p. 176.
26. Truscott, *Command Missions*, p. 544.
27. Ibid., p. 545.
28. Charles B. MacDonald, *The Might Endeavor: American Armed Forces in the European Theater in World War II* (New York: Oxford University Press, 1969), p. 189.
29. Mauldin, *Up Front*, pp. 132–35.
30. Stewart is quoted in Ellis, *The Sharp End*, p. 47.
31. Ibid., p. 109.
32. Interview with author, May, 1981. Millett's reference to "floating" occurs with some regularity as heroes attempt to recount their actions during combat. Two Vietnam veterans, both decorated for heroism, used similar imagery. One recalled, "I blacked out at the end. I think I left my body. I didn't know what to make of the guy—me, it was." The other vet said virtually the same thing. "We went right to it, and to tell you the truth, I don't remember too much after that, because I was sort of sprung from myself, you could say." (See Robert Coles, "The Psychology of Heroism," in Manning, *Above and Beyond*, pp. 274–75).
33. Paul Fussell, "My War," *Harper's* 264 (January, 1982): 43. Fussell was an infantry officer during the war who fought through much of the same country in southern France as Murphy. He joined the combat line on November 11 at Saint Die. After Fussell was wounded, he was invalided to the rear in February for trench foot. He returned to the line in March and was wounded once more at Ingwiller.
34. See Simpson, *Murphy*, p. 137.
35. John W. Appel, "Prevention of Manpower Loss from Psychiatric Disorders: Report of a Trip to North African Theater of Operations, 17 May–29 July 1944," MSS in possession of the author.
36. Jones, *WW II*, pp. 51–52.
37. Russell F. Weigley, dean of American military historians, accepts this view uncritically, repeating complaints of higher commanders whose wartime objectives were a good deal more rarified than those of the ordinary soldier. Even Omar Bradley, revered as the "soldier's general," could not understand why American soldiers would not use the tactic called "marching fire," in which soldiers would deploy in line and fire their weapons in unison as they assaulted enemy positions. Even if it were tactically feasible, the fighting men would seldom accept such parade-ground tactics. Weigley and many others also accept S. L. A. Marshall's contention that only 25 to 30 percent of all infantry soldiers fired their weapons in combat during the war, a contention not proved. Many writers appear to be enamored of the stylishness of the German way of war, which has not produced a military victory since 1871 (Russell F. Weigley, *Eisenhower's Lieutenants: The Campaigns of France and Germany, 1944–45* [Bloomington: Indiana University Press, 1981], p. 26). See also S. L. A. Marshall, *Men against Fire: The Problem of Battle Command in Future War* (Washington, D.C.: Infantry Journal Press, 1947; reprint, Gloucester, Mass.: Peter Smith, 1976), p. 54.

38. Mauldin, *Up Front*, p. 46.
39. Murphy, *To Hell and Back*, p. 15.
40. See Taggart, *Third Infantry Division*, pp. 34, 76, and especially 102.
41. Murphy, *To Hell and Back*, pp. 106–107.
42. Taggart, *Third Infantry Division*, p. 97.
43. Simpson, *Murphy*, pp. 85–86, 95.
44. Ibid., p. 121; Murphy, *To Hell and Back*, pp. 166, 174–75.
45. Murphy, *To Hell and Back*, p. 209.
46. Swank and Marchand, "Combat Neurosis," pp. 238–39, 243. See also Samuel A. Stouffer et al., *The American Soldier*, vol. 2: *Combat and Its Aftermath* (Princeton, N.J.: Princeton University Press, 1949), pp. 284–86. This classic study postulated roughly the same curve for the onset of combat fatigue but found that the soldier's effectiveness peaked at the fourth month in combat. This calculation, however, depended upon the views of the platoon leader toward his own men, while Swank and Marchand dealt with soldiers who had been declared combat ineffective. But both studies agreed that "additional combat experience brought with it greater knowledge and skill on the one hand, and the *cumulative* effects of combat stress on the other" [emphasis added].

Combatant nations in the European theater had different requirements for the tours of combat assigned to their infantry men. The British rested their combat troops four days for every twelve in the line and calculated that these troops could last for four hundred combat days. The Americans commonly remained in the line for thirty days; but, as infantry shortages increased, combat time without relief could stretch to eighty or ninety days. The *Wehrmacht*, on the other hand, preferred to rotate whole units out of the line for what both the British and Americans would have regarded as extended periods of training and refitting. See Edward J. Drea, "Unit Reconstitution: A Historical Perspective," *CSI Report* 3 (December, 1983): 16–19.

47. Fussell, "My War," p. 264.
48. *Generalmajor* Wolf Ewet, "The 338th Division in the Bridgehead of Alsace," *Foreign Military Studies* MS no. B–074 (n.p., United States Army, Europe, 1948 [?]): 6,8.
49. Simpson, *Murphy*, p. 136.
50. Ibid., p. 137.
51. On this point see John Ellis, *The Sharp End*, p. 74.
52. Stephen Crane, *The Red Badge of Courage: An Episode of the American Civil War* (New York: D. Appleton & Co., 1895; new ed., New York: Penguin American Library, 1984), p. 46. Murphy played Henry Fleming in the film version of this war. "I had the best time on that film," he said later, and no wonder. Crane's psychological study of fear has much to offer students of the combat soldier in twentieth-century war. Murphy is quoted in Thomas Morgan, "The War Hero," *Fifty Who Made the Difference* (New York: Villard Books, 1980), p. 531.
53. Murphy, *To Hell and Back*, p. 7. See also U.S. Army, "Enlistment Record of Audie Leon Murphy, 29 June 1942," p. 2, in "201 File: Audie Leon Murphy, service number 0692509," National Personnel Records Center, Saint Louis, Missouri.
54. Murphy, *To Hell and Back*, p. 8.
55. Fighting in the Pacific theater of the war was physically harder than fighting in Europe, although the battle casualties were lower. See Stouffer, *The American Soldier*, p. 70.
56. "I had always wanted to be a soldier," Murphy recalls in *To Hell and Back*,

Notes to Pages 151–166 ★ 233

p. 4, and prepares the reader for his initiation into battle with a reminiscence of his life in Hunt County. As for the state of Texas, its legislature passed a resolution before Murphy returned home that read, "By his courage and determination to win . . . [Audie Murphy] has handed down to all Texans the glory and courage that has made Texas soldiers the greatest fighters in the world" (see Simpson, *Murphy*, p. 219).

57. See n. 66, below.
58. See n. 66, below.
59. Audie Murphy to Haney Lee, November 3, 1944, in Simpson, *Murphy*, p. 119. See also Stouffer, *The American Soldier*, p. 89, for an example.
60. Simpson, *Murphy*, p. 229, n. 16.
61. Ibid., p. 224.
62. See Morgan, "The War Hero," pp. 532–33; and Simpson, *Murphy*, p. 229.
63. Simpson, *Murphy*, pp. 257–58.
64. See Morgan, "The War Hero," p. 535.
65. "Audie Murphy, War Hero, Killed in Plane Crash," *New York Times*, June 1, 1971, p. 1.
66. Morgan, "The War Hero," p. 532.

Chapter 10

1. Antonio López de Santa Anna, "Manifesto Relative to His Operations in the Texas Campaign and His Capture," in *The Mexican Side of the Texas Revolution*, trans. Carlos E. Castaneda, 2nd ed. (1928; Austin: Graphic Ideas, 1970), p. 20.
2. Ibid., p. 32.
3. See W. W. Newcomb, Jr., *The Indians of Texas: From Prehistoric to Modern Times* (Austin: University of Texas Press, 1961), p. 347.
4. See Sam W. Haynes, *Soldiers of Misfortune: The Somervell and Mier Expeditions* (Austin: University of Texas Press, 1990).
5. For an excellent account of the Snively Expedition, see Stephen B. Oates, *Visions of Glory: Texans on the Southwestern Frontier* (Norman: University of Oklahoma Press, 1970), pp. 3–24.
6. Walter Webb, *The Texas Rangers* (Boston: Houghton Mifflin, 1935), p. 99.
7. A discussion of some films about the Alamo is provided in Susan P. Schoelwer, *Alamo Images: Changing Perceptions of a Texas Experience* (Dallas: DeGolyer Library and Southern Methodist University Press, 1985).
8. Quoted in Paul Horgan, *Great River: The Rio Grande in North American History* (New York: Rinehart, 1954), p. 536.
9. Antonio López de Santa Anna, "Manifesto Relative to His Operations," p. 20.
10. Ibid., p. 17.
11. T. R. Fehrenbach, *Lone Star: A History of Texas and the Texans* (New York: Collier Books, 1980), p. 471.
12. John H. Lenihan, *Showdown: Confronting Modern America in the Western Film* (Urbana: University of Illinois Press, 1980), pp. 28–30.
13. See Don Graham, *No Name on the Bullet: A Biography of Audie Murphy* (New York: Viking, 1989).
14. Don Graham, *Cowboys and Cadillacs: How Hollywood Looks at Texas* (Austin: Texas Monthly Press, 1983).

Chapter 11

1. Peter Aichinger, *The American Soldier in Fiction, 1880–1963: A History of Attitudes toward Warfare and the Military Establishment* (Ames: Iowa State University Press, 1975), p. ix.
2. John Gunther, in *Inside U.S.A.* (New York: Harper, 1947), p. 815, says that before America's entry into World War II, Texas was "the least isolationist state in the union, and certainly the most interventionist in the West. So many Texans went to Canada to enlist before Pearl Harbor that Montreal wags talked of 'the Royal Canadian Texan Air Force.'"
3. Aichinger, *American Soldier in Fiction*, p. viii.
4. Eisenhower's famous farewell address of January 18, 1961, has been reprinted in many collections, including Walter Millis, ed., *American Military Thought* (Indianapolis: Bobbs-Merrill Co., 1966), pp. 508–14.
5. John Bainbridge, *The Super-Americans* (New York: Holt, Rinehart and Winston, 1961). Bainbridge argues that Texas's importance lies in the manner in which it anticipates and exaggerates tendencies in the United States as a whole.
6. George Sessions Perry, *The Story of Texas A&M* (New York: McGraw-Hill, 1951).
7. A. T. Myrthe, "By a Texian," *Mexico versus Texas: A Descriptive Novel, Most of the Characters of Which Consist of Living Persons* (Philadelphia: N. Siegfried, 1838), p. vii.
8. Amelia E. Barr, *Remember the Alamo* (New York: Dodd, Mead, 1888); Augusta J. Evans, *Inez: A Tale of the Alamo* (1855; reprint, New York: G. W. Carleton, 1871), pp. 270–71.
9. Karle Wilson Baker, *Star of the Wilderness* (New York: Coward-McCann, 1942); Lon Tinkle, *Thirteen Days to Glory* (New York: McGraw-Hill, 1958); James A. Michener, *Texas* (New York: Random House, 1985).
10. John W. Thomason, Jr., *Lone Star Preacher* (New York: Scribner's Sons, 1941); John W. Thomason, Jr. *Fix Bayonets* (New York: Scribner's Sons, 1926).
11. Thomason, *Lone Star Preacher*, p. vii. Subsequent references to the book are included in the text parenthetically.
12. Elmer Kelton, *The Wolf and the Buffalo* (New York: Doubleday, 1980; reprint, Fort Worth: Texas Christian University Press, 1986), p. 44. Subsequent references to the book are included in the text parenthetically.
13. Quoted in Colonel Red Reeder, *The Mackenzie Raid* (New York: Bantam, 1955), p. vi. Reeder's novel is a formula "shoot-'em-up" and cannot be taken seriously as literature.
14. Max Crawford's *Lords of the Plain* (New York: Atheneum, 1985) borrows its title from Ernest Wallace and E. A. Hoebel's standard history, *The Comanches: Lords of the South Plains* (Norman: University of Oklahoma Press, 1952).
15. Tom Lea, *The Wonderful Country* (Boston: Little, Brown & Co., 1952), p. 304. A subsequent reference to the book is included in the text parenthetically.
16. See Stephen B. Oates, *Visions of Glory: Texans on the Southwestern Frontier* (Norman: University of Oklahoma Press, 1970), pp. 25–52. James A. Michener, in *Texas*, pp. 513–67, paints an even more unflattering portrait of the Rangers in Mexico.
17. Larry McMurtry, *Lonesome Dove* (New York: Simon and Schuster, 1985), pp. 662–66.
18. Andrew Jolly, *A Time of Soldiers* (New York: Dutton, 1976; reprint, New

York: Avon, 1977), p. 156. Subsequent references to the book are included in the text parenthetically.

19. Quoted in Lance Bertelsen, "How Texas Won the Second World War," *Southwest Review* 76 (1991): 330–31.

20. Norman Mailer, *The Naked and the Dead* (New York: Rinehart, 1948), p. 17. A subsequent reference to the book is included in the text parenthetically.

21. Norman Mailer, *Why Are We in Vietnam?* (New York: Putnam, 1967), pp. 34–35. Subsequent references to the book are included in the text parenthetically.

22. Don Graham, *Cowboys and Cadillacs: How Hollywood Looks at Texas* (Austin: Texas Monthly Press, 1983), pp. 71–72.

Epilogue

1. T. R. Fehrenbach, "The Americanization of Texas," *Texas Monthly* 3 (January, 1975): 62, 68. I was initially tempted to succumb to the current trend of entering a personal note and frame a montage of popular cultural images and experiences that shaped my sense of Texas's martial spirit. These include Tom Mix radio shows, A- and B-grade films, anecdotes, the sports pages, and especially those University of Texas graduates who—along with those from the University of Wisconsin—comprised a large portion of ROTC Military Police officers in the late 1950s. After becoming a Texas resident a generation later, I was amazed to discover how many people in the United States and Europe saw Texas as a distinct region, more so than the other American states. Upon reflection, as those perspectives were thrown into relief by the varied views of the contributors, I decided upon a clinical, third-person perspective.

2. Walter Prescott Webb, *The Great Frontier* (Boston: Houghton Mifflin, 1952). For another perspective on this complex phenomenology, see Anthony Goodman and Anthony Tuck, eds., *War and Border Societies* (London: Routledge & Kegan Paul, 1992).

3. For example, see A. J. Sowell, *Rangers and Pioneers* (New York: Argosy-Antiquarian, 1964).

4. See Hilary Mills, *Mailer: A Biography* (New York: Empire, 1982), pp. 76–81.

5. William H. McNeill, "Mythistory, or Truth, Myth, History, and Historians," *American Historical Review* 91 (February, 1986): 1–11.

6. John D. Weaver, *The Brownsville Raid* (New York: Norton, 1970; reprint, College Station: Texas A&M University Press, 1992).

7. Twenty-nine were born in the British Isles. See "Remember the Alamo: Everyone Has Heard of It, but Did You Know Twenty-nine Britons Were Involved?" *Soldier* 40 (April 23, 1984): 16.

8. Other notable sieges include Babylon, Jerusalem, Masada, Troy, Syracuse, Athens, Carthage, Paris, Saint-Jean-d'Acre, Chateau Gaillard, Constantinople, Vienna, Gibraltar, Fort Pitt, Sevastapol, Vicksburg, Lucknow, Cameron, Rorke's Drift, Khartoum, Chitral, Peking, Kimberley, Mafeking, Mukden, Musa Dagh, Kut-al-Amara, the Alcazar, Westerplatte, Brest-Litovsk, Tobruk, Malta, Demyansk, Leningrad, Kohima-Imphal, Dien Bien Phu, and Khe Sanh.

9. For popular cultural perspectives, see F. Romer, *Makers of History: The Story of the Development of the History of Our Country and the Part Played in It by the Colt* (Hartford, Conn.: Colt's Patent Firearms Manufacturing Co., 1926); and David Nevin,

The Old West: The Soldiers (New York: Time-Life Books, 1973).

10. Ellsworth S. Grant, *The Colt Legacy: The Story of the Colt Armory in Hartford, 1855–1980* (Providence: Mowbray Co., 1982), pp. 7–8.

11. Joseph H. Lehmann, *The Modern Major-General: A Biography of Sir Garnet Wolseley* (Boston: Houghton Mifflin, 1964), p. 123.

12. "State is No. 3 in Military Pacts; Wright's County Gets a Fat Slice," *Houston Chronicle*, March 31, 1989, 14A. Looking at that pattern in the mid-1980s, *Atlantic Monthly* correspondent Nicholas Lemann saw Texas as "strongly supportive of the military . . . out of conviction rather than economic interest . . . because the great lesson of Texas history is that strength and force are the foundations of their society" (Nicholas Lemann, "Power and Wealth," *The Texas Humanist* 7 [January–February, 1985]: 12).

13. Sherrod is quoted in J. Robert Moskin, *The U.S. Marine Corps Story* (New York: McGraw-Hill, 1982), p. 294.

14. See Grady C. Durham, "The T-Patchers' River Hell," *Houston Chronicle Magazine*, March 18, 1984, p. 7.

15. Frido von Senger und Etterlin, *Neither Fear nor Hope*, trans. George Malcolm (New York: Dutton, 1964), p. 193.

16. Harry C. Butcher, *My Three Years with Eisenhower* (New York: Simon and Schuster, 1946), pp. 419–20.

17. With respect to the purge of the 32nd Division in the Buna campaign, see Edward T. Laner, *Thirty-second Infantry Division in World War II* (Madison: Bureau of Purchase, n.d. [ca. 1956], pp. 80–86, 126.

18. Lawrence Wright, "Remembrance of Things Primitive," *Texas Monthly* 21 (February, 1993): 198.

CONTRIBUTORS

ROGER A. BEAUMONT IS PROFESSOR OF HISTORY AT TEXAS A&M University. He served a term on the U.S. Army Historical Advisory Committee, was Secretary of the Navy Fellow at the U.S. Naval Academy, and has given invited lectures at the U.S. Army Command and General Staff College and the U.S. Marine Corps Command and General Staff College. He is the author of *Military Elites* (1974), *Sword of the Raj: The British Army in India, 1747–1947* (1977), *Special Operations and Elite Units, 1939-88* (1988), and *Joint Military Operations* (1993).

Martin Blumenson served for much of his career as a historian with the U.S. Army and for ten years was senior historian in the Office of the Chief of Military History in Washington, D.C. He has written many books, including *Breakout and Pursuit* (1961) and *Salerno to Cassino* (1969), significant volumes in *U.S. Army in World War II,* the army's Green Books series. His other works include *Anzio: The Gamble That Failed* (1963), *Kasserine Pass* (1967), *The Duel for France* (1963), *The Patton Papers,* 2 vols. (1972-74), *Mark Clark* (1984), and *Patton: The Man behind the Legend* (1985).

James E. Crisp is assistant professor of history at North Carolina State University. His articles and reviews have been published in historical journals and reference works.

Thomas W. Cutrer is associate professor of American Studies at Arizona State University–West at Phoenix and editor of *The Journal of the Rocky Mountains American Studies Association.* He is the author of *Parnassus on the Mississippi: The Southern Review and the Baton Rouge Literary Community, 1935–42* (1984) and *Ben McCulloch and the Frontier Military Tradition* (1993).

Joseph G. Dawson III is associate professor of history and director of the Military Studies Institute at Texas A&M University. He is the author of *Army Generals and Reconstruction: Louisiana, 1862–77* (1982). He compiled *The Late Nineteenth-Century U.S. Army: A Research Guide* (1990). He was associate editor of *The Dictionary of American Military Biography*, 3 vols. (1984) and edited *The Commanders in Chief: Presidential Leadership in Modern Wars* (1993).

Don B. Graham is J. Frank Dobie Regents Professor in American and English literature at the University of Texas at Austin. He has contributed numerous articles to literary and historical journals and chapters to various edited books. His major works include *The Fiction of Frank Norris: The Aesthetic Context* (1978), *Cowboys and Cadillacs: How Hollywood Looks at Texas* (1983), and *No Name on the Bullet: A Biography of Audie Murphy* (1989).

Paul Andrew Hutton is associate professor of history at the University of New Mexico, where he also served for several years as the editor of the *New Mexico Historical Review*. He is the author of *Phil Sheridan and His Army* (1985). He is editor of several works, including *Soldiers West: Biographies from the Military Frontier* (1987), *The Custer Reader* (1992), and the series *Eyewitness to the Civil War* (1991–92).

William H. Leckie was professor of history at the University of Toledo, where he also served as dean of the graduate school. He is the author of *The Military Conquest of the Southern Plains* (1963) and *The Buffalo Soldiers: A Narrative of the Negro Cavalry in the West* (1967). He is coauthor, with Shirley A. Leckie, of *Unlikely Warriors: General Benjamin H. Grierson and His Family* (1984).

Sandra L. Myres (1932–91) was professor of history at the University of Texas–Arlington. She was the author of *Westering Women and the Frontier Experience* (1982). She edited *Cavalry Wife: The Diary of Eveline M. Alexander* (1977), *Army Letters from an Officer's Wife*, by Frances Roe (1984), and *Ho for California: Women's Overland Diaries from the Huntington Library* (1980).

Tom Pilkington is University Scholar for Literature and professor of English at Tarleton State University, Stephenville, Texas. Pilkington is the author of several books, including *My Blood's Country: Studies in Southwestern Literature* (1973) and *Imagining Texas: The Literature of the Lone Star State* (1981). He is editor and coeditor of other works, such as *The Texas Literary Tradition* (1983), *A Literary History of the American West* (1987), and *Range Wars: Heated Debates, Sober Reflections, and Other Assessments of Texas Writing* (1989).

Joseph C. Porter has served as curator of western American history and ethnology at the Joslyn Art Museum, Omaha, Nebraska, and director of publications for the Missouri Historical Society in Saint Louis. He is the author of *Paper Medicine Man: John Gregory Bourke and His American West* (1986).

Roger J. Spiller is George C. Marshall Professor of Military History at the U.S. Army Command and General Staff College, Fort Leavenworth, Kansas. He was deputy director of the Combat Studies Institute there from 1986 to 1991. He is also historian to the chief of staff of the U.S. Army. He is the author of *Not War but Like War: The American Intervention in Lebanon, 1958* (1981) and was editor of *The Dictionary of American Military Biography*, 3 vols. (1984).

Ralph A. Wooster established his career as professor of history at Lamar University in Beaumont, Texas, where he also served as dean of graduate studies and associate vice president and dean of faculties. He is the author of *Secession Conventions of the South* (1962), *The People in Power: Courthouse and Statehouse in the Lower South* (1969), and *Politicians, Planters, and Plain Folk: Courthouse and Statehouse in the Upper South* (1975). He was coeditor of *Texas Vistas* (1987).

INDEX

Acuña, Rudy, 19
Adobe Walls, Tex.: battle of, 189
African Americans, 6, 12; and Brownsville incident, 7, 188, 190; as buffalo soldiers, 88–89, 95, 173–76; in Civil War, 86; as soldiers in Texas, 86–96, 187–88. *See also* slavery
Agua Nueva, Mex., 64, 65, 66, 67, 6S, 69, 70
Alabama, 71, 128
Alamo, 4, 5, 9, 10, 16, 48, 68, 97, 161, 165, 168, 170; battle of, 14, 57, 158–59, 190 ; fiction about, 169–70; films about, 19, 22, 25, 28, 157-60, 165, 166; and historiography, 3, 15, 22–29, 170 ; symbolism of, 14–31, 187, 188
Alamo: The Price of Freedom (film), 19, 28
Alamo, The (film), 19, 22, 25, 165
Alexander, Eveline, 111
Allen, James, 23
American Revolution, 3, 86, 97, 160
Ampudia, Pedro de, 58, 59, 63
Andrews, Emily, 101, 102, 104, 107
Anzio, It.: battle of, 8, 133, 134, 144, 148
Apache Canyon, N. Mex.: battle of , 77
Arkansas, 49, 82, 83
Arizona, 75, 76, 77, 89, 91, 111, 114, 115, 116, 177
Arista, Mariano, 54
Army of Northern Virginia, 5, 73, 172, 189

Austin, Stephen F., 18, 39, 43, 44, 50, 55
Austin, Tex., 49, 95, 101, 107, 180, 191
Austria, 136, 139

Babbitt, Bruce, 20-21
Banado, Manuel, 119-20
Banks, Nathaniel P., 81-83
Barker, Eugene C., 45, 46
Barry, Buck, 59, 60, 61, 63
Battle of San Pietro, The (film), 186
Battle of the Bulge, 186
Baugh, Virgil E., 28
Baylor, John R., 75, 76
Beaumont, Tex., 81
Bee, Hamilton P., 73, 83
Beeville, Tex., 11
Benavides, Santos, 97
Biddle, Ellen, 100
Binkley, William C., 45
Birkhead, Claude V., 129, 130
"Black Legend," 35–36, 39
Blair, Walter, 28
Bliss, William W. S., 56, 57, 64
Blumenson, Martin, 7, 8, 184, 190, 191
Bois de Riedwihr: battle in, 137, 138, 142, 144, 150, 152
Bonham, James B., 21
Bonilla, Ruben, 21
Bourke, John G., 7; as author, 117, 123, 126; as ethnologist, 115–16; as folklorist, 115–17, 124–26; as frontier army officer, 113–27

242 ★ INDEX

Bowie, Jim, 3, 4, 14, 16, 18, 21, 22, 170
Bowles, Chief, 156
Boyd, Frances, 97, 100, 101, 102, 104, 105, 111, 112
Brackett, Albert G., 51
Bradburn, Juan D., 34
Bradley, Omar N., 9, 130
British army, 131, 133, 141, 143, 146
Brown, J. D., 52, 54
Brownsville, Tex., 72, 82, 85, 123, 126. *See also* African Americans
Brownwood, Tex., army camp, 129
Buell, George, 95
Buena Vista, Mex.: battle of, 67–69, 70
Buenger, Walter, 71
Buffalo soldiers. *See* African Americans
Burke, James W., 28

California, 46, 69, 77, 128
Camargo, Mex., 54, 55, 58, 101
Camp Bowie, Tex., 128, 129, 130
Camp Mabry, Tex., 190
Campbell, Randolph B., 5
Canales, Antonio, 54, 55
Canby, E. R. S., 76, 77
Carr, Eugene A., 86
Chickamauga, Ga.: battle of, 73, 84, 114
Chipman, Donald, 12
Chivington, John, 77
Civil War, 5, 6, 86, 87, 93, 111, 114, 128, 145, 169, 173, 184, 189; Texans in, 71–85, 157, 170–71
Clark, Edward, 72, 73, 74
Clark, Mark, 8–9, 130, 131, 133
Clarksville, Tex., 61
Clausewitz, Carl von, 186
Coffee, John, 51, 69
Cold War, 10, 163, 165, 190–91
Collins, J. Lawton, 134
Colmar Pocket, Fr. : battle of, 136, 150
Colorado, 77, 115, 186
Confederate States of America, 5, 71–72, 74, 170, 171
Connor, Seymour V., 45
Corpus Christi, Tex., 11, 21, 27, 49, 52, 53, 78, 79, 82, 102, 122, 126

Cortina, Júan, 72
Cos, Martín Perfecto de, 18, 160
Crane, Stephen, 150–51
Crawford, Max, 175
Crisp, James, 3, 4, 187, 188
Crockett, David, 3, 4, 14, 33, 51, 157, 158, 170; books about, 24, 28; death of, 23–30
Crook, George, 113, 114–15, 117
Cruz y Arocha, Antonio, 18
Custer, Elizabeth, 97, 98, 99, 106, 107, 108, 112
Custer, George A., 14, 30, 86, 87, 97, 108, 175
Cutrer, Thomas. 4–5, 185, 189

Dahlquist, John, 135
Dallas, Tex., 11, 28, 84, 153, 183, 191
Dana, Richard H., 39
Daughters of the Republic of Texas, 25, 27, 29, 31
Davis, Edmund J., 84
Davis, Jefferson, 72, 75
Dawley, Earnest, 131
Dawson, Joseph G., III, 185, 190
Dawson, Nicholas M., 55, 57
Debray Xavier B., 80, 83
De León, Arnoldo, 12, 34–36, 41–44, 46–47
Diaz, Porfirio, 113, 118, 119
Dickinson, Susannah, 23, 158
Disney, Walt, 25
Dobie, J. Frank, 22, 23, 127
Dowling, Richard W., 81–82
Dr. Strangelove (film), 165–66, 191

Eisenhower, Dwight D., 9, 130, 168
Ellis, Edward S., 24
Ellis, Richard, 110
El Paso, Tex., 10, 75, 76, 77, 91, 92, 101, 175, 177, 180, 191
Encarnación, Mex., 65, 66, 69

Fannin, James, 4, 18, 21, 57, 155, 170
Fehrenbach, T. R., 160, 184

Fiction. *See* literature
Films, 4, 10, 45, 153, 155–66, 186, 187, 191; about the Alamo, 19, 22, 25, 28, 157–60, 165, 166. *See also individual films*
Flipper, Henry, 94
Florida, 71, 116, 130
Flying Tigers, 190
Foner, Jack, 110
Ford, John, 162, 163
Ford, John S. ("Rip"), 72, 75, 79, 82, 85, 157
Foreman, Gary, 28
Fort Bliss, Tex., 75, 76, 77, 91, 101, 104, 175, 179
Fort Brown, Tex., 54, 72, 91, 103
Fort Clark, Tex., 91, 100, 101, 104
Fort Concho, Tex., 90, 92, 94, 95, 96, 173, 175
Fort Craig, N. Mex., 76, 77, 114, 117
Fort Davis, Tex., 87, 91, 94, 101, 104
Fort Duncan, Tex., 101, 102
Fort Griffin, Tex., 81–82
Fort Inge, Tex., 10, 100
Fort Leavenworth, Kan., 87
Fort McIntosh, Tex., 117, 118, 120, 121
Fort McKavett, Tex., 87
Fort Quitman, Tex., 93
Fort Richardson, Tex., 91
Fort Ringgold, Tex., 100, 117, 118, 119, 121, 122, 123, 124, 126
Fort Sam Houston, Tex., 11, 117
Fort Sill, Okla., 89
Fort Stockton, Tex., 101
Fort Sumter, S.C., 72, 74, 84
Fort Union, N. Mex., 77
Fort Worth, Tex., 10, 11
France: fall of, 129; invasion of southern, 135, 136, 144, 149. *See also* individual cities; Normandy campaign
Franklin, John Hope, 5
Franklin, William B., 81, 82
Frantz, Joe, 27
Frederickson, George, 40, 43
Fremantle, Arthur, 73
Fussell, Paul, 146–47, 150

Gainesville, Tex., 84–85
Gallant Legion (film), 162, 164
Galveston, Tex., 64, 74, 78, 79, 85, 105, 189; battles of, 79–81
Garza, Catarino, 117–23, 126–27
Garza, Maria, 124
Garza, Tomás, 120
Garzistas, 118–23, 127
Georgia, 71, 72, 83, 84, 184
German army, 8, 10, 131, 133, 134, 135, 137, 138, 141, 144, 147–50, 161, 191
Geronimo, 115, 116
Gettysburg, Pa.: battle of, 73, 84, 146, 172, 189
Gillespie, Richard A., 56, 59
Glorieta Pass, N. Mex.: battle of, 77
Goliad, Tex., 4, 18, 34, 44, 49, 57, 68, 155, 159, 160, 170, 190
Gonzales, Tex., 32, 49, 52, 69
Graham, Don, 4, 10, 183, 186, 187
Granbury, Hiram, 5, 84, 85
Green, Thomas J., 17, 76, 77, 80, 83
Greene, Graham, 153
Grierson, Alice, 100
Grierson, Benjamin, 87–91, 93–96
Griffith, D. W., 45, 158
Guerrero, Vincente, 40

Hatch, Edward, 87–89, 91–93, 95
Hauck, Richard B., 28
Hays, John C., 49, 51, 52, 53, 59, 60, 62, 63, 70, 157
Hébert, Paul O., 78, 79
Henson, Margaret S., 34
Hispanics, 7, 12, 18, 19, 20, 33, 40, 105, 106, 121–23, 163, 167, 187; lifestyles of, 116, 119, 124–26 : and Texas Revolution, 35–48. See also *Tejanos;* Juan Sequin
Hitchcock, Ethan A., 51
Hobby, Oveta Culp, 190
Hood, John Bell, 5, 73–74, 84, 85, 97, 172
Houston, Sam, 4, 18, 28, 32, 51, 70, 71, 84, 97, 155, 156, 157, 159, 169, 170, 171, 178

Houston, Tex., 7, 72, 73, 78, 81
Huston, John, 163, 186
Hutton, Paul A., 3, 29–30, 187, 188

Illinois, 122
Indian territory, 74, 83, 88, 89, 92, 115
Indians, 4, 6, 7, 10, 37, 38, 40, 44, 51, 74, 88, 89, 102–106, 111, 116, 156, 157, 161, 168, 169, 173; Apaches, 7, 89, 91, 93, 114–17, 123, 163, 176, 177; Arapahos, 89 ; Cherokees, 156; Cheyennes, 88, 89, 92, 93, 115; Chickasaws, 74 ; Comanches, 50, 55, 74, 88, 89, 92, 104, 157, 162, 173–75, 187, 189 ; Delawares, 97; Kickapoos, 88, 89, 175; Kiowas, 50, 74, 88, 89; Lakotas, 115; Lipans, 88; Utes, 115
Italy: campaign for, 131–34, 136, 137, 146–49, 191. *See also individual cities*

Jackson, Andrew, 51
Jackson, Jack, 19
Jenkins, John H., 32–33, 34, 35, 47, 48
Johnson, Lyndon, 183, 190, 191
Johnston, Albert S., 5, 73, 83–84, 97
Johnston, Eliza, 101, 102, 109
Jolly, Andrew, 177–80
Jones, James, 147

Kansas, 88, 156, 187
Kelton, Elmer, 173–75
Kendall, George, 55, 58, 60
Kentucky, 73
Keyes, Geoffrey, 8, 133–34
Kilgore, Dan, 27, 29, 30, 33
Korean War, 141, 146, 163, 169, 190
Kovic, Ron, 9

Lack, Paul D., 43
Lamar, Mirabeau B., 44, 156, 178
Laredo, Tex., 117, 126
Lane, Lydia, 97, 99, 100, 102, 104, 107
Last Command, The (film), 22, 25
Lea, Tom, 175–76
League of United Latin-American Citizens, 21

Leckie, William H., 6, 187
Lee, Robert E., 5, 73, 79, 85, 97, 172, 178, 189
LeMay, Alan, 163
Lenihan, John, 163
Lincoln, Abraham, 72, 86
Literature, 10, 150, 167–83, 186, 187. *See also individual works*
Lofaro, Michael, 28–30
Lone Star Preacher (Thomason), 171–72
Lord, Walter, 15, 23, 25 .
Los Tejanos: The True Story of Juan Sequin (Jackson), 19
Lowrie, Samuel H., 45–46
Louisiana, 12, 20, 52, 71, 74, 75, 78, 82, 83, 84, 87, 129, 173
Lubbock, Francis R., 74
Lubbock, Tex., 10

MacArthur, Douglas, 9
Mackenzie, Ranald S., 89, 95, 97, 157, 175
McCord, James E., 74
McCulloch, Ben, 4, 5; in Civil War, 72; description of, 52; in Mexican War, 49–70, 186
McCulloch, Henry, 72
McCullough, Samuel, 97
McDonald, Archie, 33
McLean, Malcolm D., 34, 35, 38
McMurtry, Larry, 176
McNair, Lesley J., 129–30
Magruder, John B., 79–82, 85
Mailer, Norman, 180–83, 186
Mangus, Chief, 91
Mansfield, La.: battle of, 83
Marshall, George C., 9, 130
Marshall, S. L. A., 141
Massachusetts, 130, 184
Matamoros, Mex., 52, 53, 54, 56, 126
Mattes, Merrill, 112 .
Mauldin, Bill, 138, 142, 145–46, 147
May, Charles A., 65, 68, 69
May, Robert E., 6
Meade, George G., 61, 62
Medal of Honor, 9, 88, 136, 139, 141, 142, 143, 144, 146, 149, 152, 154, 165, 191
Meuse-Argonne, Fr.: battle of, 128

Mexican army, 119, 156, 161, 176, 190; in Mexican War, 55–63, 66–70; in Texas Revolution, 14, 25–26, 155, 159–60, 169. *See also* Santa Anna, Antonio Lopez de
Mexican War (1846–48), 4, 12, 47, 72, 76, 105, 156, 190; Texas Rangers in, 49–70, 183
Mexico, 4, 5, 12, 36–40, 43, 49, 50, 64, 82, 91, 118, 119, 168; and Constitution of 1824, 19–20
Mexico City, 39, 40, 46, 65
Michener, James A., 170
Midway: battle of, 190
Mier Expedition, 4, 5, 17, 51, 52, 57, 62, 63, 68, 69, 156, 190
Miles, Nelson A., 86, 90
Miller, Char, 11
Minnesota, 186
Miñón, José V., 64, 65
Mississippi, 71, 78
Missouri, 49, 109, 111
Montana, 115
Monte Artemisio, It.: battle of, 134, 136
Monte Cassino, It.: battle of, 134
Montejano, David, 12
Montelimar, Fr.: battle of, 135, 136
Monte Lungo, It.: battle of, 132, 148
Monterrey, Mex., 54–56, 65; battle of, 58–63, 70
Moore, Edwin N., 4
Murphy, Audie, 9, 10, 137–40, 142–43, 146–54, 164–65, 186, 191
Murrah, Pendleton, 74
Myres, Sandra L., 7, 38, 187

Najera, Juan, 60
Naked and the Dead, The (Mailer), 180–81, 186
National Guard, 7, 128, 129, 130, 136, 180, 186, 187
Navarro, José A., 44, 45
Nebraska, 115, 177
Neches, Tex.: battle of, 156
New Jersey, 133
New Mexico, 30, 44, 46, 73, 75, 76, 77, 78, 89, 91, 92, 102, 107, 111, 114, 116, 117, 156, 157, 177, 178, 187
New Orleans Greys, 20
New York, 6, 12, 76, 87, 112, 130, 133, 180, 185, 191
Nichols, Ebenezer B., 72–73
Nichols, Roger, 110
Nimitz, Chester W., 9–10
Normandy campaign, 10, 135, 141, 149
Norris, James M., 74
North Africa campaign, 130, 141, 144, 145
North Carolina, 85
Nugent, Walter, 35

Oates, Stephen, 76
Ohio, 59, 76, 128
Oklahoma, 12, 174

Palmito Ranch, Tex.: battle of, 85, 97
Palo Alto, Tex.: battle of, 53, 56
Palo Duro Canyon, Tex.: battle of, 175
Parker, Fess, 25
Parker, Quanah, 97
Patch, Alexander, 135, 139
Patton, George, 130, 150
Peña, José Enrique de la, 25–26
Penalosa, Eufemia, 97
Pennsylvania, 136
Pennybacker, Anna, 22
Perry, Carmen, 25–27, 29, 30
Perry, George S., 168
Philippines, 164, 190
Pilkington, Tom, 10, 186, 187
Pleasant Hill, La.: battle of, 83
Plum Creek, Tex.: battle of, 50, 51
Pointe du Hoc, Fr.: battle at, 10
Polignac, Camille, 83
Polk, James K., 49, 64
Porter, Joseph C., 7, 187
Potter, E. B., 9
Potter, Reuben M., 19

Railroads, 41, 87, 110, 111
Rapido River, It.: battle of, 8–9, 133–34, 136, 191
Reconstruction, 6, 173, 187
Red Badge of Courage, The (Crane), 150–51, 153

Red River, 74, 83, 95, 156
Red River War, 89, 92, 95
Reid, Samuel C., 52, 61, 63
Reily, James, 76
Resaca de la Palma, Tex.: battle of, 53, 56
Retamal, Tex.: skirmish at, 120, 121
Riley, Glenda, 38
Rio Grande, 4, 49, 52, 54, 55, 70, 72, 74, 75, 76, 82, 84, 86, 88, 89, 91, 95, 106, 107, 114, 116, 117, 118, 119, 121, 123, 124, 125, 163
Rio Grande City, Tex., 118, 121, 124, 125
Roberts, Lou, 100
Robertson, Sterling C., 34
Robinson, Cecil, 46
Rogers, William P., 74
Rome, It.: battle for, 133, 134, 136
Roosevelt, Theodore, 24, 167
Rose, Lewis ("Moses"), 22, 23
Ross, Lawrence S., 5, 84, 189
Rough Riders, 167
Rudder, James Earl, 10
Runaway Scrape, 155

Sabine Pass, Tex., 78, 79, 81–82, 97
Salado Creek, Tex., 55
Salerno, It.: battle of, 8, 9, 131, 136, 148
Salt War, 92
San Angelo (Saint Angela), Tex., 10, 95, 96, 173, 177
San Antonio, Tex., 4, 10, 11, 12, 14, 20, 28, 44, 45, 49, 50, 55, 57, 72, 76, 77, 87, 91, 101, 105, 117, 120, 122, 123, 125, 129, 143, 158, 167, 177, 181, 186
San Jacinto, Tex.: battle of, 4, 10, 19, 41, 43, 48, 51, 57, 76, 97, 155, 159, 160, 169, 170, 171
San Luis Potosí, Mex., 65
San Pietro, It.: battle of, 9, 133, 136
Santa Anna, Antonio Lopez de, 14, 18, 20, 23, 24, 25, 41, 57, 62, 66, 67, 68, 70, 155, 159, 160, 170
Santa Fe, N. Mex., 5, 76, 77, 97
Santa Fe Expedition, 44, 156
Schmidt, Eric von, 28
Schoelwer, Susan P., 28

Scott, Winfield, 51
Scurry, William R., 66, 67, 70, 76, 77
Searchers, The (film), 162–63, 187
Seguín, Juan: in Mexican War, 55–58; in Texas Revolution, 18-19, 21, 41–42, 44–45, 48, 97
Selective Service Act, 129
Shackford, James, 28
Shafter, William R., 92, 94
Sharpsburg, Md.: battle of, 73, 84
Shaw, Jim, 97
Sheridan, Philip H., 86, 89, 117
Sherman, William T., 84, 86, 93, 110, 111
Shiloh, Tenn.: battle of, 5, 74, 83
Sibley, Henry Hopkins, 5, 73, 75–77
Sicily: campaign for, 130, 138, 143, 144, 147–48
Slavery, 20, 31, 43, 44, 46, 71, 78, 95
Smith, Edmund Kirby, 85
Smith, John W., 23
Smith, Ashbel, 74
Smith, Richard P., 24
Smith, Thomas T., 10
Smithsonian Institution, 28, 117
Somervell Expedition, 156
Smyrl, Frank, 84
Snively, Jacob, 156
South Carolina, 71, 185
South Dakota, 115
Spanish-American War, 167, 177
Spain, 12, 35–37, 39
Spiller, Roger J., 9, 186, 191
Steele, Frederick, 83
Steele, William, 76
Steinbeck, John, 146

Tarawa: battle of, 191
Taylor, Edward T., 36, 38–40
Taylor, Richard, 83
Taylor, Zachary, 4, 49, 51, 52, 54, 55, 56, 57, 58, 59, 63, 64, 65, 69, 70, 157
Tejanos, 18–21, 42, 44, 45, 47, 48, 118
Tennessee, 49, 51, 79, 83, 114
Terry's Texas Rangers, 5, 73
Texas A&M University, 10, 12, 164, 167, 168, 184
Texas military units: 1st Hvy. Artillery

Regt., 78, 82; 1st Inf. Regt., 73; 1st Mounted Rifles, 72; 1st Mounted Riflemen, 49, 52, 59; 2nd Cav. Regt., 75; 2nd Inf. Regt., 74; 2nd Mounted Rifles, 73; 3rd Artillery Bn., 78; 4th Cav. Regt., 73, 76; 4th Inf. Regt., 73, 78; 5th Cav. Regt., 73, 76; 5th Inf. Regt., 73, 172; 7th Cav. Regt. 13, 76; 8th Cav. Regt., 5, 73; 11th Cav. Regt., 74; 26th Cav. Regt., 80; 36th Inf. Div, 7–9, 128–36; 46th Cav. Regt., 74; Frontier Regt., 74; Granbury's Tex. Brig., 84, 85; Hood's Tex. Brig., 5, 73–74, 84, 97, 172; Lane Rangers, 85; Polignac's Tex. Brig., 83; Walker's Tex. Div., 83;

Texas navy, 4

Texas Rangers, 4–5, 72, 92, 97, 100, 121, 160, 189; compared to other military groups, 185–86; fiction about, 176–77; films about, 161–63; and lack of discipline, 5, 50–51, 55, 57, 176; in Mexican War, 49–70, 157, 183, 189; murder of Mexicans, 56–57, 69–70

Texas Republic, 4, 5, 44–45, 51

Texas Revolution, 3, 4, 17, 19, 20, 27, 32–33, 155, 160, 161, 184, 189; fiction about, 169–70; films about, 157, 159; racism and, 35–48, 187–88

Thermopylae, 14, 17

Thomason, John W., Jr., 171–72

Tijerina, Andrew, 47

Time of Soldiers, A (Jolly), 177–80

Tinkle, Lon, 170

To Hell and Back (Murphy), 149, 164

To Hell and Back (film), 164, 186

Torrejon, Anastasio, 58, 68

Travis, William B., 3, 4, 14, 16–20, 24, 33, 34, 158; and line in sand, 21–23

Truscott, Lucien, 134, 135, 144, 145

Tunisia, 130, 152

Twiggs, David E., 72

Unforgiven, The (film), 163, 187

United States Army, 6, 7, 9, 10, 11, 50, 52, 156–57, 163, 178; African Americans in, 86–96, 173–76, 187–88; dragoons, 50, 55, 63, 65, 68, 75, 76; in Mexican War, 52, 56, 61, 63; Rangers, 10. *See also* World War I; World War II

————units: Fifth Army, 8, 131, 133, 134; Seventh Army, 130, 135; II Corps, 8, 130, 133, 134; VI Corps 130, 131, 134, 135, 145; VII Corps, 134; 1st Inf. Div., 130; 3rd Inf. 135, 137–38, 142, 144–45, 148; 9th Inf. Div., 130, 189; 25th Inf. Div., 147; 27th Inf. Div., 191; 36th Inf. Div., 7–9, 128–36, 185, 189, 190, 191; 45th Inf. Div. 130, 131, 135, 147; 49th Armor Div., 190; 2nd Cav. Regt., 175; 4th Cav. Regt., 88, 89, 95; 6th Cav.Regt., 90, 93; 7th Cav Regt., 87; 7th Inf. Regt., 144; 9th Cav. Regt., 86–91, 95; 10th Cav. Regt., 86–95, 176; 11th Inf. Regt., 94; 15th Inf. Regt., 137; 24th Inf. Regt., 86, 88, 91, 92; 25th Inf. Regt. 86, 88, 91, 92; 30th Inf. Regt., 137, 144; 40th Inf. Regt., 86; 41st Inf. Regt., 86; 112th Armor Cav. Regt., 180, 186; 141st Inf. Regt., 130, 134; 142nd Inf. Regt., 130, 131, 134; 143rd Inf. Regt., 130, 131, 134

United States Marine Corps, 9, 143, 151, 171, 191

United States Military Academy (West Point), 6, 51, 56, 75, 76, 78, 94, 108, 111, 114, 117

United States Naval Academy, 9, 78

United States Navy air stations, 11

United States War Department, 72, 117, 120

University of Texas at Austin, 178

Up Front (Mauldin), 145–46

Upton, Emory, 111

Utley, Robert, 111, 112

Valverde, N. Mex.: battle of, 76, 77

Van Dorn, Earl, 78

Vera Cruz, Mex.: 40, 65

Victoria Cross, 139, 141, 143, 144

Victorio, Chief, 91, 92, 93, 94

Vidor, King, 161

Viele, Egbert, 99, 111
Viele, Teresa, 97, 99, 100, 101, 102, 104, 105, 106, 109, 111
Vietnam War, 9, 144, 153, 167, 169, 177, 179, 181–83, 190
Villa, Pancho, 178
Virginia, 12, 39, 40, 73, 79, 81, 83, 136, 171, 185
Vosges Mountains campaign, 135–36, 149

Waco, Tex., 84, 192
Walker, Fred L., 7, 8, 130, 131, 133, 134, 135
Walker, John G., 5
Walker, Samuel H., 53, 189
Warfield Expedition, 156
Wayne, John, 9, 19, 22, 26, 27, 30, 162, 163, 165
Webb, Walter P., 51, 185, 187
Weber, David J., 19, 33, 35–39, 46–47
West Point. *See* United States Military Academy
We've Never Been Licked (film), 164
Why Are We in Vietnam? (Mailer), 181–82
Wigfall, Louis T., 73

Wild Bunch, The (film), 160–61
Williams, Amelia, 22
Wisconsin, 184, 191
With Santa Anna in Texas (Peña), 25
Wolf and the Buffalo, The (Kelton), 173–76
Woll, Adrian, 51
Women, 7, 12, 38, 40, 97; and frontier army, 97–112, 187
Women's Army Corps, 190
Wonderful Country, The (Lea), 175–76
Wool, John E., 68
Wooster, Ralph A., 5, 189
Wooster, Robert, 10
World War I, 130, 152, 164, 169, 177; Texans in, 11, 128, 129, 165
World War II, 7–9, 10, 11, 164, 167, 169, 172, 190; Texans in, 128–40, 142–44, 147–54, 168, 178, 191
Worth, William J., 58, 59, 60, 61, 62, 97

Young, William C., 74

Zavala, Lorenzo de, 19
Zuber, William P., 22, 23
Zulus, 141

www.ingramcontent.com/pod-product-compliance
Lightning Source LLC
Chambersburg PA
CBHW030313080526
44584CB00012B/548